The Story of Lee

Volume 3

by Seán Michael Wilson
& Piarelle

nbm GRAPHIC NOVELS

Nantier · Beall · Minoustchine
NEW YORK

ISBN: 978-1-68112-195-6
©2019 Seán Michael Wilson & Piarelle
Library of Congress Control Number: 2010941038

1st printing, February 2019

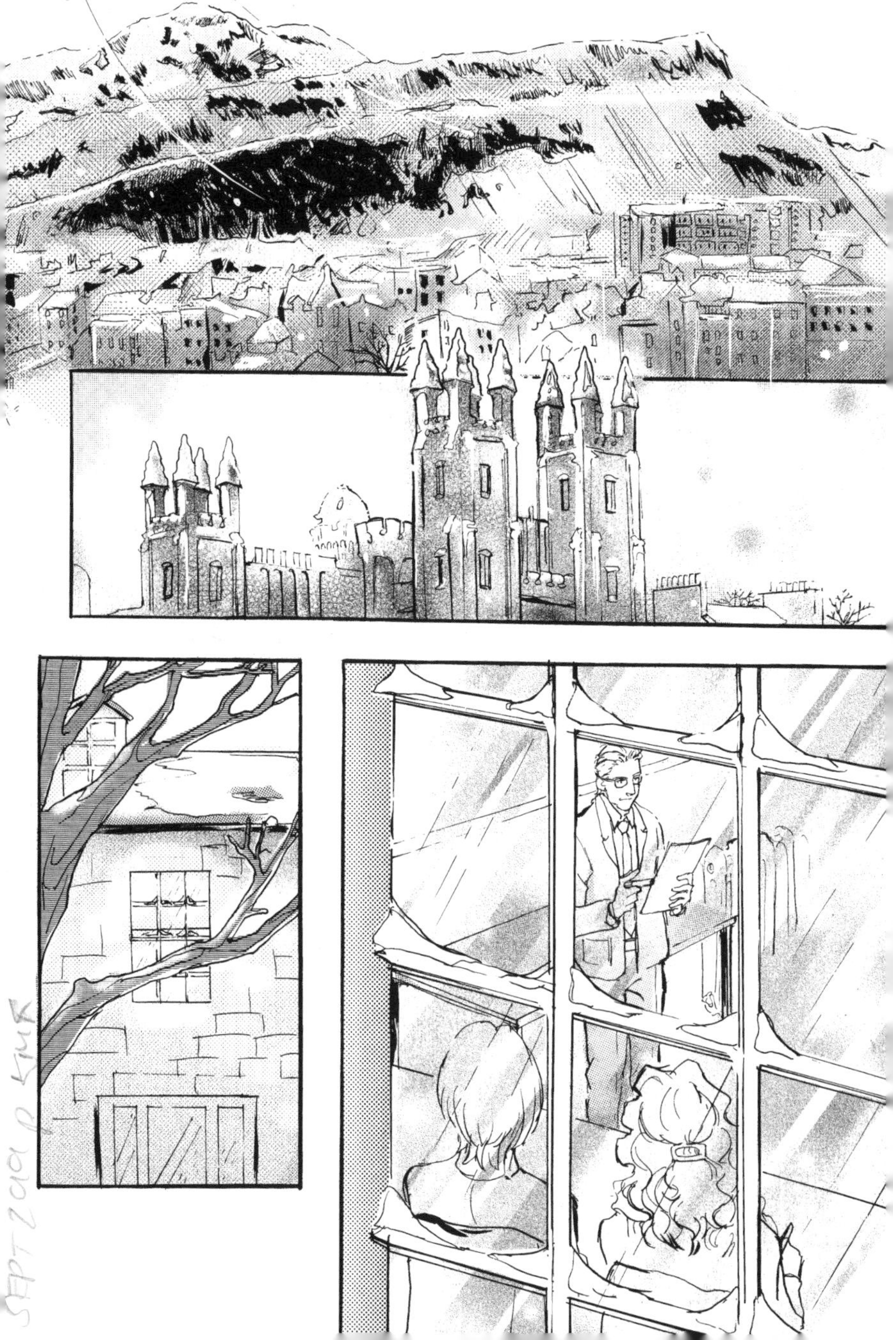

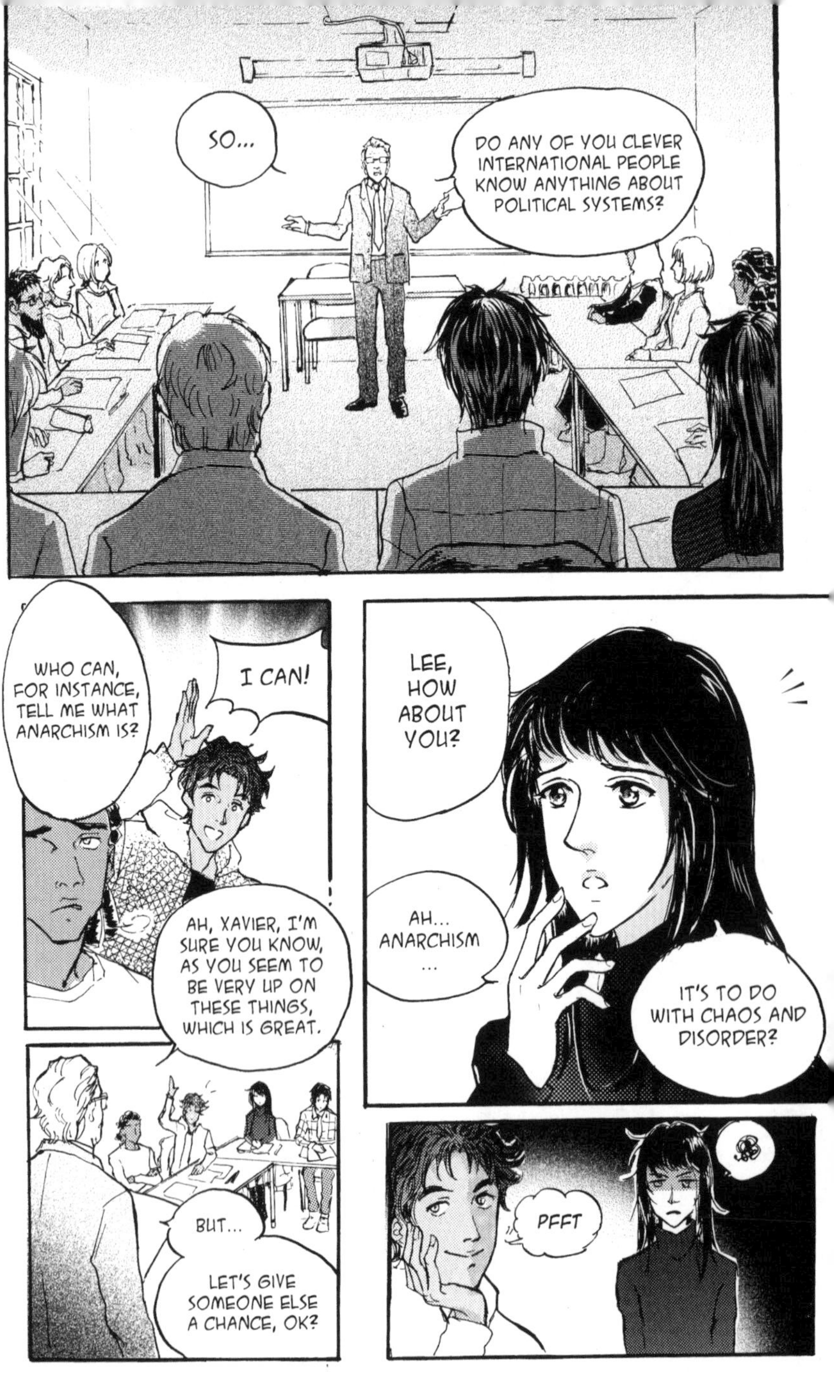
SO...
DO ANY OF YOU CLEVER INTERNATIONAL PEOPLE KNOW ANYTHING ABOUT POLITICAL SYSTEMS?
WHO CAN, FOR INSTANCE, TELL ME WHAT ANARCHISM IS?
I CAN!
AH, XAVIER, I'M SURE YOU KNOW, AS YOU SEEM TO BE VERY UP ON THESE THINGS, WHICH IS GREAT.
BUT...
LET'S GIVE SOMEONE ELSE A CHANCE, OK?
LEE, HOW ABOUT YOU?
AH... ANARCHISM ...
IT'S TO DO WITH CHAOS AND DISORDER?
PFFT

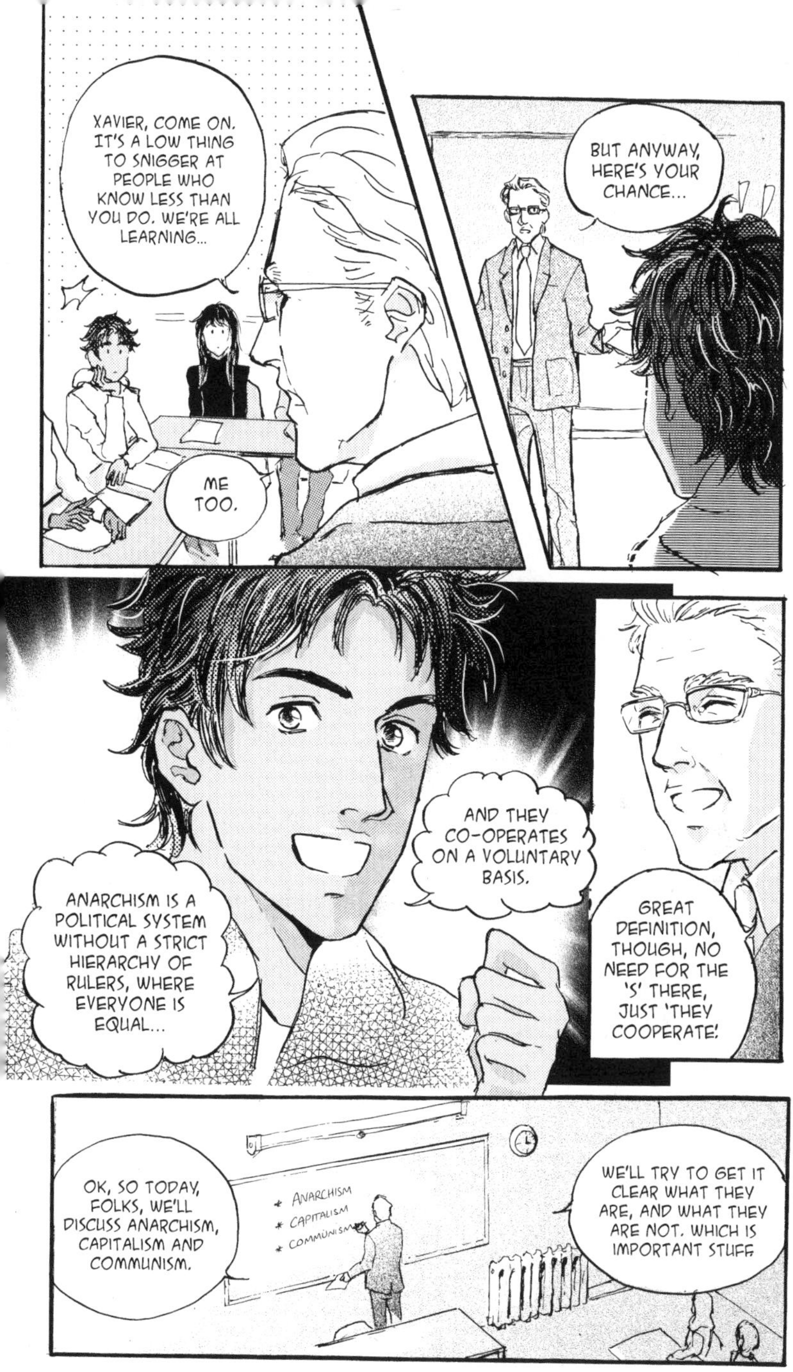
XAVIER, COME ON. IT'S A LOW THING TO SNIGGER AT PEOPLE WHO KNOW LESS THAN YOU DO. WE'RE ALL LEARNING...
ME TOO.
BUT ANYWAY, HERE'S YOUR CHANCE...
ANARCHISM IS A POLITICAL SYSTEM WITHOUT A STRICT HIERARCHY OF RULERS, WHERE EVERYONE IS EQUAL...
AND THEY CO-OPERATES ON A VOLUNTARY BASIS.
GREAT DEFINITION, THOUGH, NO NEED FOR THE 'S' THERE, JUST 'THEY COOPERATE'.
OK, SO TODAY, FOLKS, WE'LL DISCUSS ANARCHISM, CAPITALISM AND COMMUNISM.
* ANARCHISM
* CAPITALISM
* COMMUNISM
WE'LL TRY TO GET IT CLEAR WHAT THEY ARE, AND WHAT THEY ARE NOT. WHICH IS IMPORTANT STUFF

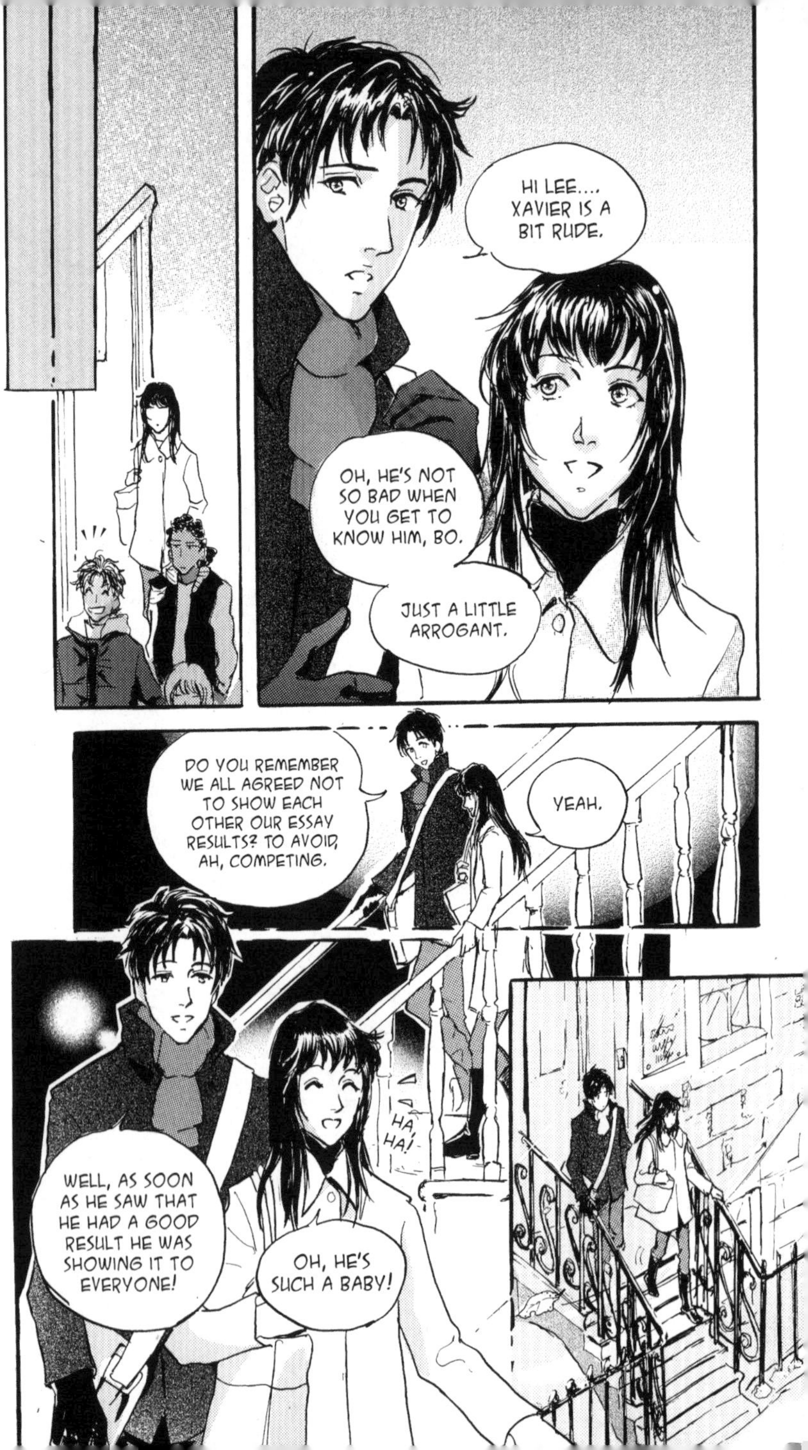
HI LEE.... XAVIER IS A BIT RUDE.
OH, HE'S NOT SO BAD WHEN YOU GET TO KNOW HIM, BO.
JUST A LITTLE ARROGANT.
DO YOU REMEMBER WE ALL AGREED NOT TO SHOW EACH OTHER OUR ESSAY RESULTS? TO AVOID, AH, COMPETING.
YEAH.
WELL, AS SOON AS HE SAW THAT HE HAD A GOOD RESULT HE WAS SHOWING IT TO EVERYONE!
HA, HA!
OH, HE'S SUCH A BABY!

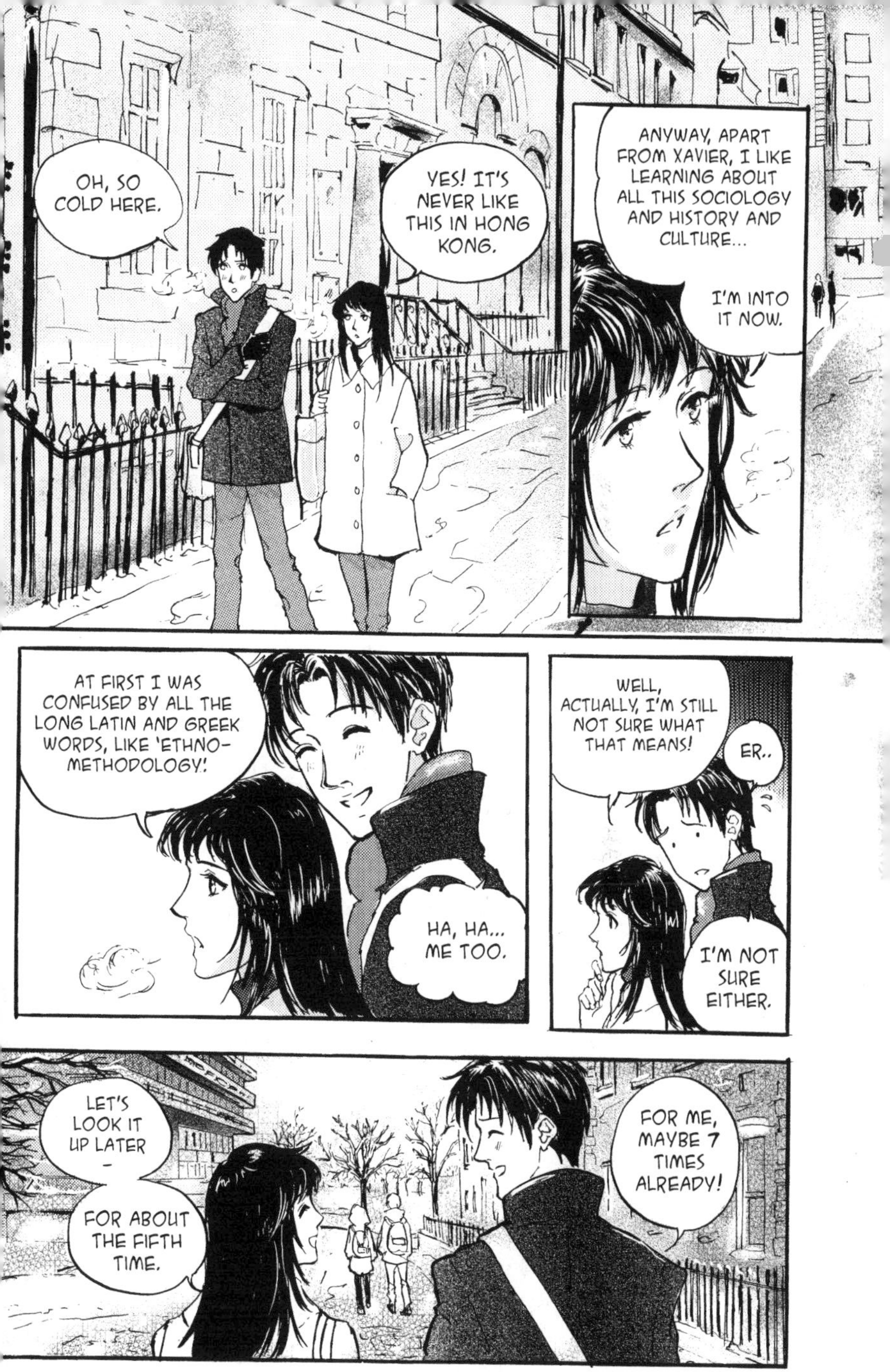
OH, SO COLD HERE.
YES! IT'S NEVER LIKE THIS IN HONG KONG.
ANYWAY, APART FROM XAVIER, I LIKE LEARNING ABOUT ALL THIS SOCIOLOGY AND HISTORY AND CULTURE...
I'M INTO IT NOW.
AT FIRST I WAS CONFUSED BY ALL THE LONG LATIN AND GREEK WORDS, LIKE 'ETHNO-METHODOLOGY'.
HA, HA... ME TOO.
WELL, ACTUALLY, I'M STILL NOT SURE WHAT THAT MEANS!
ER..
I'M NOT SURE EITHER.
LET'S LOOK IT UP LATER -
FOR ABOUT THE FIFTH TIME.
FOR ME, MAYBE 7 TIMES ALREADY!

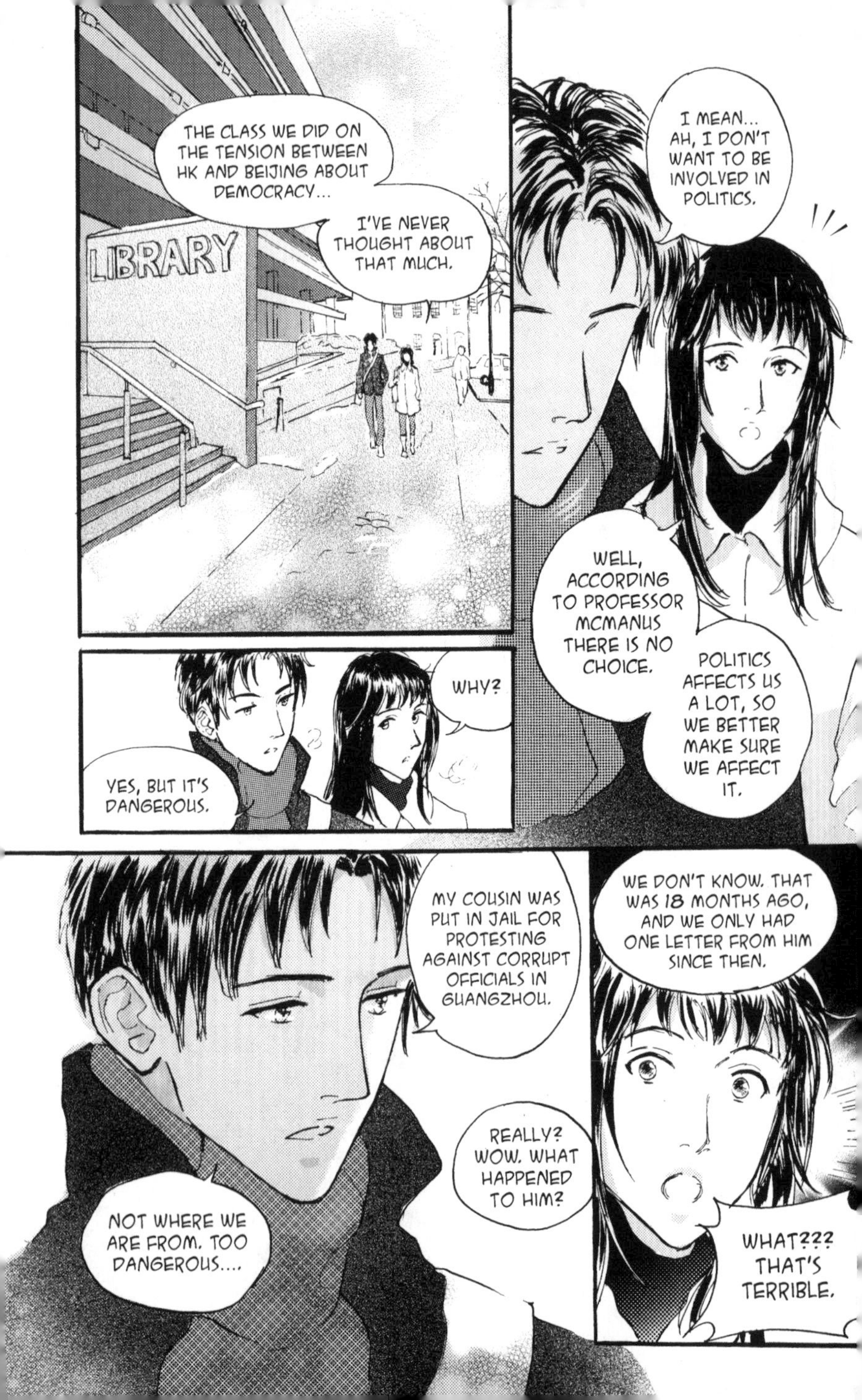
THE CLASS WE DID ON THE TENSION BETWEEN HK AND BEIJING ABOUT DEMOCRACY...
I'VE NEVER THOUGHT ABOUT THAT MUCH.
LIBRARY
I MEAN... AH, I DON'T WANT TO BE INVOLVED IN POLITICS.
WHY?
YES, BUT IT'S DANGEROUS.
WELL, ACCORDING TO PROFESSOR MCMANUS THERE IS NO CHOICE.
POLITICS AFFECTS US A LOT, SO WE BETTER MAKE SURE WE AFFECT IT.
NOT WHERE WE ARE FROM. TOO DANGEROUS....
MY COUSIN WAS PUT IN JAIL FOR PROTESTING AGAINST CORRUPT OFFICIALS IN GUANGZHOU.
WHAT??? THAT'S TERRIBLE.
REALLY? WOW. WHAT HAPPENED TO HIM?
WE DON'T KNOW. THAT WAS 18 MONTHS AGO, AND WE ONLY HAD ONE LETTER FROM HIM SINCE THEN.

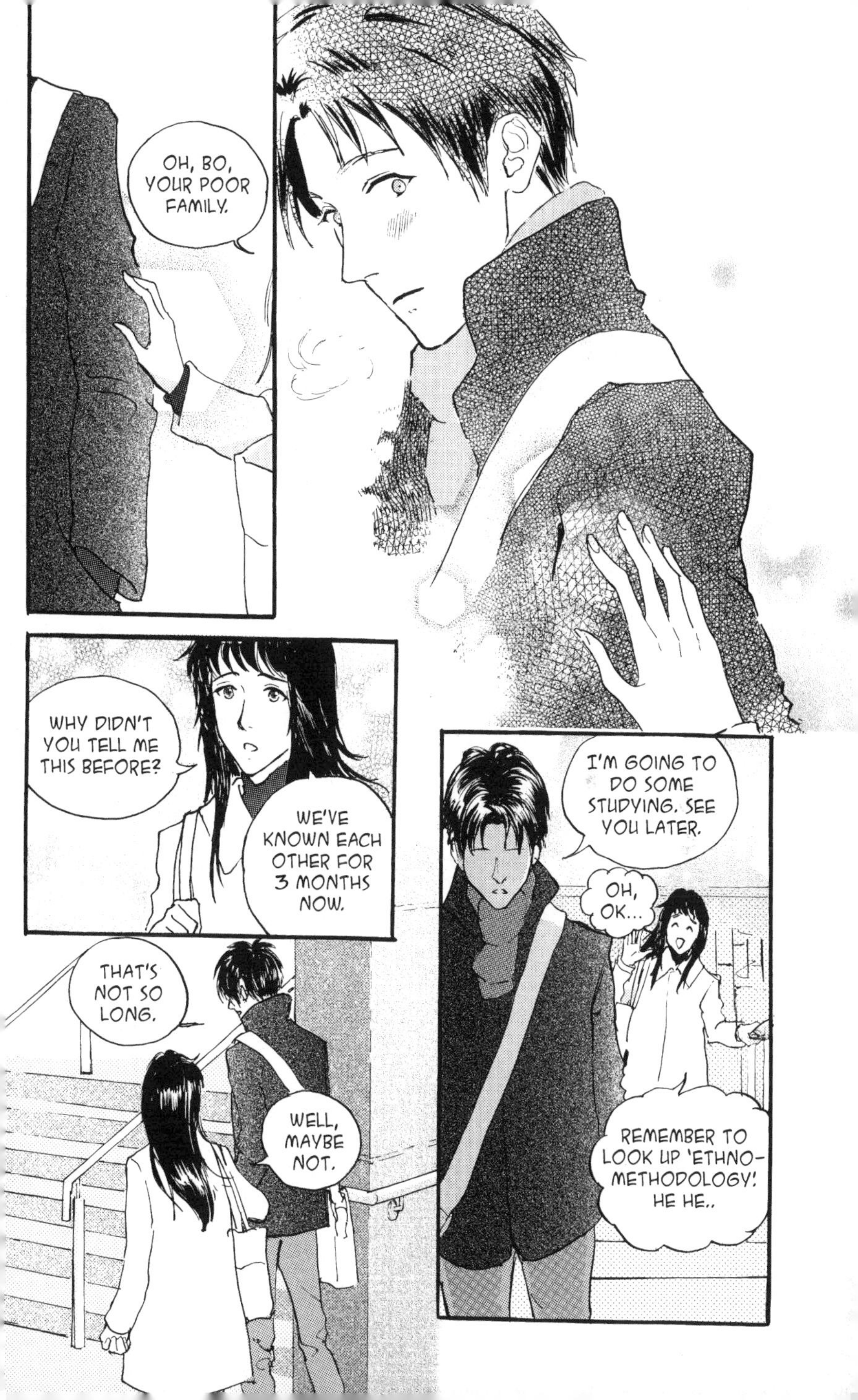
OH, BO, YOUR POOR FAMILY.
WHY DIDN'T YOU TELL ME THIS BEFORE?
WE'VE KNOWN EACH OTHER FOR 3 MONTHS NOW.
THAT'S NOT SO LONG.
WELL, MAYBE NOT.
I'M GOING TO DO SOME STUDYING. SEE YOU LATER.
OH, OK...
REMEMBER TO LOOK UP 'ETHNO-METHODOLOGY'! HE HE..

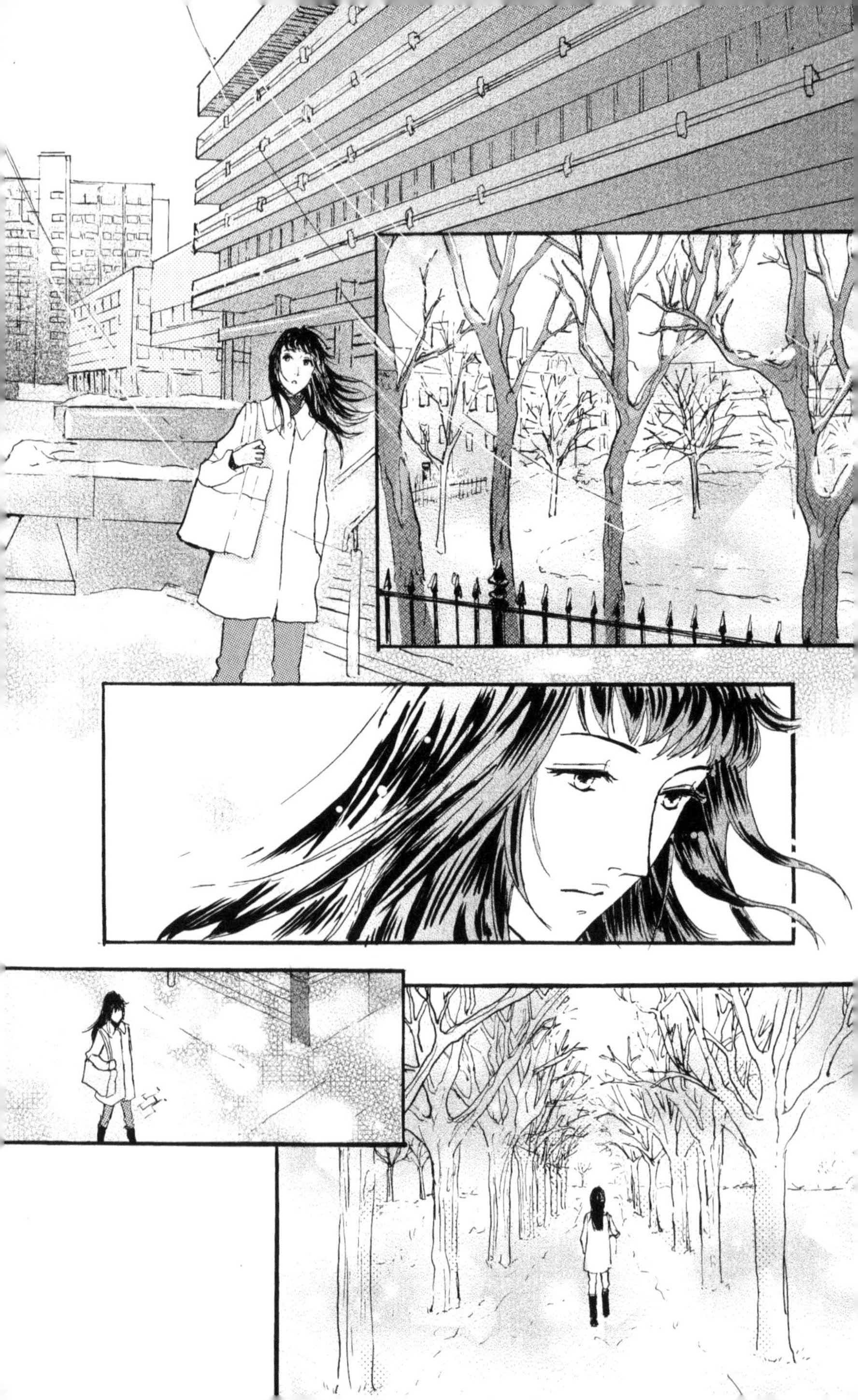

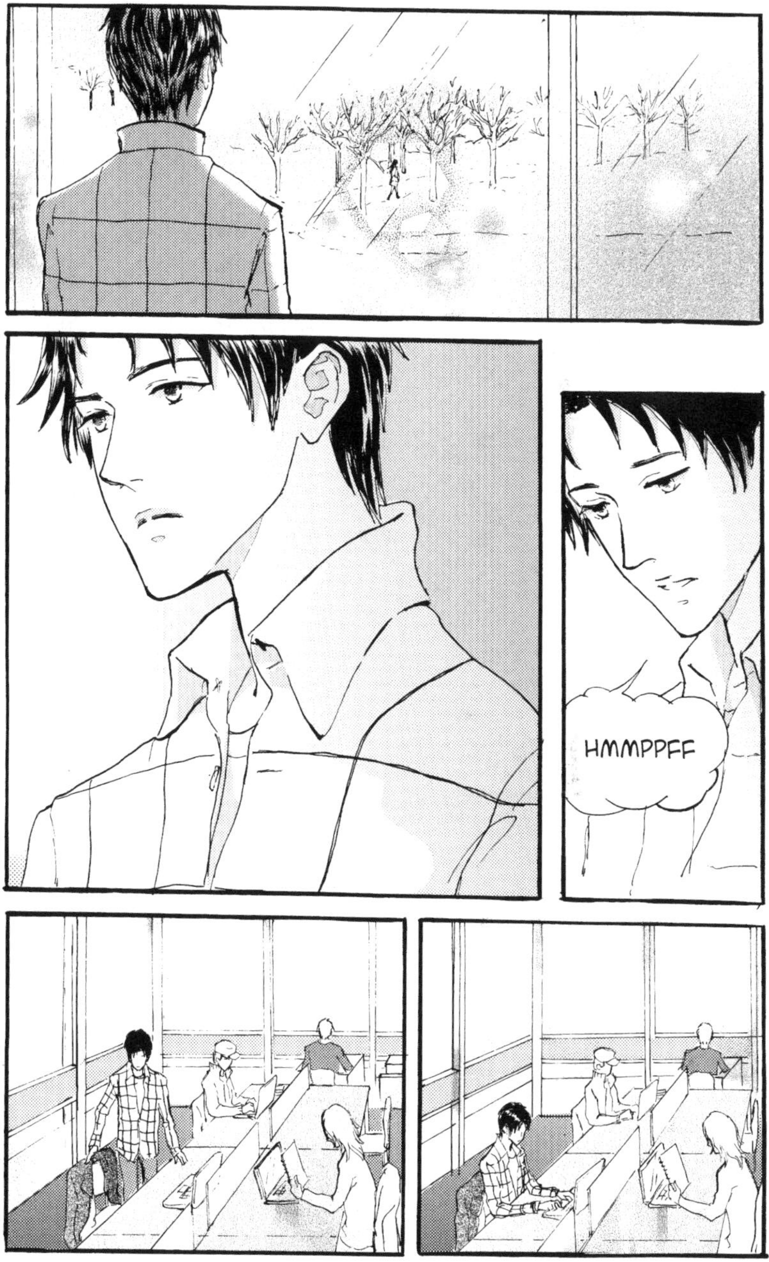
HMMPPFF

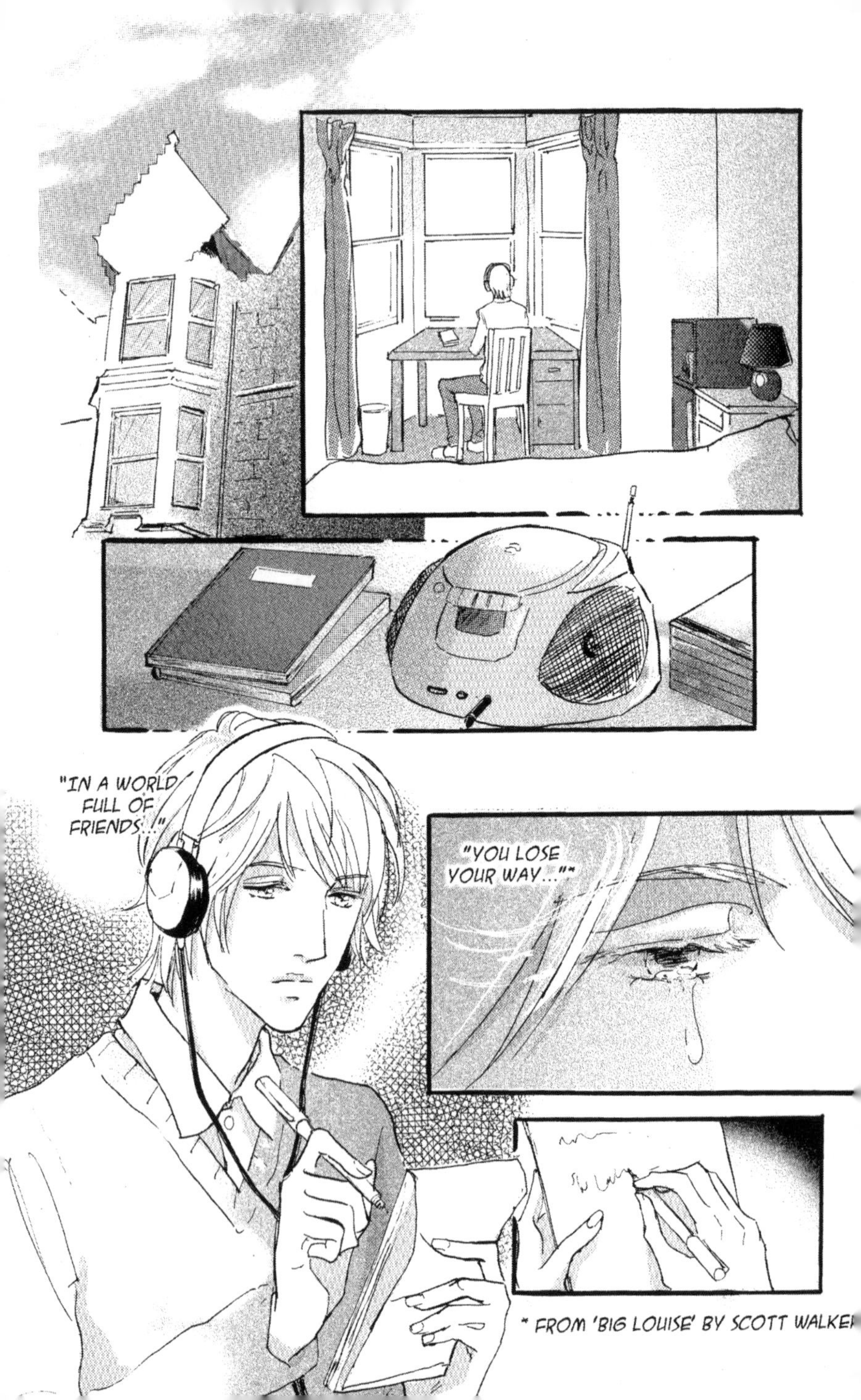
"IN A WORLD FULL OF FRIENDS..."
"YOU LOSE YOUR WAY..."*
* FROM 'BIG LOUISE' BY SCOTT WALKER

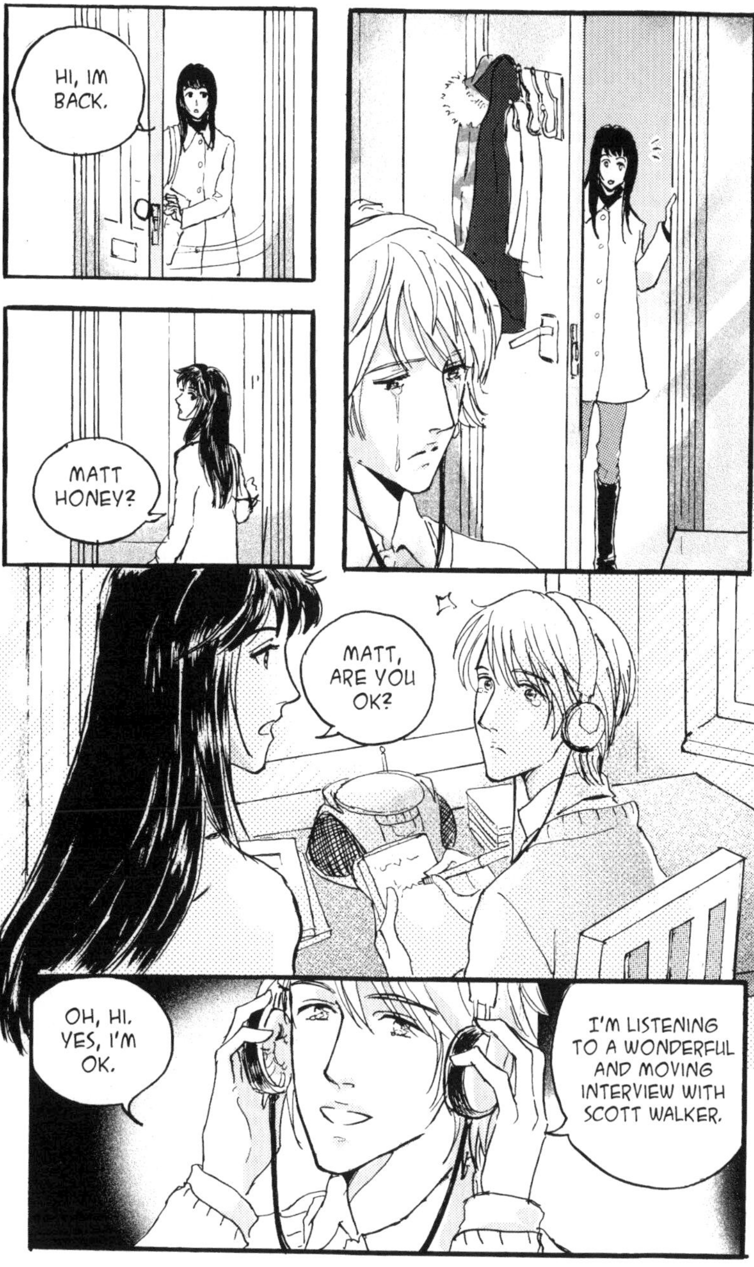
HI, IM BACK.
MATT HONEY?
MATT, ARE YOU OK?
OH, HI. YES, I'M OK.
I'M LISTENING TO A WONDERFUL AND MOVING INTERVIEW WITH SCOTT WALKER.

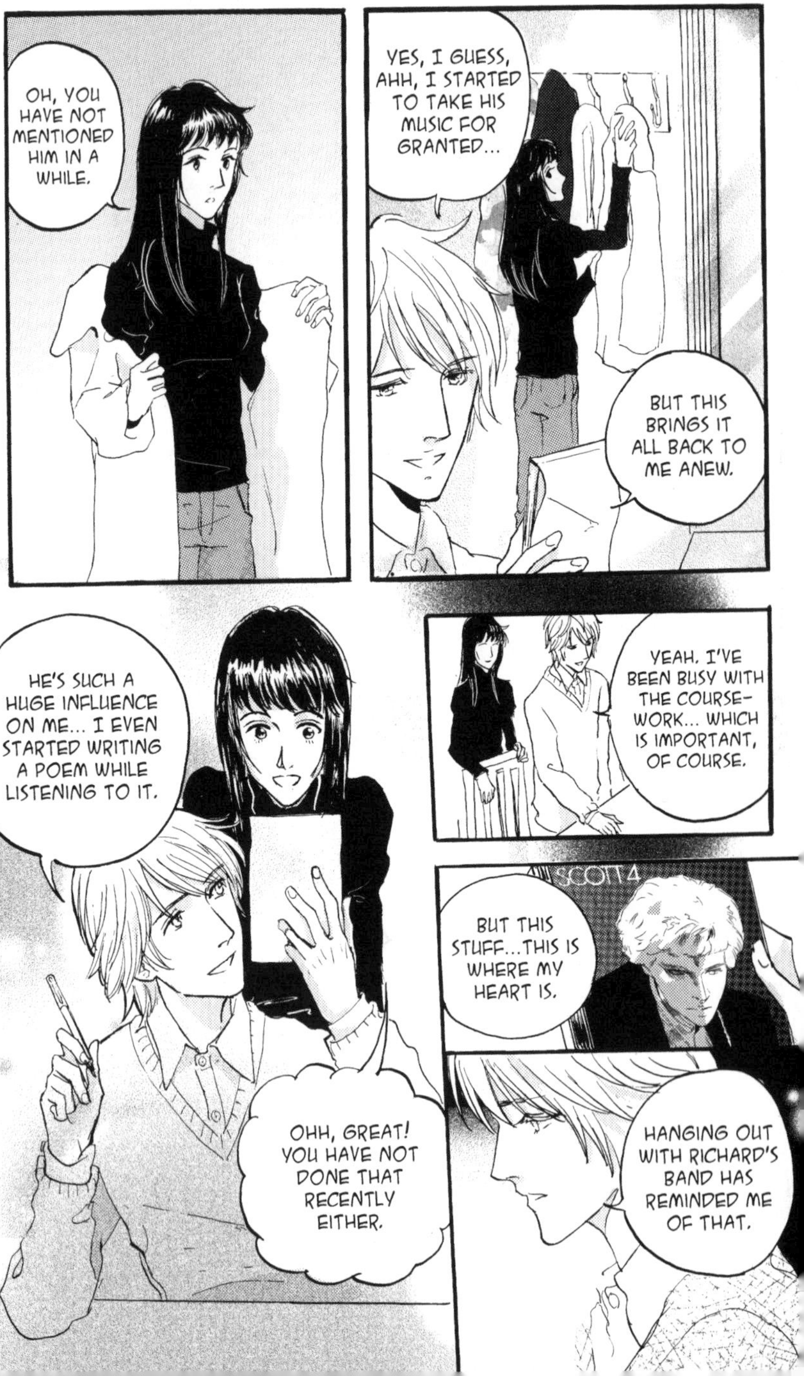
OH, YOU HAVE NOT MENTIONED HIM IN A WHILE.
YES, I GUESS, AHH, I STARTED TO TAKE HIS MUSIC FOR GRANTED...
BUT THIS BRINGS IT ALL BACK TO ME ANEW.
HE'S SUCH A HUGE INFLUENCE ON ME... I EVEN STARTED WRITING A POEM WHILE LISTENING TO IT.
OHH, GREAT! YOU HAVE NOT DONE THAT RECENTLY EITHER.
YEAH. I'VE BEEN BUSY WITH THE COURSE-WORK... WHICH IS IMPORTANT, OF COURSE.
SCOTT 4
BUT THIS STUFF...THIS IS WHERE MY HEART IS.
HANGING OUT WITH RICHARD'S BAND HAS REMINDED ME OF THAT.

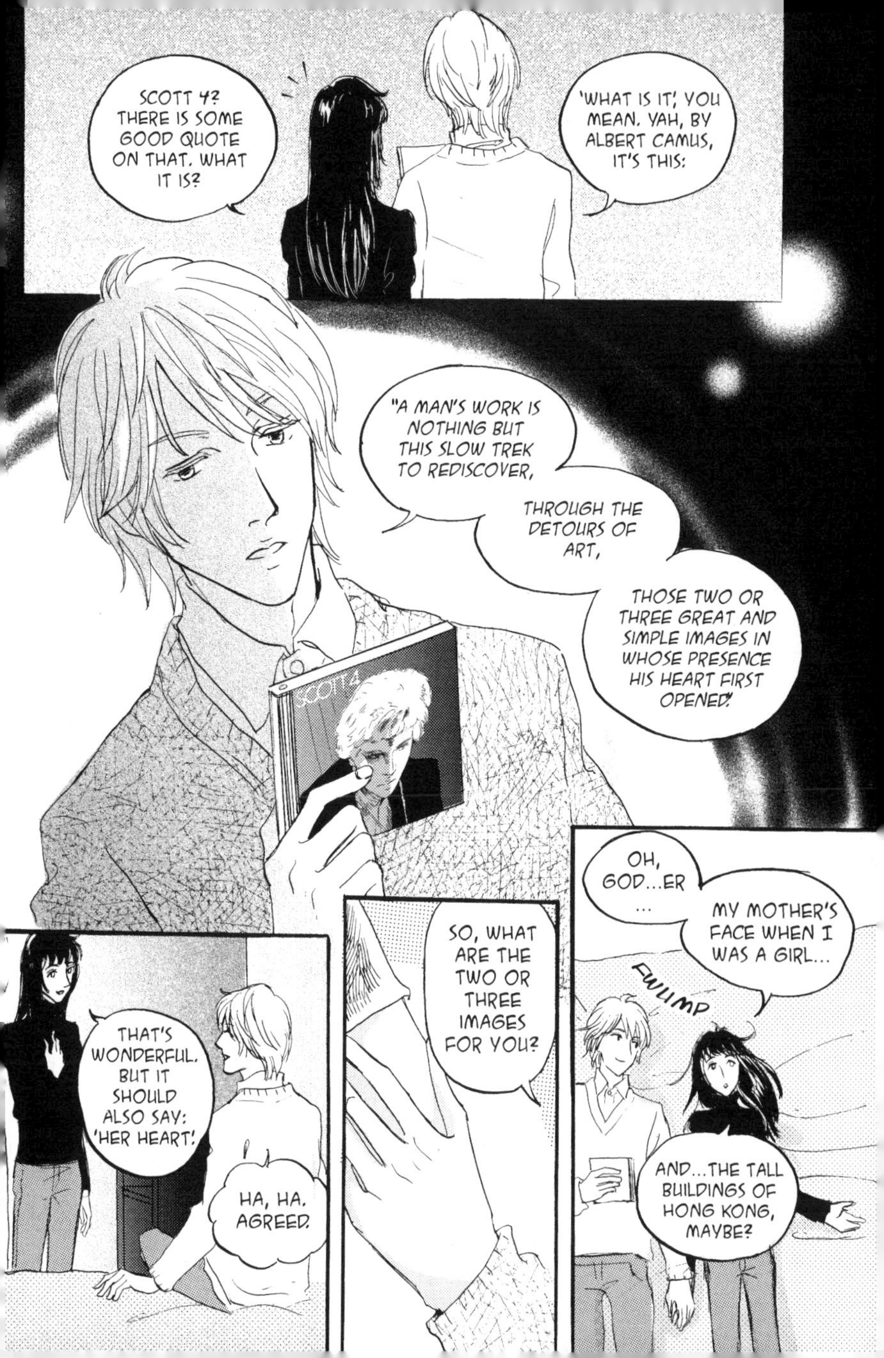
SCOTT 4? THERE IS SOME GOOD QUOTE ON THAT. WHAT IT IS?
'WHAT IS IT,' YOU MEAN. YAH, BY ALBERT CAMUS, IT'S THIS:
"A MAN'S WORK IS NOTHING BUT THIS SLOW TREK TO REDISCOVER,
THROUGH THE DETOURS OF ART,
THOSE TWO OR THREE GREAT AND SIMPLE IMAGES IN WHOSE PRESENCE HIS HEART FIRST OPENED."
SCOTT 4
THAT'S WONDERFUL. BUT IT SHOULD ALSO SAY: 'HER HEART.'
HA, HA. AGREED.
SO, WHAT ARE THE TWO OR THREE IMAGES FOR YOU?
OH, GOD...ER ...
MY MOTHER'S FACE WHEN I WAS A GIRL...
FWUMP
AND...THE TALL BUILDINGS OF HONG KONG, MAYBE?

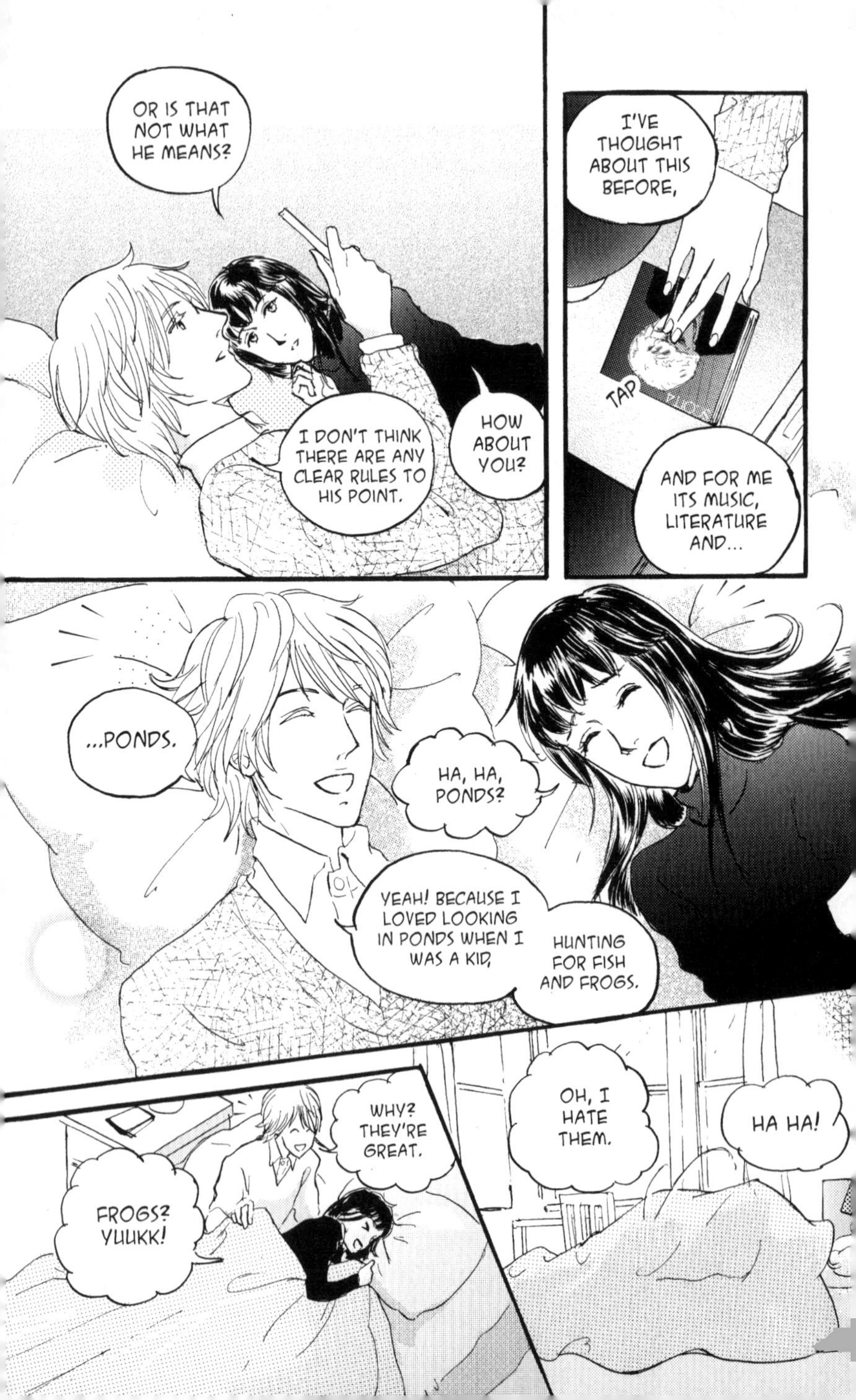
OR IS THAT NOT WHAT HE MEANS?
I DON'T THINK THERE ARE ANY CLEAR RULES TO HIS POINT.
HOW ABOUT YOU?
I'VE THOUGHT ABOUT THIS BEFORE,
TAP
AND FOR ME ITS MUSIC, LITERATURE AND...
...PONDS.
HA, HA, PONDS?
YEAH! BECAUSE I LOVED LOOKING IN PONDS WHEN I WAS A KID,
HUNTING FOR FISH AND FROGS.
FROGS? YUUKK!
WHY? THEY'RE GREAT.
OH, I HATE THEM.
HA HA!

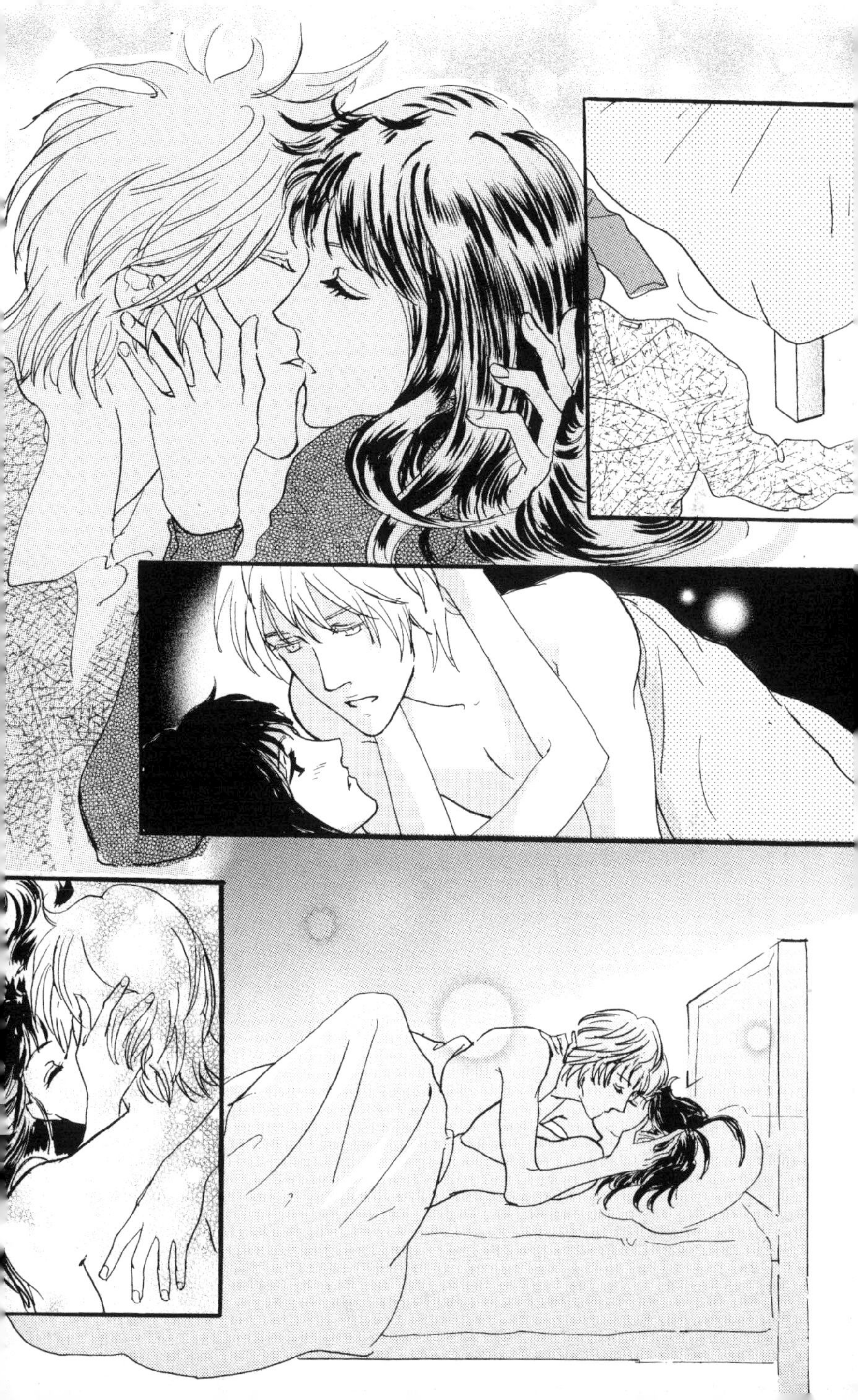

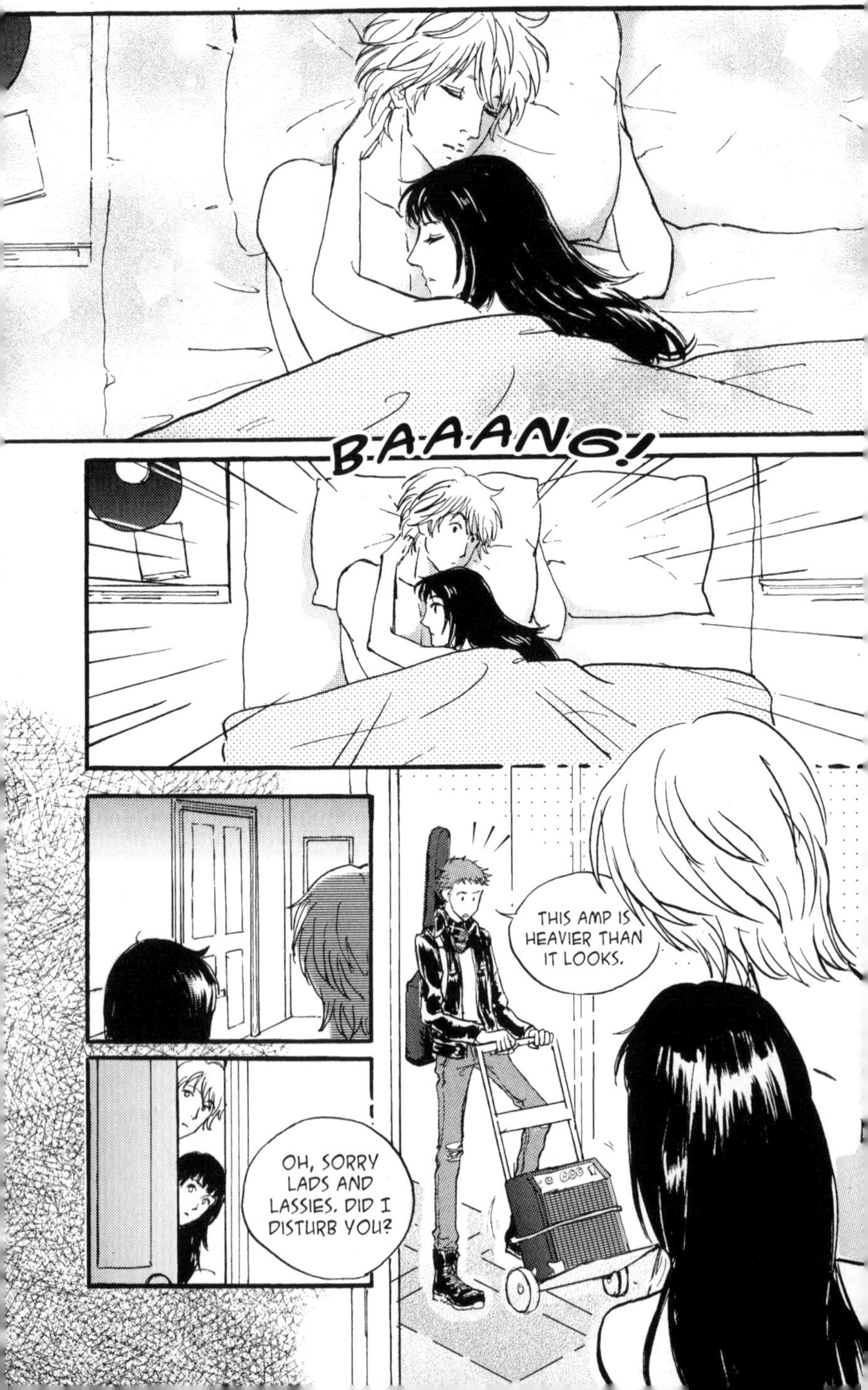
BAAANG!
THIS AMP IS HEAVIER THAN IT LOOKS.
OH, SORRY LADS AND LASSIES. DID I DISTURB YOU?

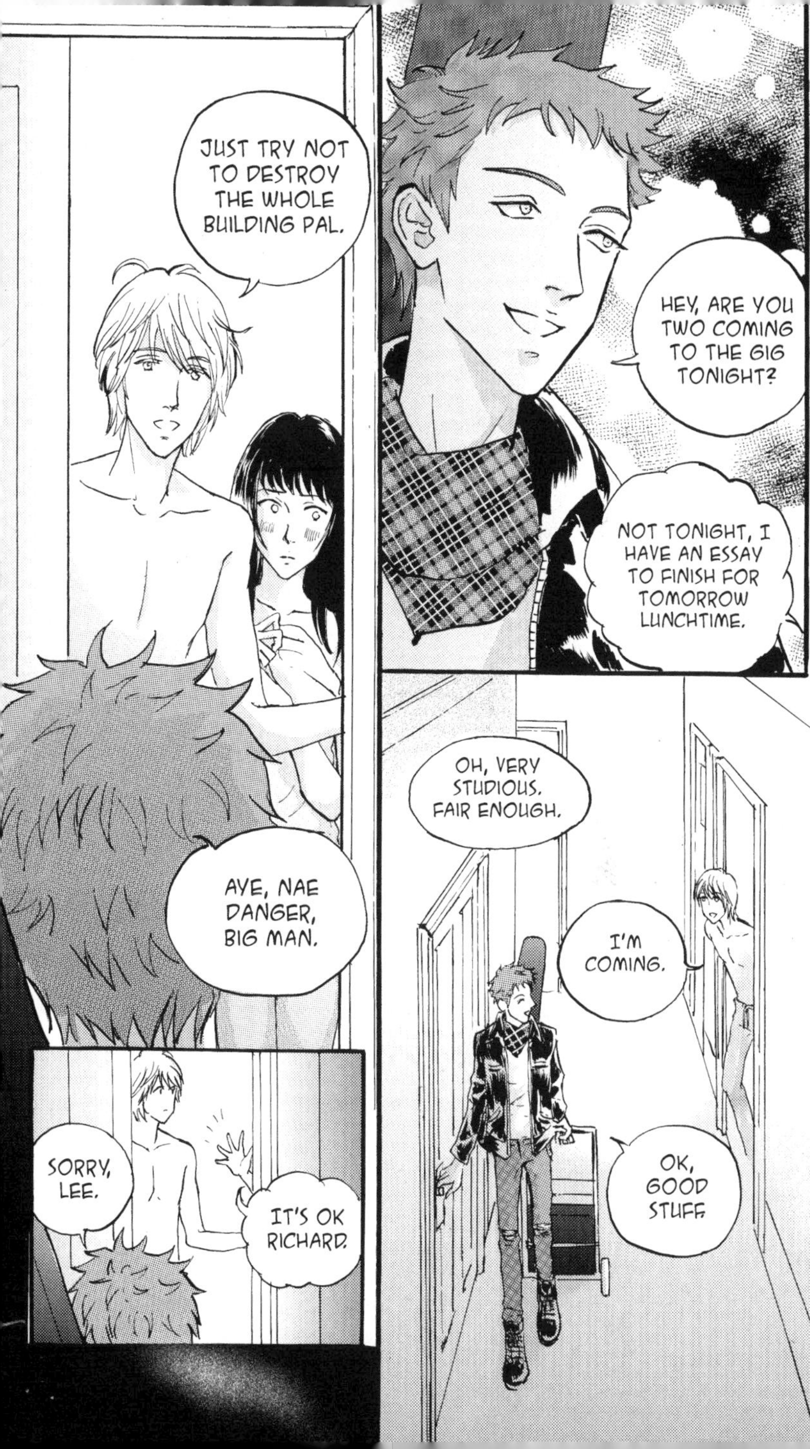
JUST TRY NOT TO DESTROY THE WHOLE BUILDING PAL.
AYE, NAE DANGER, BIG MAN.
SORRY, LEE.
IT'S OK RICHARD.
HEY, ARE YOU TWO COMING TO THE GIG TONIGHT?
NOT TONIGHT, I HAVE AN ESSAY TO FINISH FOR TOMORROW LUNCHTIME.
OH, VERY STUDIOUS. FAIR ENOUGH.
I'M COMING.
OK, GOOD STUFF.

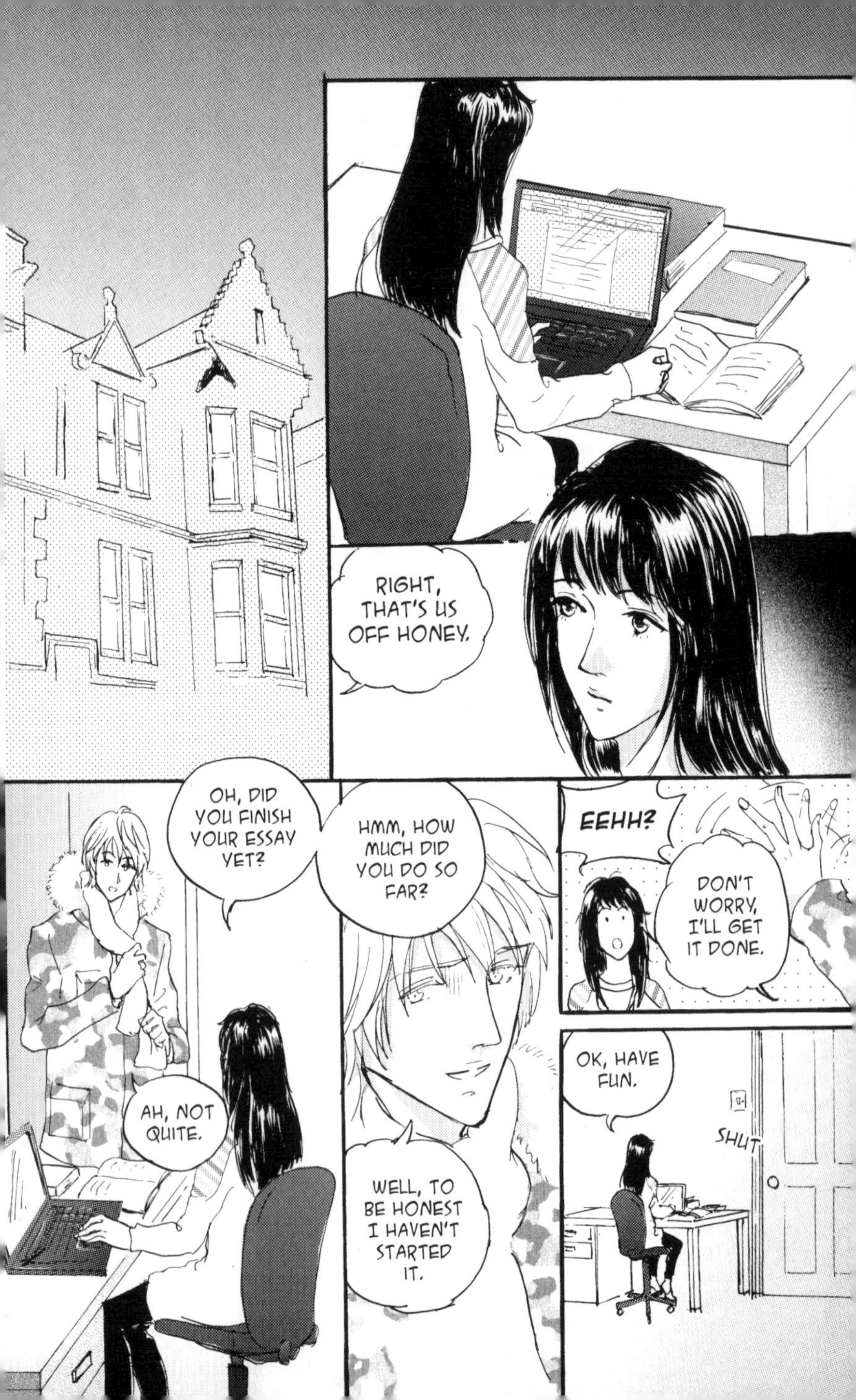
RIGHT, THAT'S US OFF HONEY.
OH, DID YOU FINISH YOUR ESSAY YET?
AH, NOT QUITE.
HMM, HOW MUCH DID YOU DO SO FAR?
WELL, TO BE HONEST I HAVEN'T STARTED IT.
EEHH?
DON'T WORRY, I'LL GET IT DONE.
OK, HAVE FUN.
SHUT

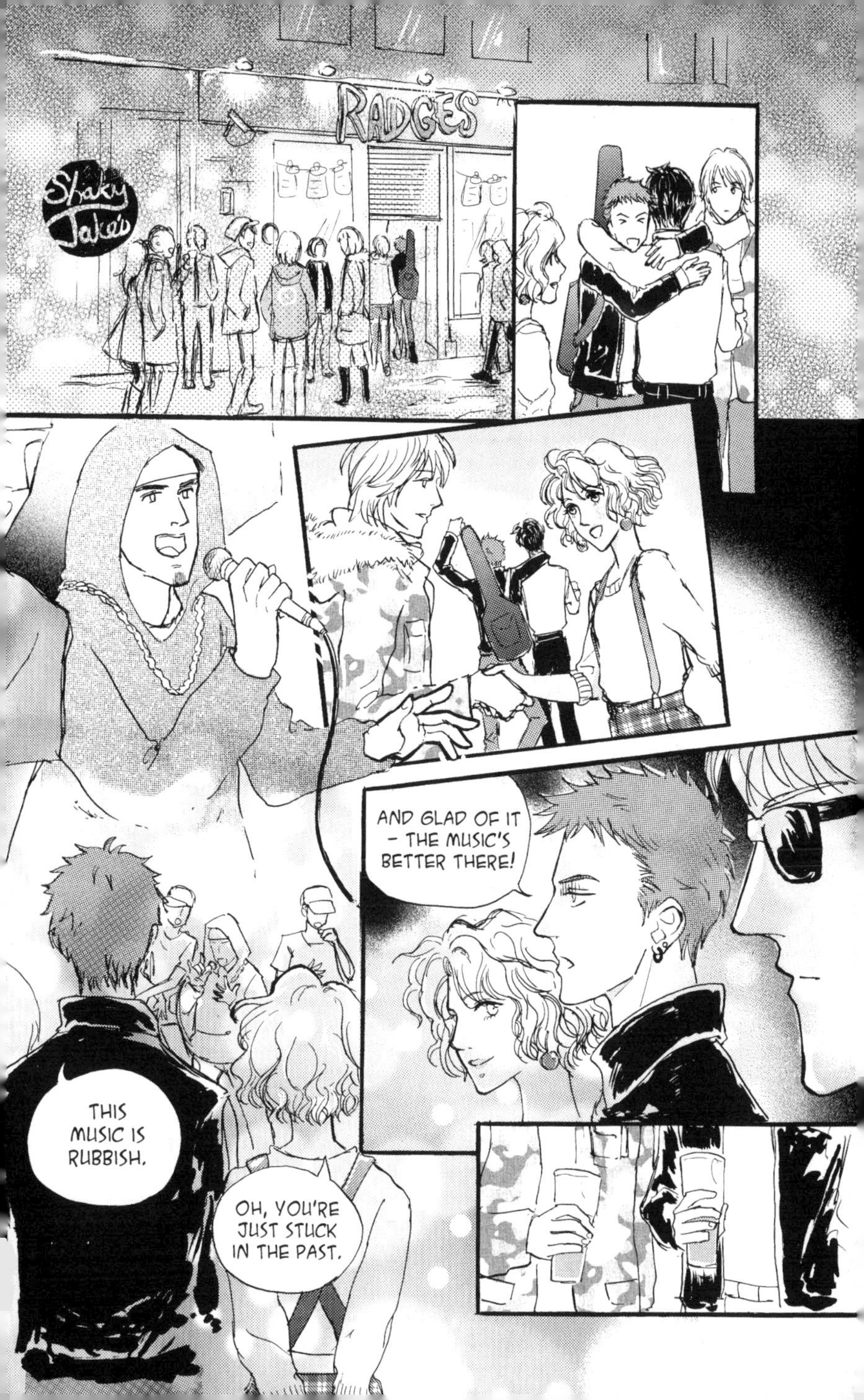
RADGES
Shaky Jake's
THIS MUSIC IS RUBBISH.
OH, YOU'RE JUST STUCK IN THE PAST.
AND GLAD OF IT - THE MUSIC'S BETTER THERE!

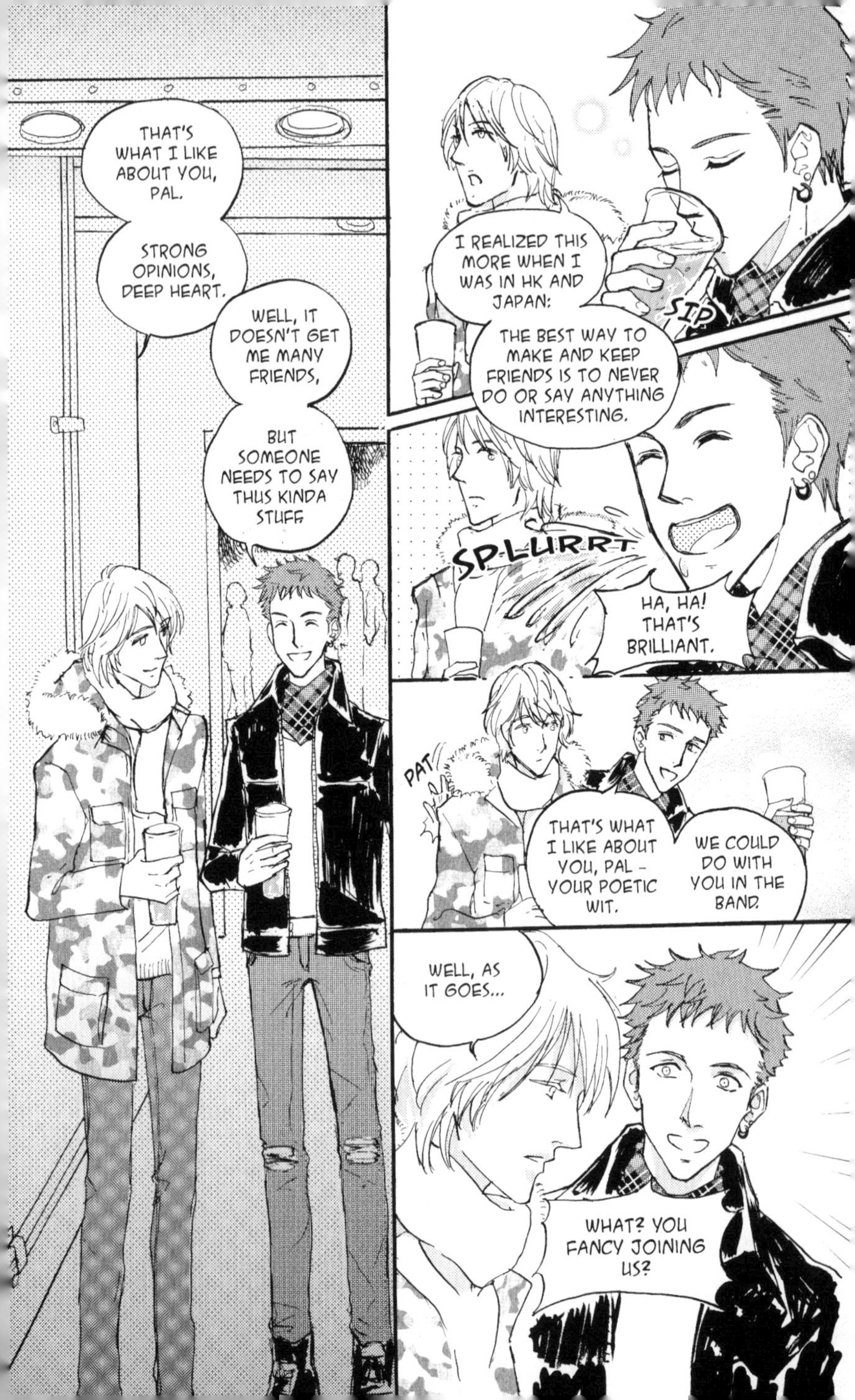
THAT'S WHAT I LIKE ABOUT YOU, PAL.
STRONG OPINIONS, DEEP HEART.
WELL, IT DOESN'T GET ME MANY FRIENDS,
BUT SOMEONE NEEDS TO SAY THUS KINDA STUFF.
I REALIZED THIS MORE WHEN I WAS IN HK AND JAPAN:
SIP
THE BEST WAY TO MAKE AND KEEP FRIENDS IS TO NEVER DO OR SAY ANYTHING INTERESTING.
SPLURRT
HA, HA! THAT'S BRILLIANT.
PAT
THAT'S WHAT I LIKE ABOUT YOU, PAL - YOUR POETIC WIT.
WE COULD DO WITH YOU IN THE BAND.
WELL, AS IT GOES...
WHAT? YOU FANCY JOINING US?

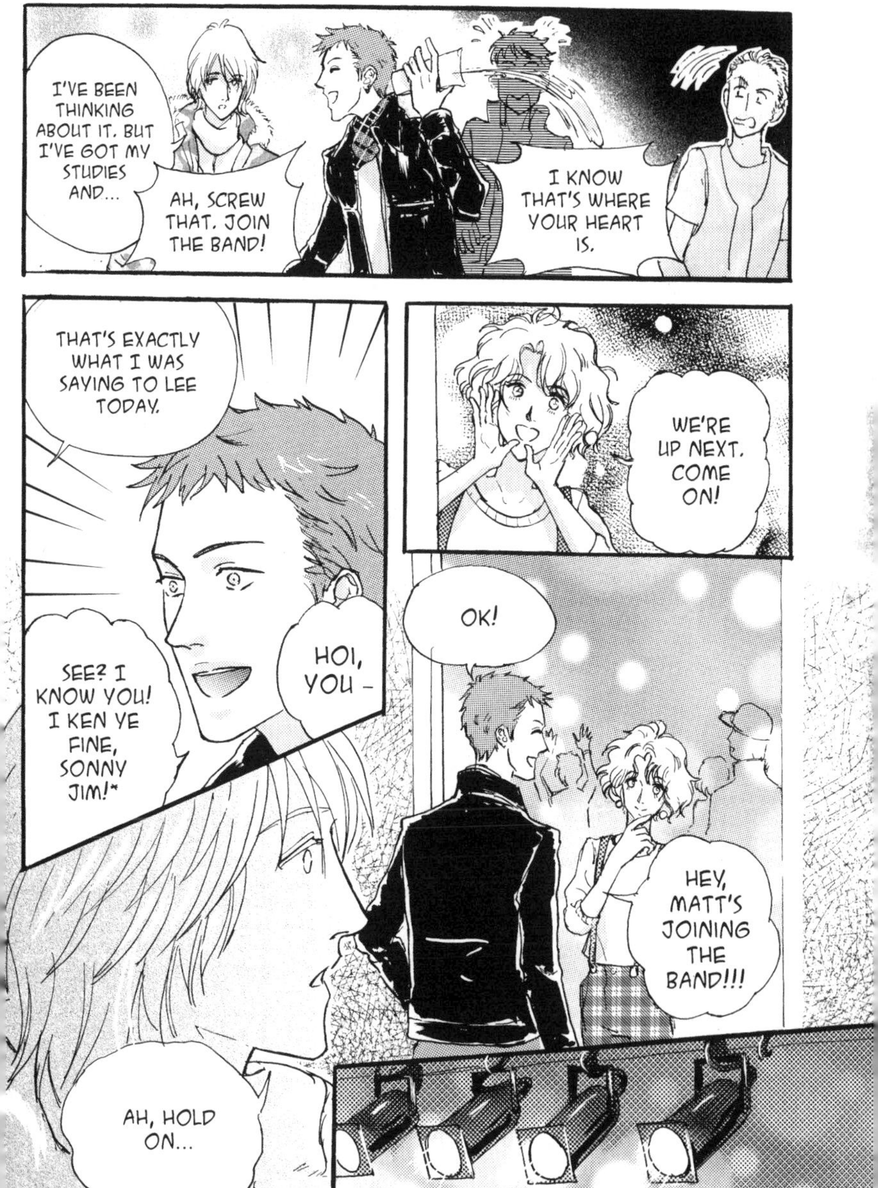
I'VE BEEN THINKING ABOUT IT. BUT I'VE GOT MY STUDIES AND...
AH, SCREW THAT. JOIN THE BAND!
I KNOW THAT'S WHERE YOUR HEART IS.
THAT'S EXACTLY WHAT I WAS SAYING TO LEE TODAY.
WE'RE UP NEXT. COME ON!
SEE? I KNOW YOU! I KEN YE FINE, SONNY JIM!*
HOI, YOU –
OK!
HEY, MATT'S JOINING THE BAND!!!
AH, HOLD ON...

*"I KEN YE FINE" A SCOTS PHRASE WHICH MEANS I UNDERSTAND YOUR PERSONALITY.

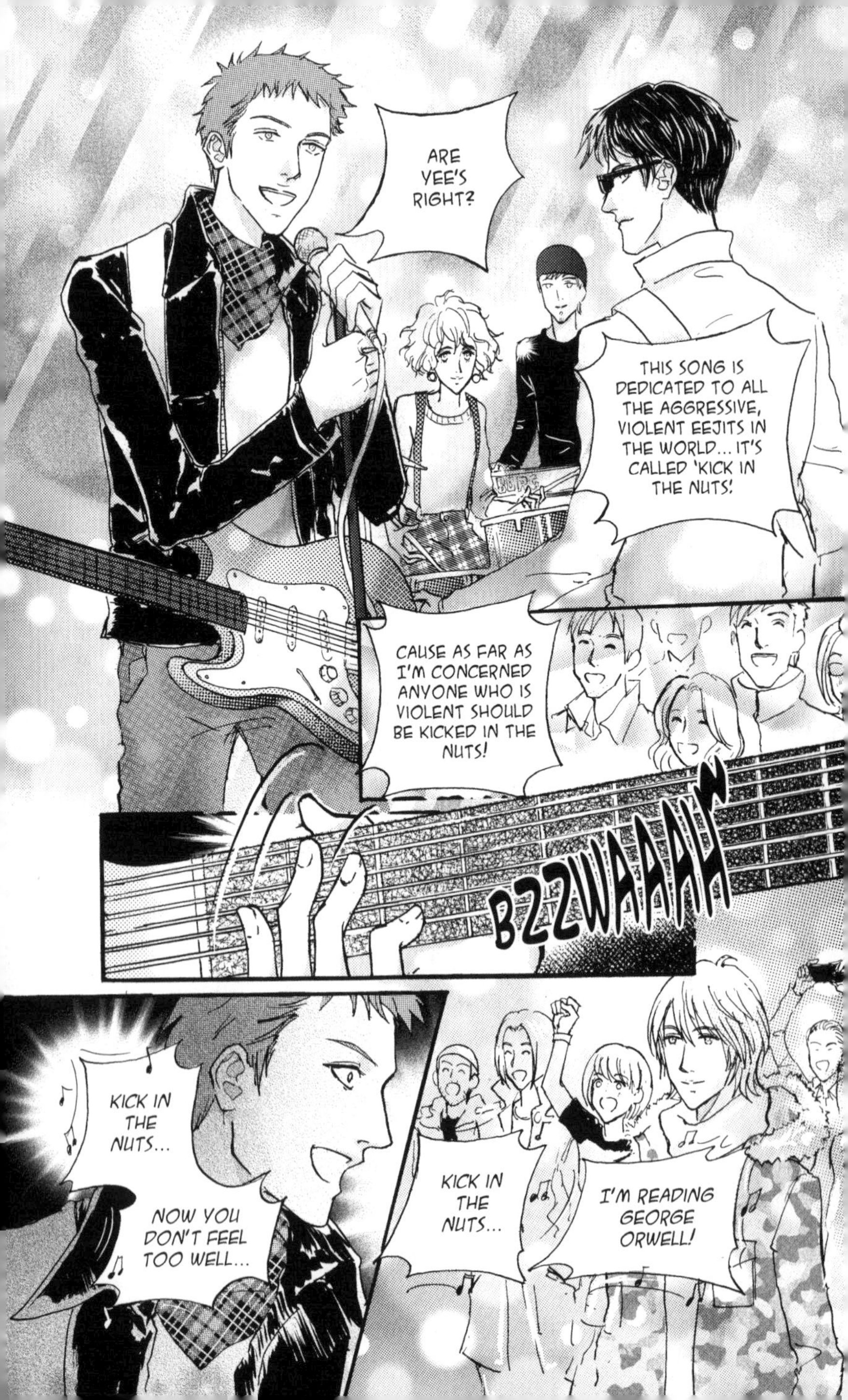

ARE YEE'S RIGHT?
THIS SONG IS DEDICATED TO ALL THE AGGRESSIVE, VIOLENT EEJITS IN THE WORLD... IT'S CALLED 'KICK IN THE NUTS!
CAUSE AS FAR AS I'M CONCERNED ANYONE WHO IS VIOLENT SHOULD BE KICKED IN THE NUTS!
BZZWAAAH
KICK IN THE NUTS...
NOW YOU DON'T FEEL TOO WELL...
KICK IN THE NUTS...
I'M READING GEORGE ORWELL!

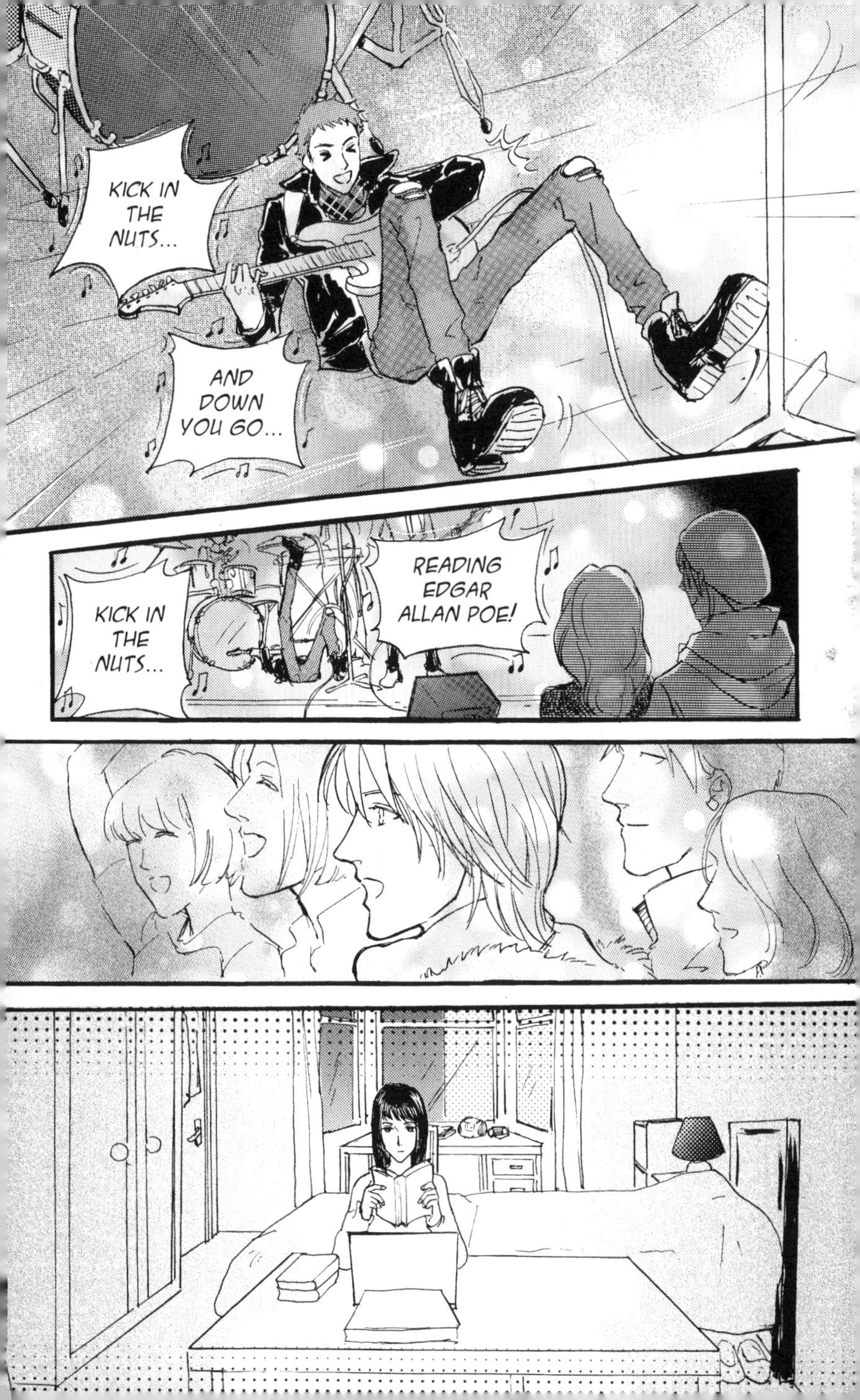
KICK IN THE NUTS...
AND DOWN YOU GO...
READING EDGAR ALLAN POE!
KICK IN THE NUTS...

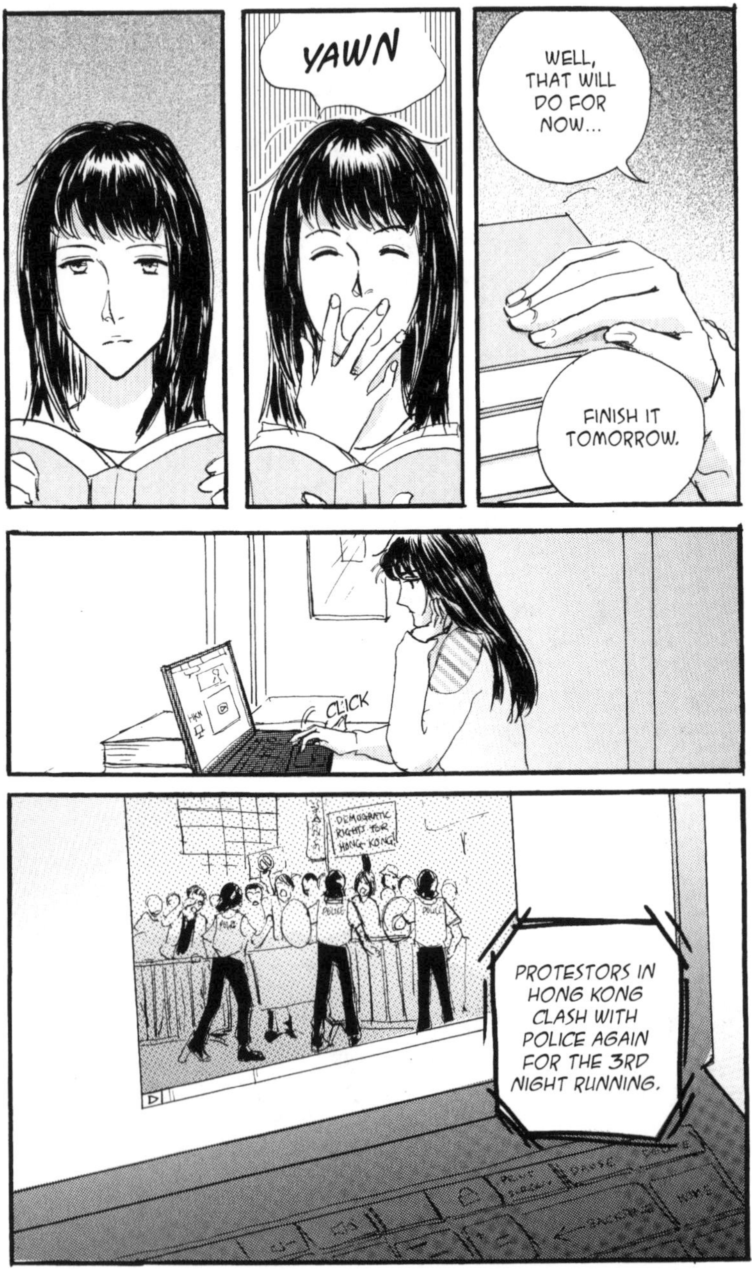
YAWN
WELL, THAT WILL DO FOR NOW...
FINISH IT TOMORROW.
CLICK
DEMOCRATIC RIGHTS FOR HONG KONG!
PROTESTORS IN HONG KONG CLASH WITH POLICE AGAIN FOR THE 3RD NIGHT RUNNING.

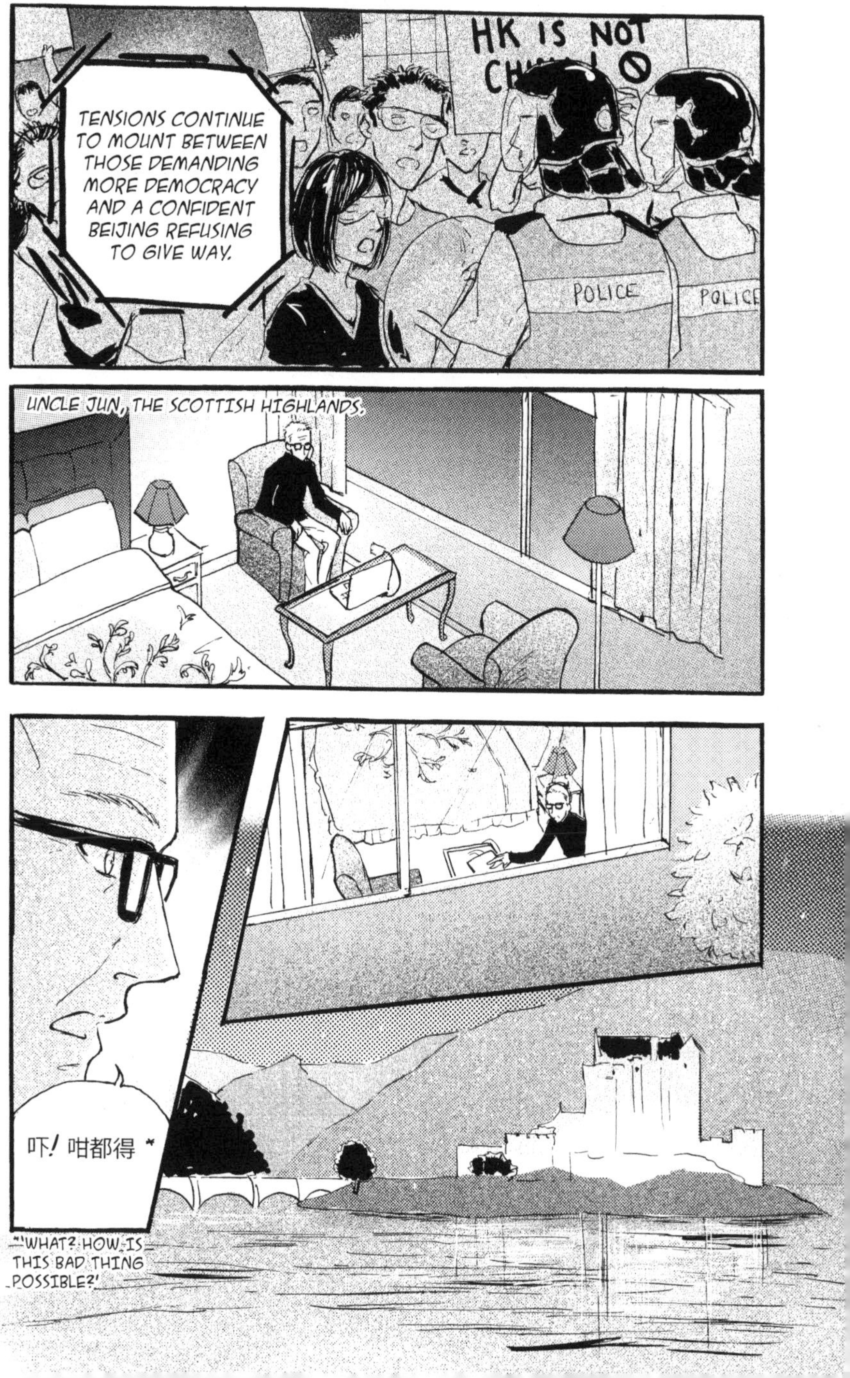
HK IS NOT
TENSIONS CONTINUE TO MOUNT BETWEEN THOSE DEMANDING MORE DEMOCRACY AND A CONFIDENT BEIJING REFUSING TO GIVE WAY.
POLICE
POLICE
UNCLE JUN, THE SCOTTISH HIGHLANDS.
吓! 咁都得 *
*'WHAT? HOW IS THIS BAD THING POSSIBLE?'

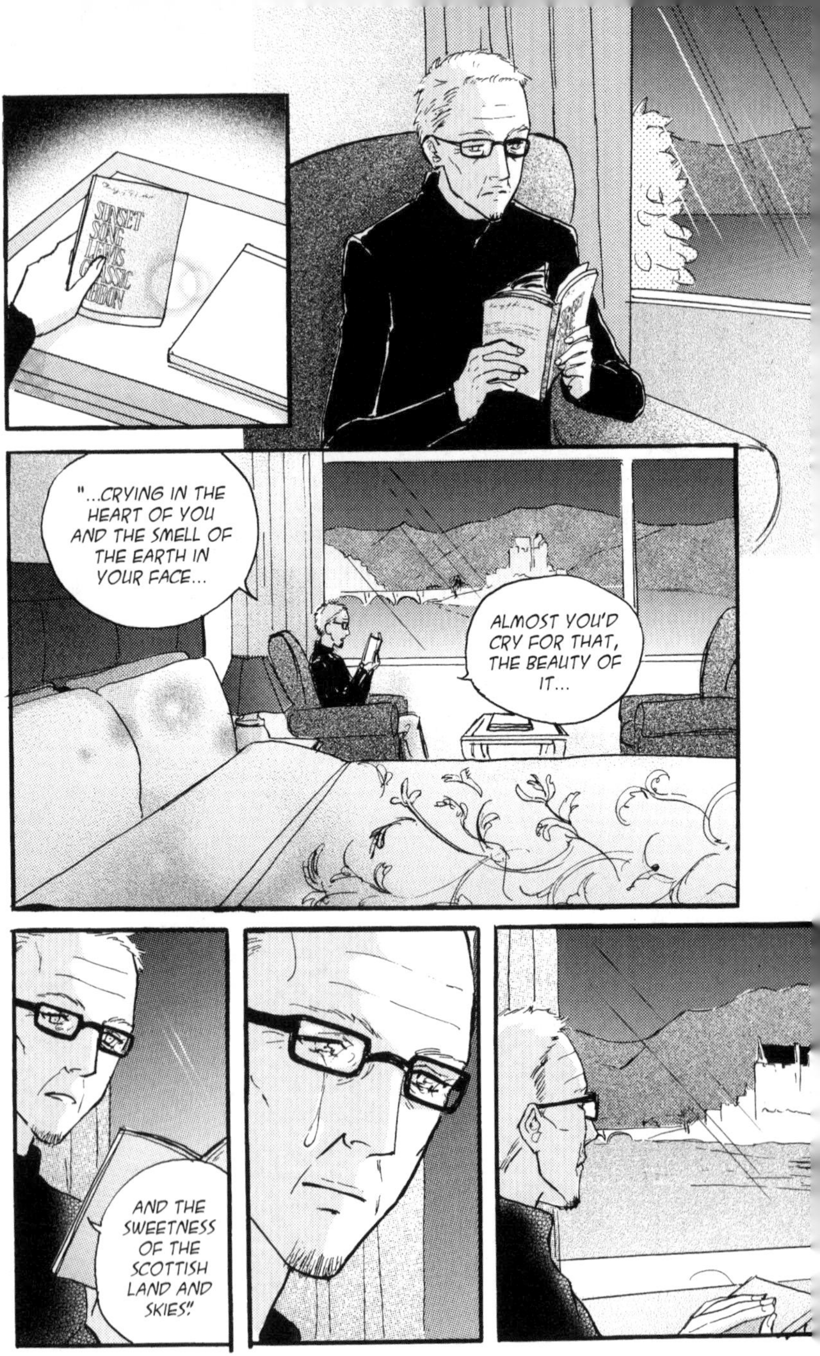
SUNSET SONG LEWIS GRASSIC GIBBON
"...CRYING IN THE HEART OF YOU AND THE SMELL OF THE EARTH IN YOUR FACE...
ALMOST YOU'D CRY FOR THAT, THE BEAUTY OF IT...
AND THE SWEETNESS OF THE SCOTTISH LAND AND SKIES."

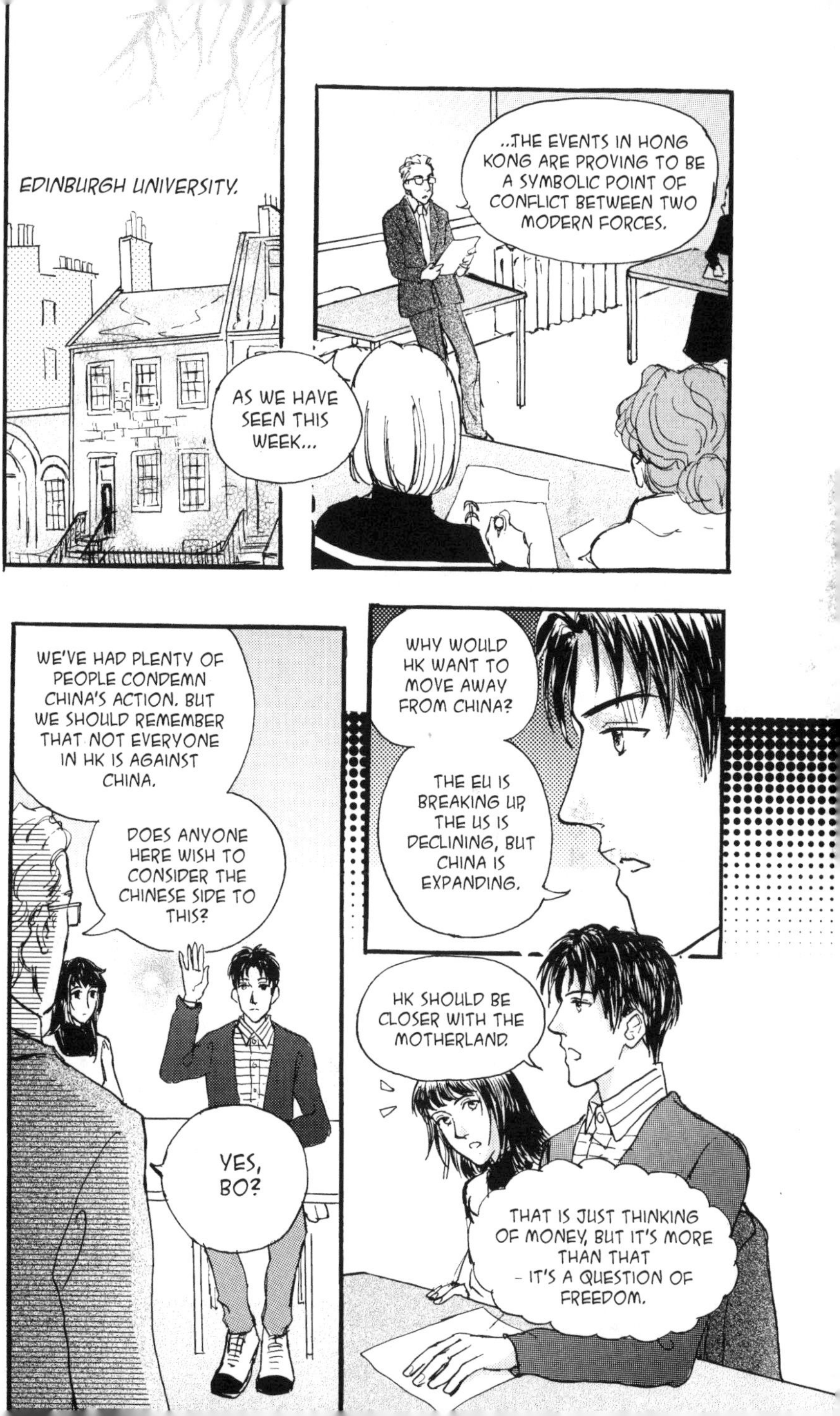
EDINBURGH UNIVERSITY.
..THE EVENTS IN HONG KONG ARE PROVING TO BE A SYMBOLIC POINT OF CONFLICT BETWEEN TWO MODERN FORCES.
AS WE HAVE SEEN THIS WEEK...
WE'VE HAD PLENTY OF PEOPLE CONDEMN CHINA'S ACTION. BUT WE SHOULD REMEMBER THAT NOT EVERYONE IN HK IS AGAINST CHINA.
DOES ANYONE HERE WISH TO CONSIDER THE CHINESE SIDE TO THIS?
YES, BO?
WHY WOULD HK WANT TO MOVE AWAY FROM CHINA?
THE EU IS BREAKING UP, THE US IS DECLINING, BUT CHINA IS EXPANDING.
HK SHOULD BE CLOSER WITH THE MOTHERLAND.
THAT IS JUST THINKING OF MONEY, BUT IT'S MORE THAN THAT - IT'S A QUESTION OF FREEDOM.

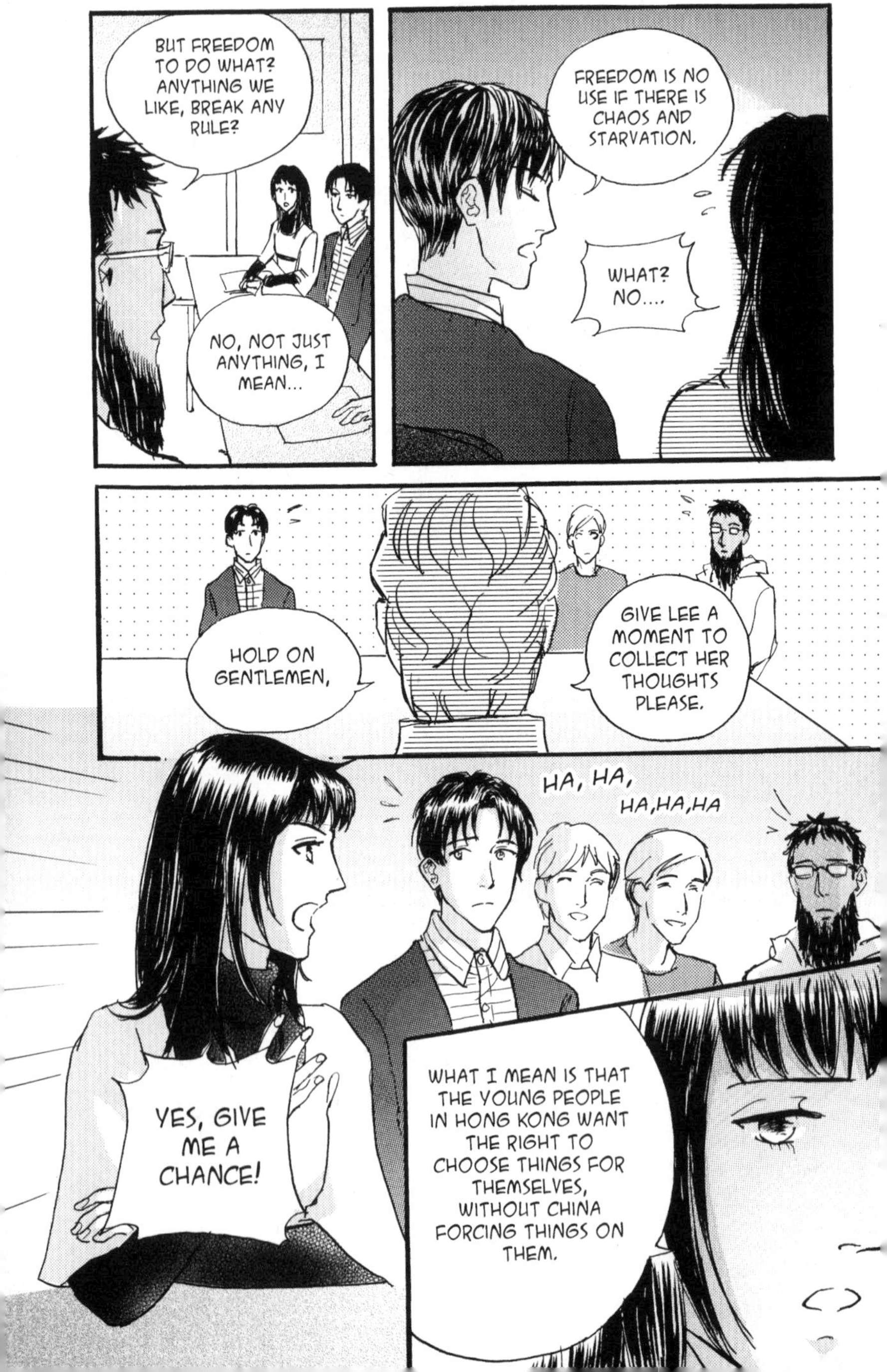
BUT FREEDOM TO DO WHAT? ANYTHING WE LIKE, BREAK ANY RULE?
NO, NOT JUST ANYTHING, I MEAN...
FREEDOM IS NO USE IF THERE IS CHAOS AND STARVATION.
WHAT? NO....
HOLD ON GENTLEMEN,
GIVE LEE A MOMENT TO COLLECT HER THOUGHTS PLEASE.
HA, HA, HA,HA,HA
YES, GIVE ME A CHANCE!
WHAT I MEAN IS THAT THE YOUNG PEOPLE IN HONG KONG WANT THE RIGHT TO CHOOSE THINGS FOR THEMSELVES, WITHOUT CHINA FORCING THINGS ON THEM.

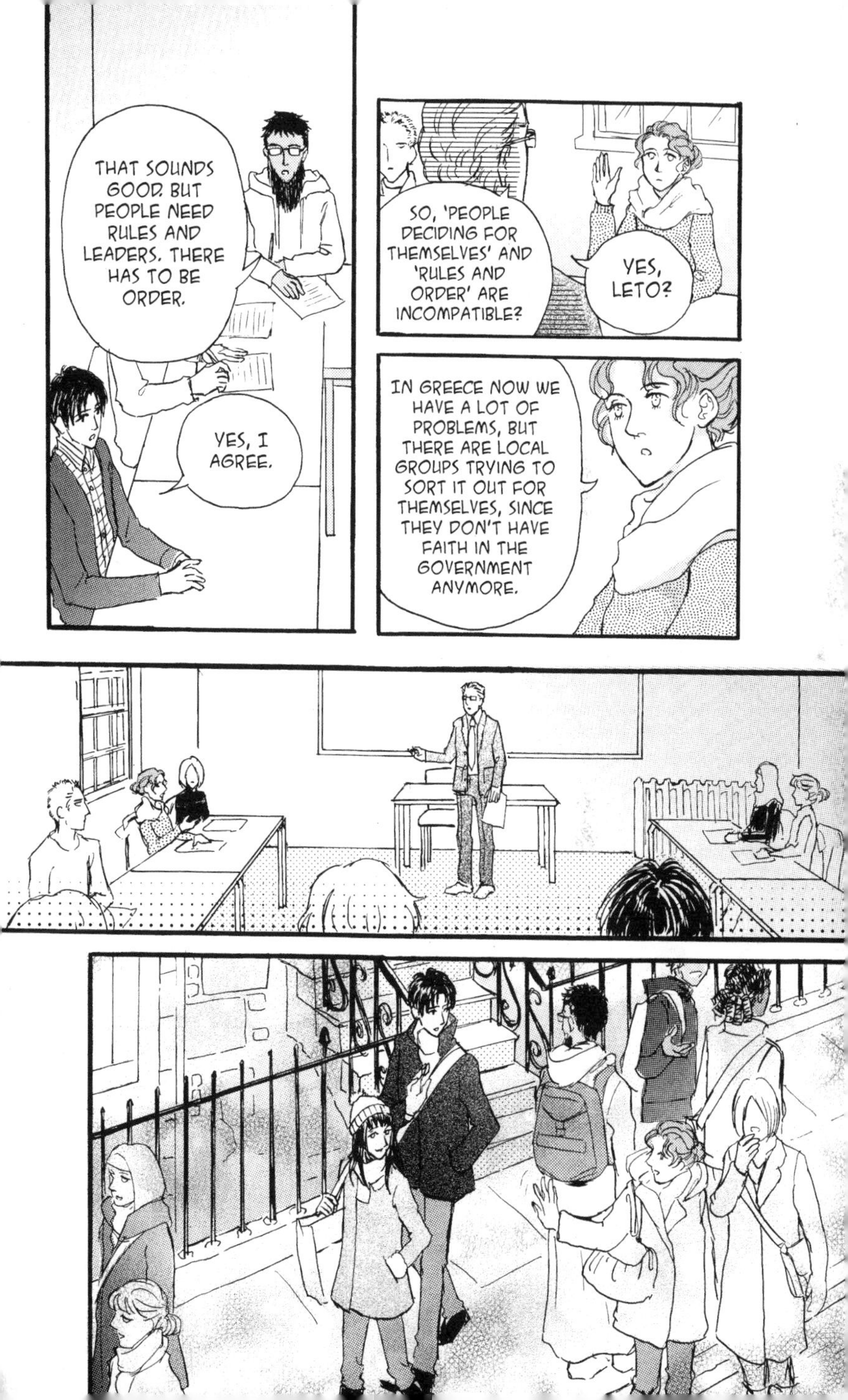
THAT SOUNDS GOOD. BUT PEOPLE NEED RULES AND LEADERS. THERE HAS TO BE ORDER.
YES, I AGREE.
SO, 'PEOPLE DECIDING FOR THEMSELVES' AND 'RULES AND ORDER' ARE INCOMPATIBLE?
YES, LETO?
IN GREECE NOW WE HAVE A LOT OF PROBLEMS, BUT THERE ARE LOCAL GROUPS TRYING TO SORT IT OUT FOR THEMSELVES, SINCE THEY DON'T HAVE FAITH IN THE GOVERNMENT ANYMORE.

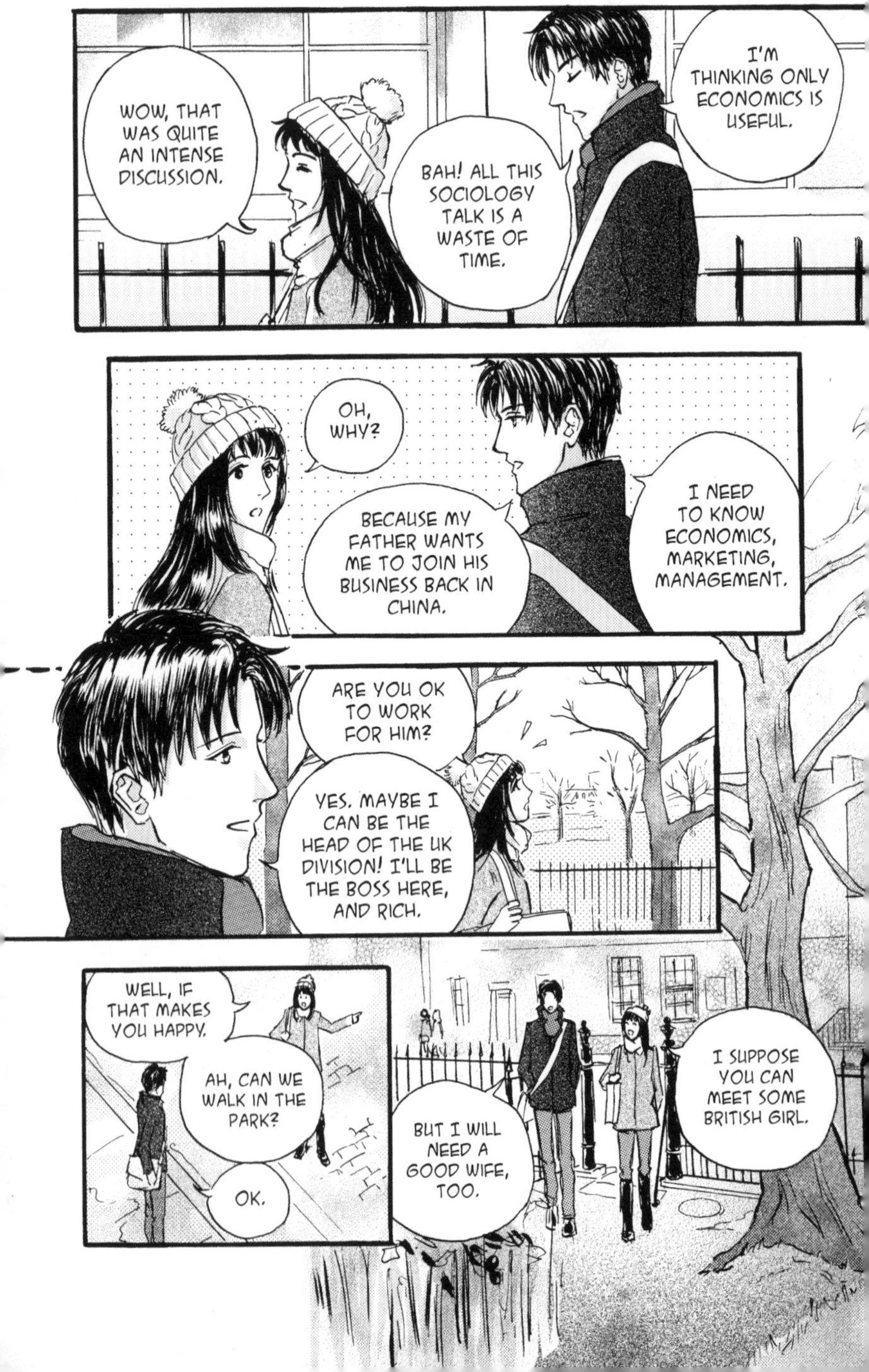
WOW, THAT WAS QUITE AN INTENSE DISCUSSION.
BAH! ALL THIS SOCIOLOGY TALK IS A WASTE OF TIME.
I'M THINKING ONLY ECONOMICS IS USEFUL.
OH, WHY?
BECAUSE MY FATHER WANTS ME TO JOIN HIS BUSINESS BACK IN CHINA.
I NEED TO KNOW ECONOMICS, MARKETING, MANAGEMENT.
ARE YOU OK TO WORK FOR HIM?
YES. MAYBE I CAN BE THE HEAD OF THE UK DIVISION! I'LL BE THE BOSS HERE, AND RICH.
WELL, IF THAT MAKES YOU HAPPY.
AH, CAN WE WALK IN THE PARK?
OK.
BUT I WILL NEED A GOOD WIFE, TOO.
I SUPPOSE YOU CAN MEET SOME BRITISH GIRL.

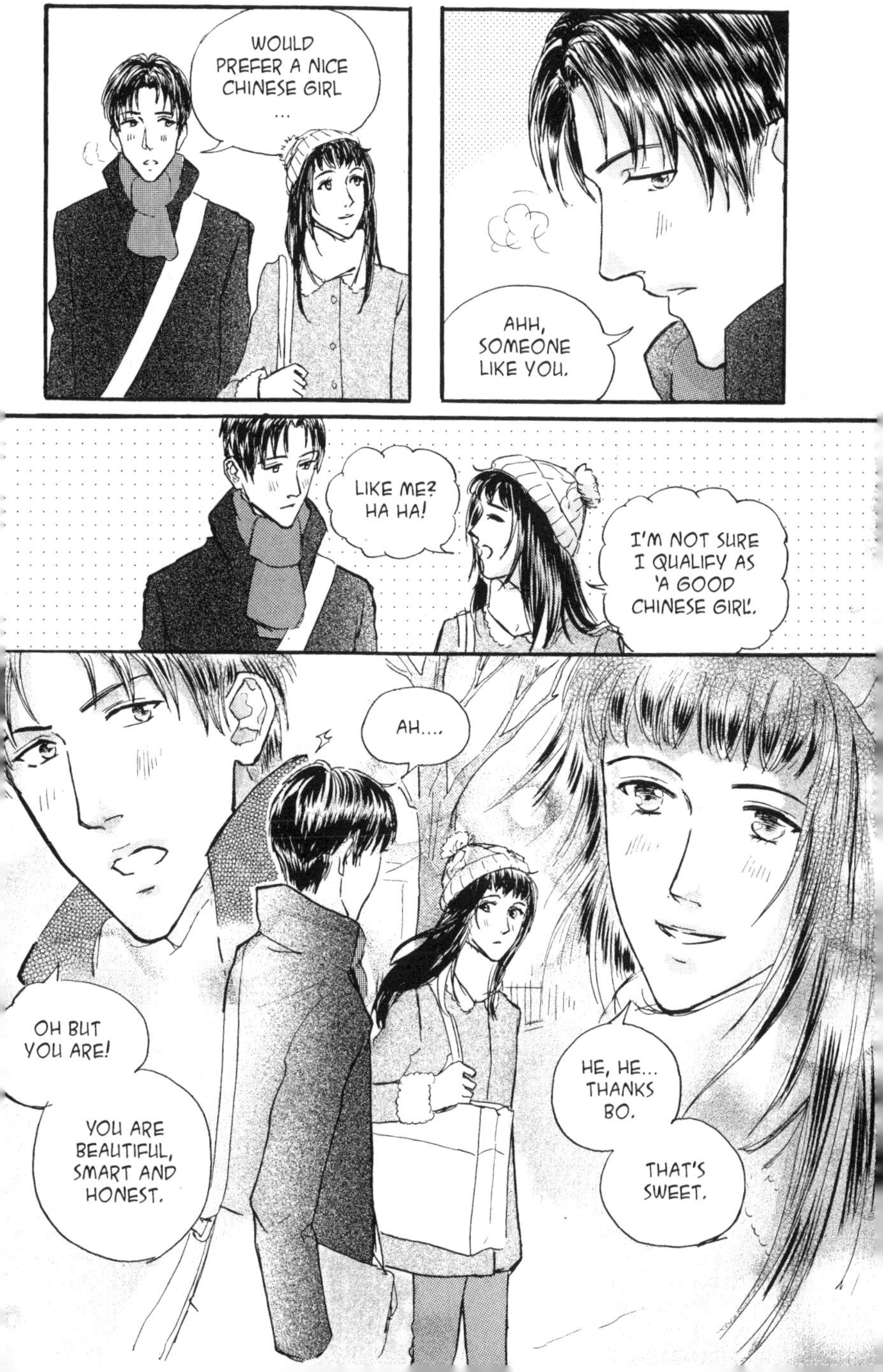
WOULD PREFER A NICE CHINESE GIRL ...
AHH, SOMEONE LIKE YOU.
LIKE ME? HA HA!
I'M NOT SURE I QUALIFY AS 'A GOOD CHINESE GIRL'.
AH....
OH BUT YOU ARE!
YOU ARE BEAUTIFUL, SMART AND HONEST.
HE, HE... THANKS BO.
THAT'S SWEET.

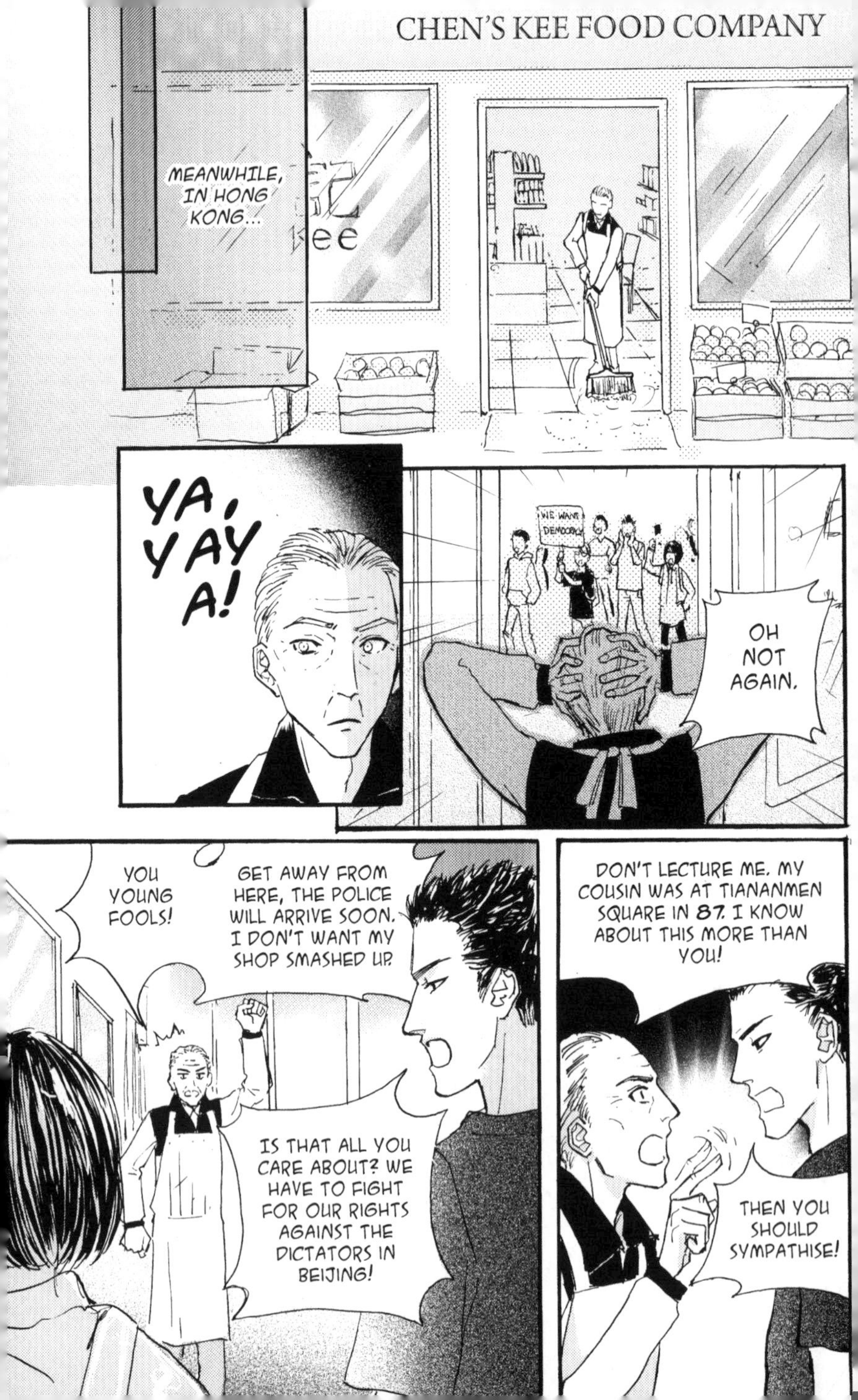
CHEN'S KEE FOOD COMPANY
MEANWHILE, IN HONG KONG...
Kee
YA, YAY A!
WE WANT DEMOCRACY
OH NOT AGAIN.
YOU YOUNG FOOLS!
GET AWAY FROM HERE, THE POLICE WILL ARRIVE SOON. I DON'T WANT MY SHOP SMASHED UP.
IS THAT ALL YOU CARE ABOUT? WE HAVE TO FIGHT FOR OUR RIGHTS AGAINST THE DICTATORS IN BEIJING!
DON'T LECTURE ME. MY COUSIN WAS AT TIANANMEN SQUARE IN 87. I KNOW ABOUT THIS MORE THAN YOU!
THEN YOU SHOULD SYMPATHISE!

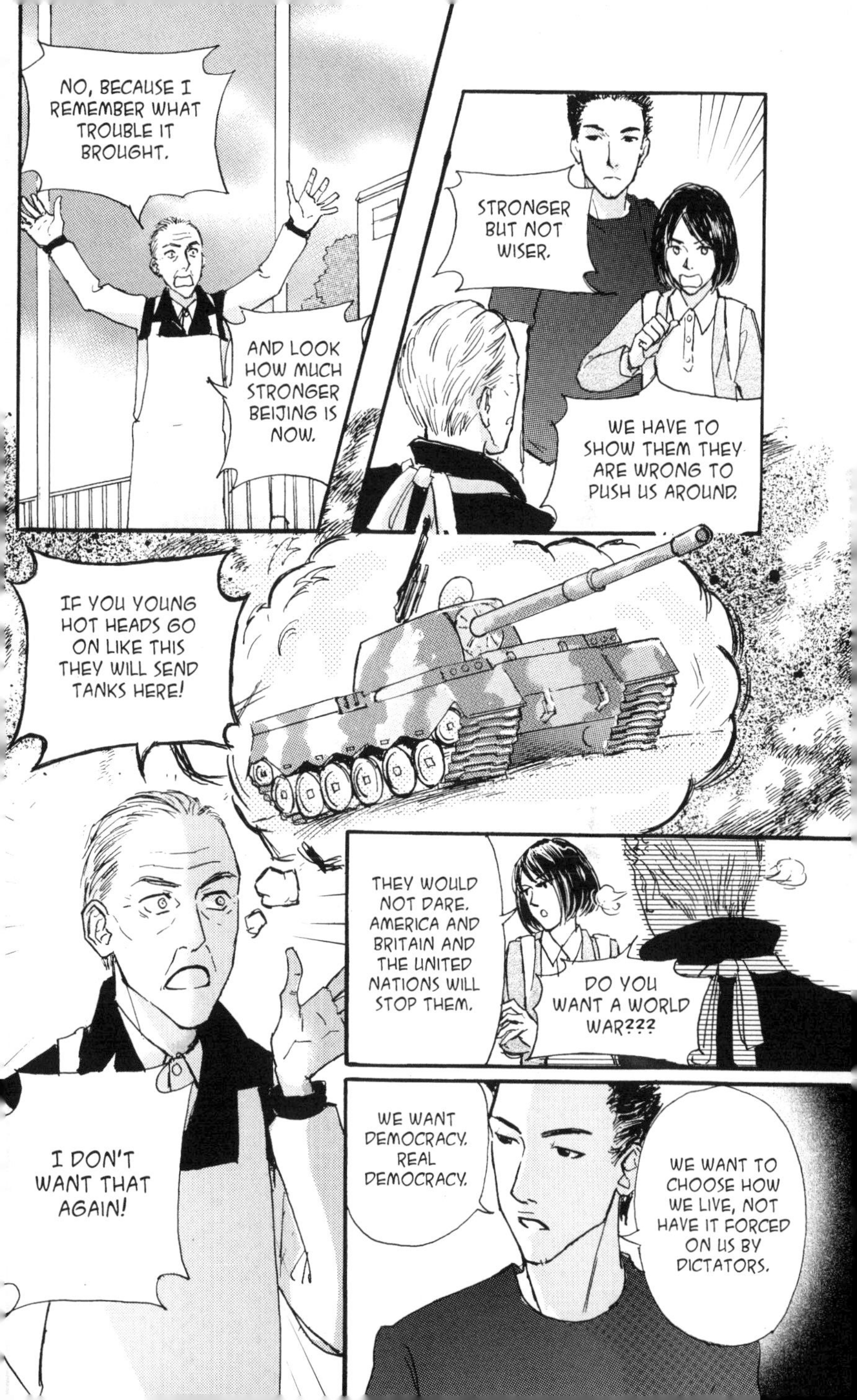
NO, BECAUSE I REMEMBER WHAT TROUBLE IT BROUGHT.
AND LOOK HOW MUCH STRONGER BEIJING IS NOW.
STRONGER BUT NOT WISER.
WE HAVE TO SHOW THEM THEY ARE WRONG TO PUSH US AROUND.
IF YOU YOUNG HOT HEADS GO ON LIKE THIS THEY WILL SEND TANKS HERE!
THEY WOULD NOT DARE. AMERICA AND BRITAIN AND THE UNITED NATIONS WILL STOP THEM.
DO YOU WANT A WORLD WAR???
I DON'T WANT THAT AGAIN!
WE WANT DEMOCRACY. REAL DEMOCRACY.
WE WANT TO CHOOSE HOW WE LIVE, NOT HAVE IT FORCED ON US BY DICTATORS.

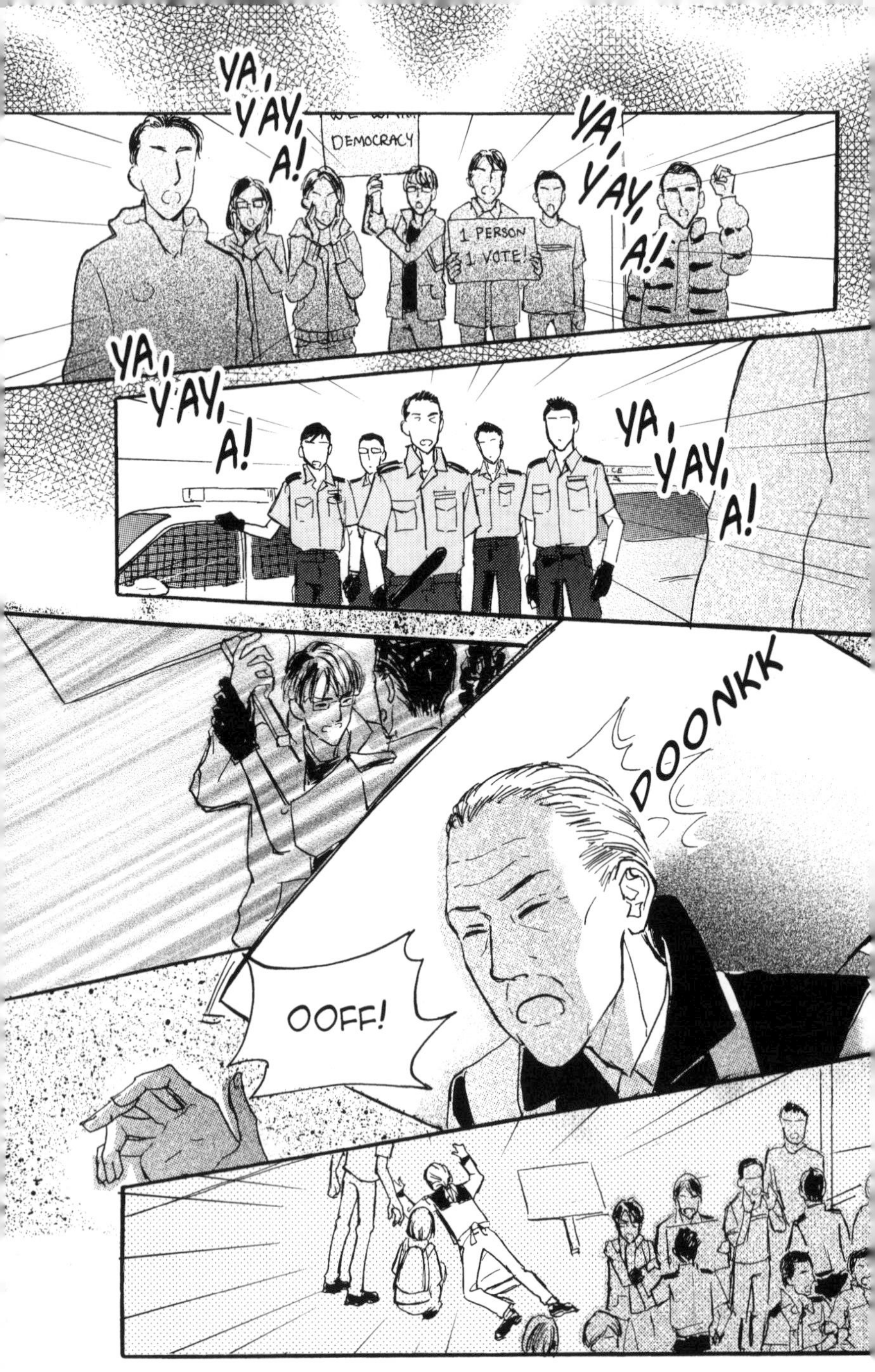
YA, YAY, A!
DEMOCRACY
1 PERSON 1 VOTE!
YA, YAY, A!
YA, YAY, A!
YA, YAY, A!
DOONKK
OOFF!

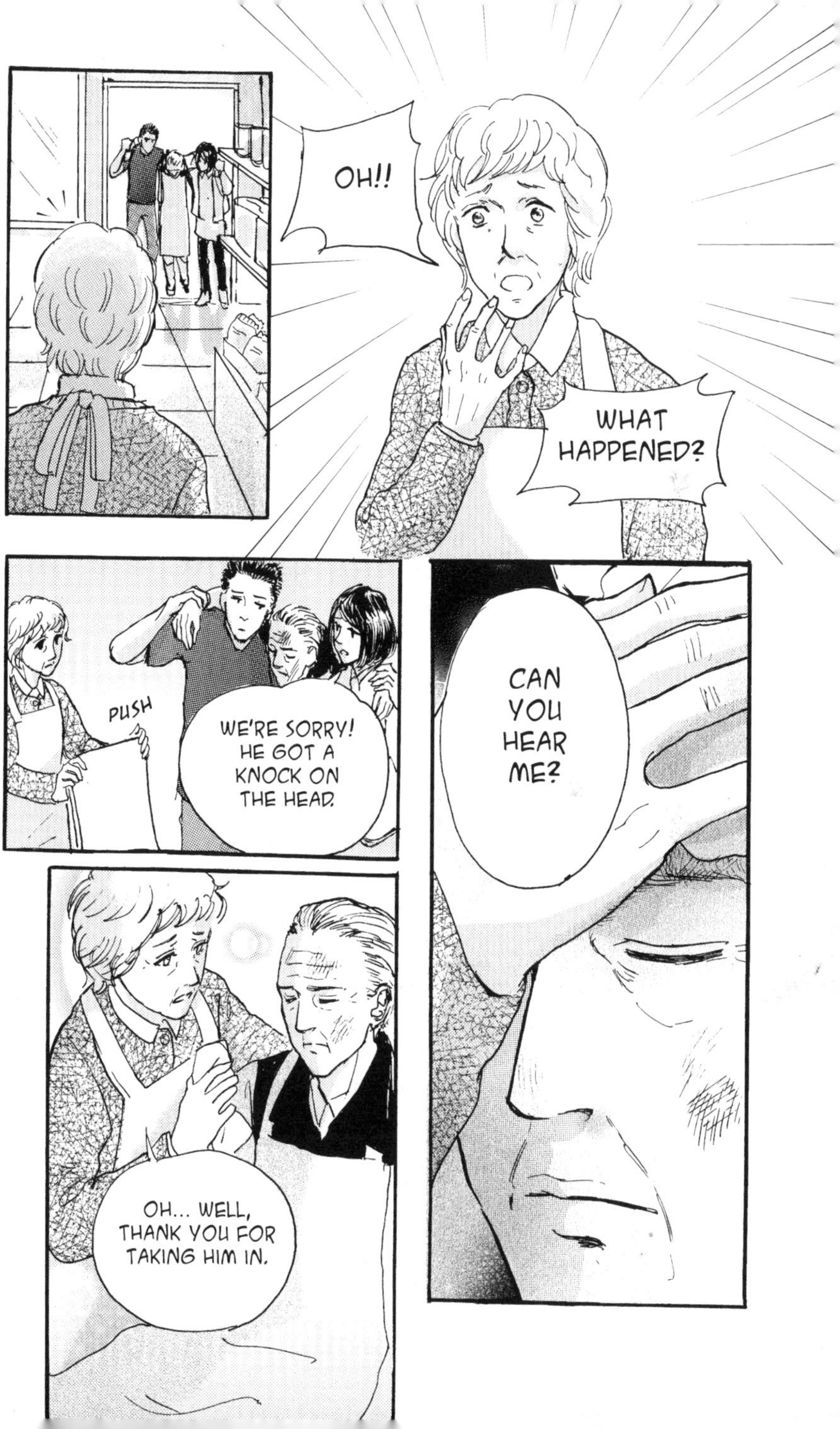
OH!!
WHAT HAPPENED?
PUSH
WE'RE SORRY! HE GOT A KNOCK ON THE HEAD.
OH... WELL, THANK YOU FOR TAKING HIM IN.
CAN YOU HEAR ME?

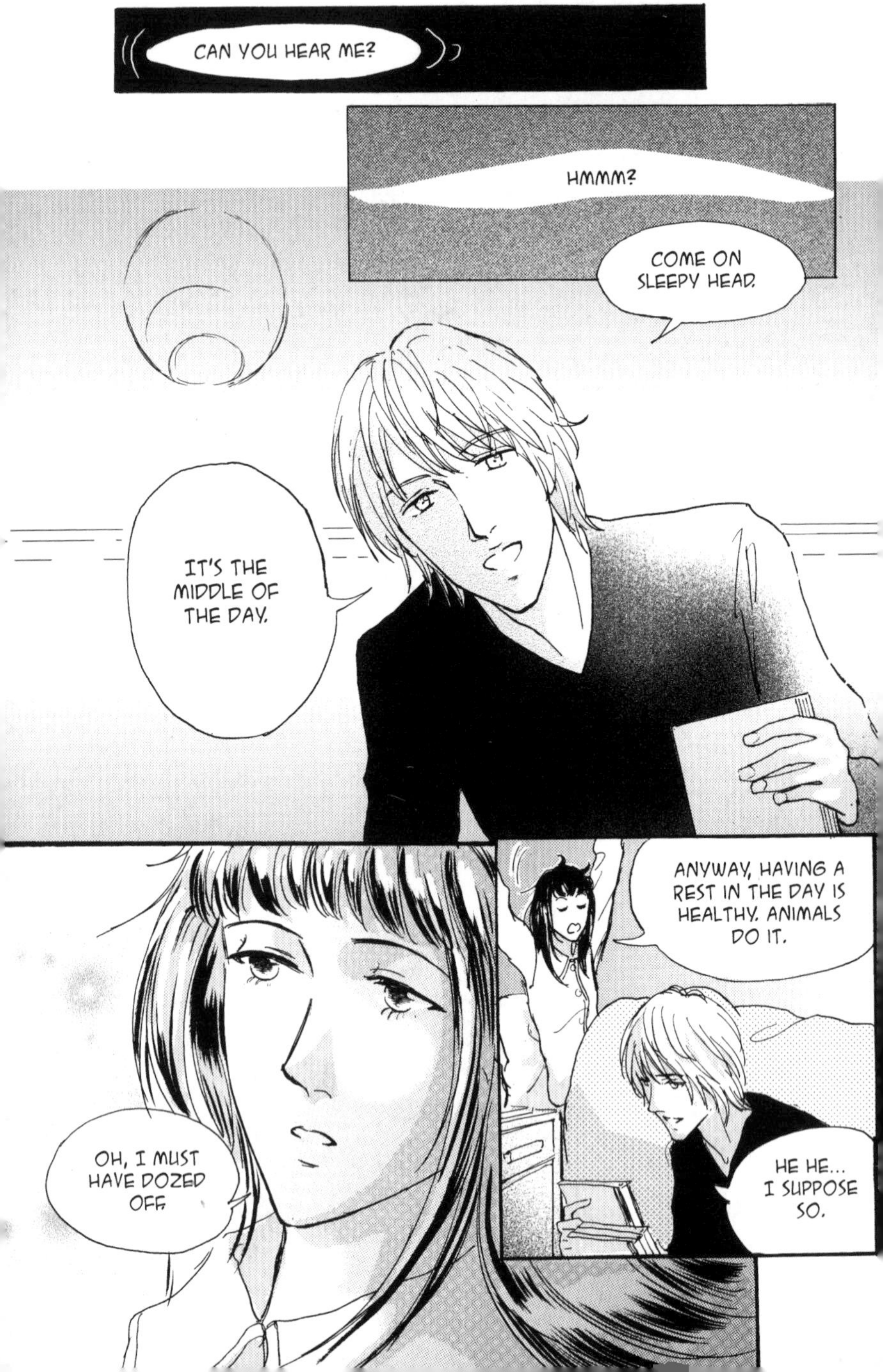
CAN YOU HEAR ME?
HMMM?
COME ON SLEEPY HEAD.
IT'S THE MIDDLE OF THE DAY.
OH, I MUST HAVE DOZED OFF.
ANYWAY, HAVING A REST IN THE DAY IS HEALTHY. ANIMALS DO IT.
HE HE... I SUPPOSE SO.

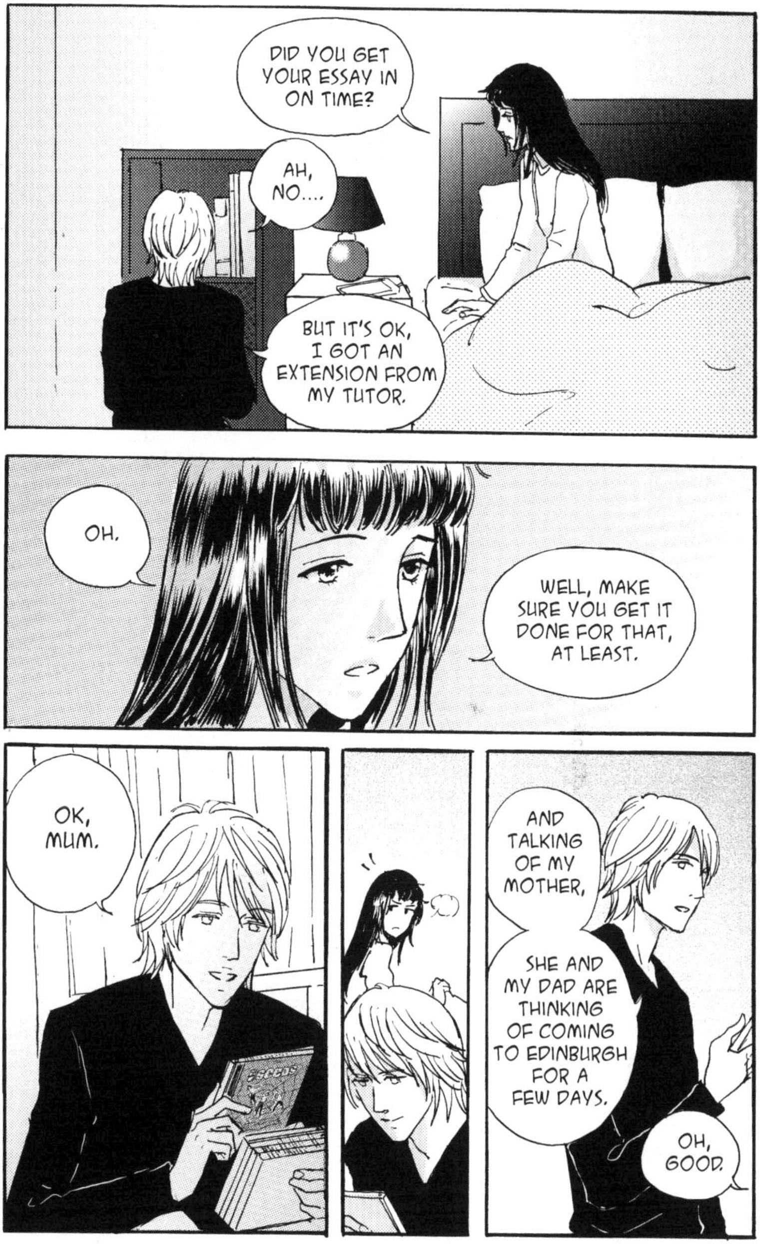
DID YOU GET YOUR ESSAY IN ON TIME?
AH, NO....
BUT IT'S OK, I GOT AN EXTENSION FROM MY TUTOR.
OH.
WELL, MAKE SURE YOU GET IT DONE FOR THAT, AT LEAST.
OK, MUM.
AND TALKING OF MY MOTHER,
SHE AND MY DAD ARE THINKING OF COMING TO EDINBURGH FOR A FEW DAYS.
OH, GOOD.

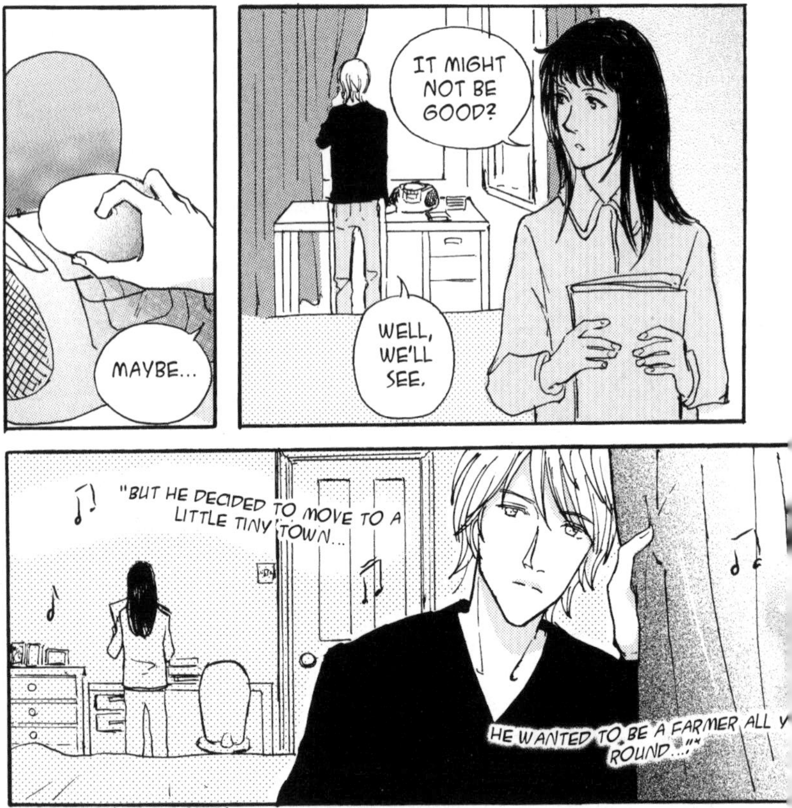
MAYBE...
IT MIGHT NOT BE GOOD?
WELL, WE'LL SEE.
"BUT HE DECIDED TO MOVE TO A LITTLE TINY TOWN...
HE WANTED TO BE A FARMER ALL Y ROUND...!"*

*'MR FARMER' BY THE SEEDS.

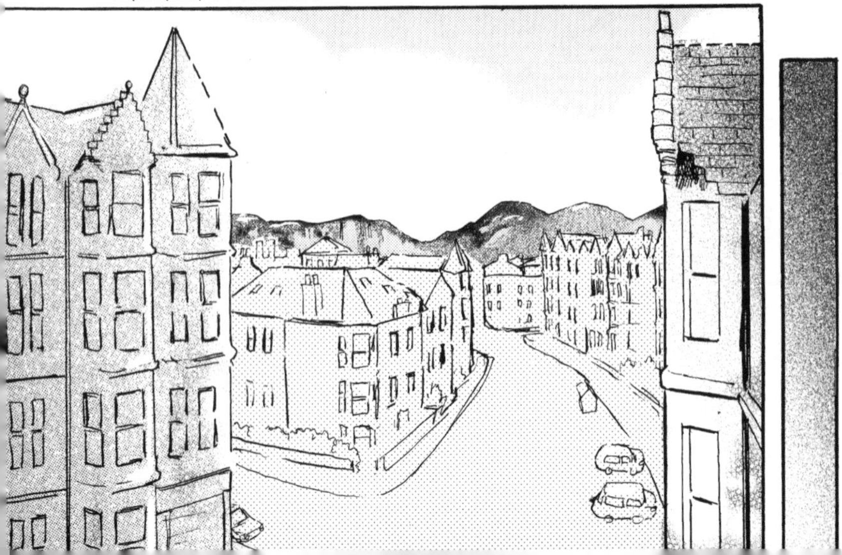

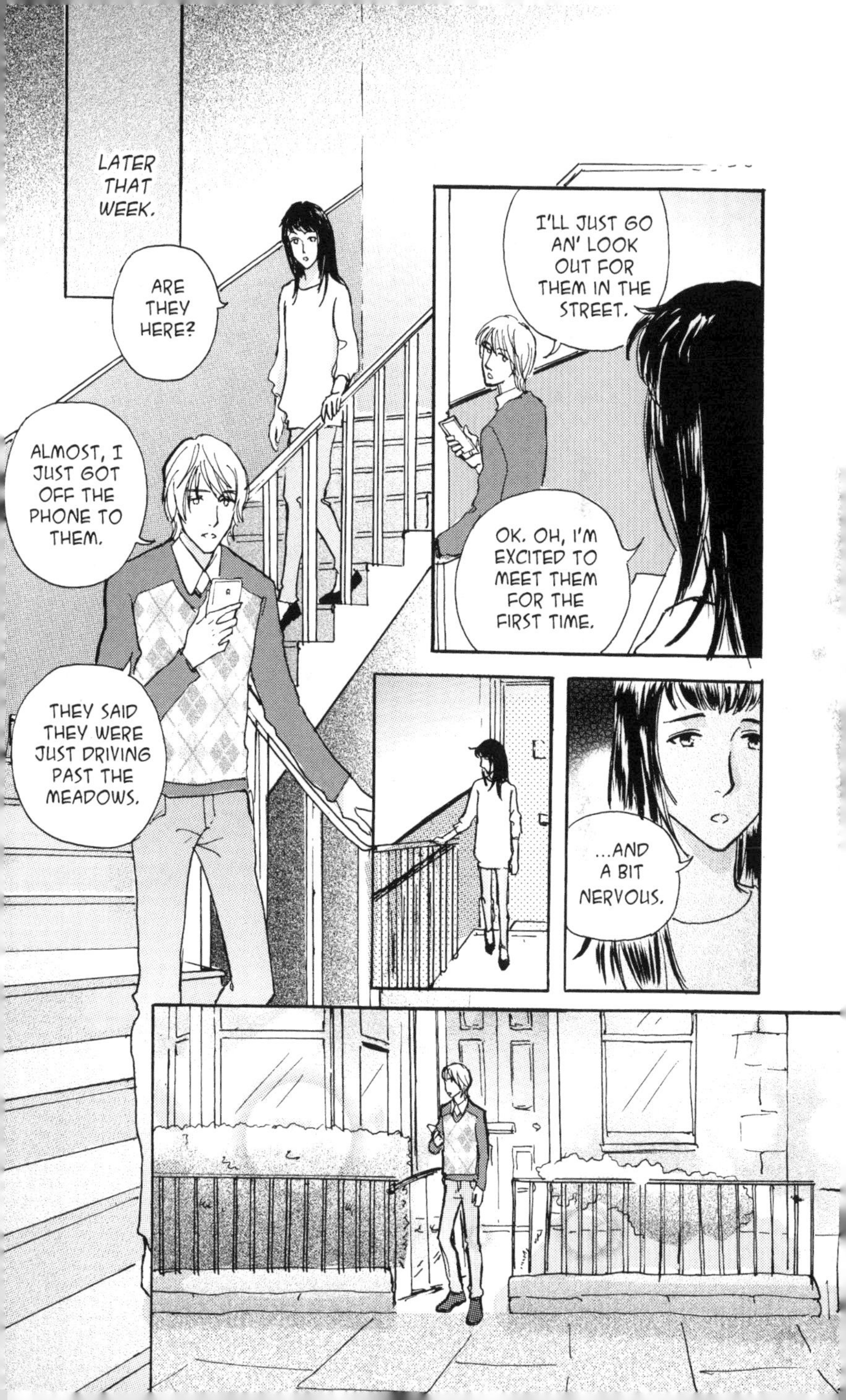
LATER THAT WEEK.
ARE THEY HERE?
ALMOST, I JUST GOT OFF THE PHONE TO THEM.
THEY SAID THEY WERE JUST DRIVING PAST THE MEADOWS.
I'LL JUST GO AN' LOOK OUT FOR THEM IN THE STREET.
OK. OH, I'M EXCITED TO MEET THEM FOR THE FIRST TIME.
...AND A BIT NERVOUS.

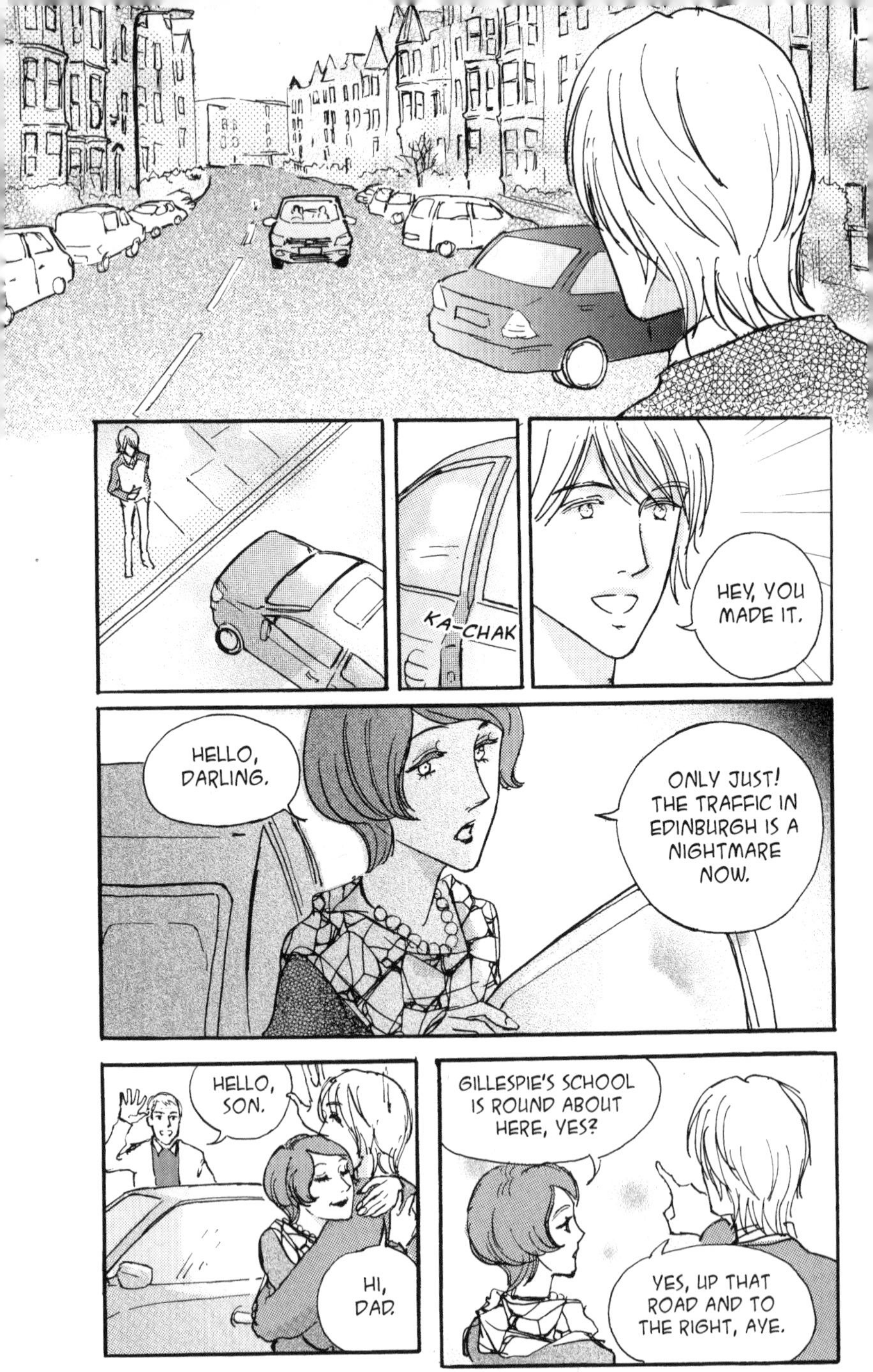
KA-CHAK
HEY, YOU MADE IT.
HELLO, DARLING.
ONLY JUST! THE TRAFFIC IN EDINBURGH IS A NIGHTMARE NOW.
HELLO, SON.
HI, DAD.
GILLESPIE'S SCHOOL IS ROUND ABOUT HERE, YES?
YES, UP THAT ROAD AND TO THE RIGHT, AYE.

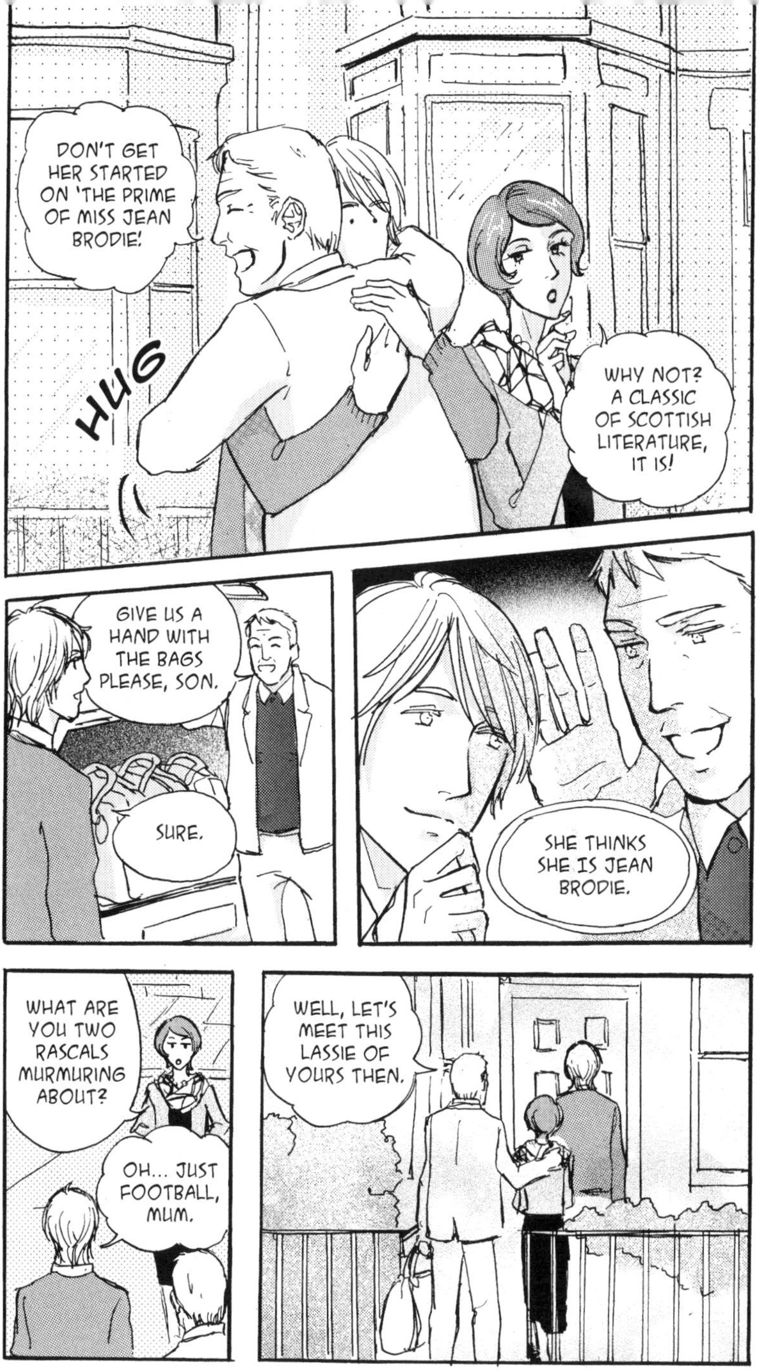
DON'T GET HER STARTED ON 'THE PRIME OF MISS JEAN BRODIE'.
HUG
WHY NOT? A CLASSIC OF SCOTTISH LITERATURE, IT IS!
GIVE US A HAND WITH THE BAGS PLEASE, SON.
SURE.
SHE THINKS SHE IS JEAN BRODIE.
WHAT ARE YOU TWO RASCALS MURMURING ABOUT?
OH... JUST FOOTBALL, MUM.
WELL, LET'S MEET THIS LASSIE OF YOURS THEN.

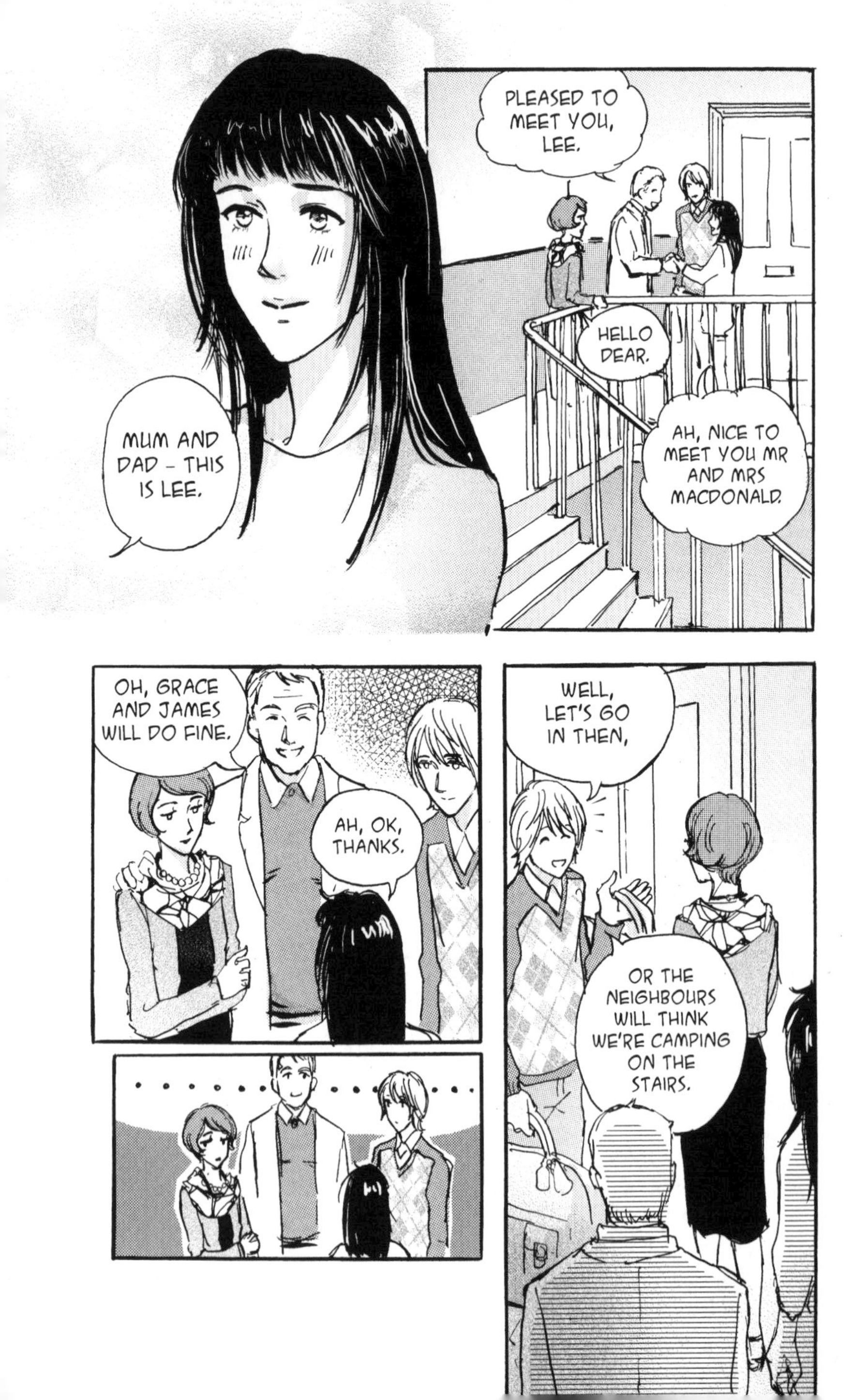
MUM AND DAD - THIS IS LEE.
PLEASED TO MEET YOU, LEE.
HELLO DEAR.
AH, NICE TO MEET YOU MR AND MRS MACDONALD.
OH, GRACE AND JAMES WILL DO FINE.
AH, OK, THANKS.
WELL, LET'S GO IN THEN,
OR THE NEIGHBOURS WILL THINK WE'RE CAMPING ON THE STAIRS.

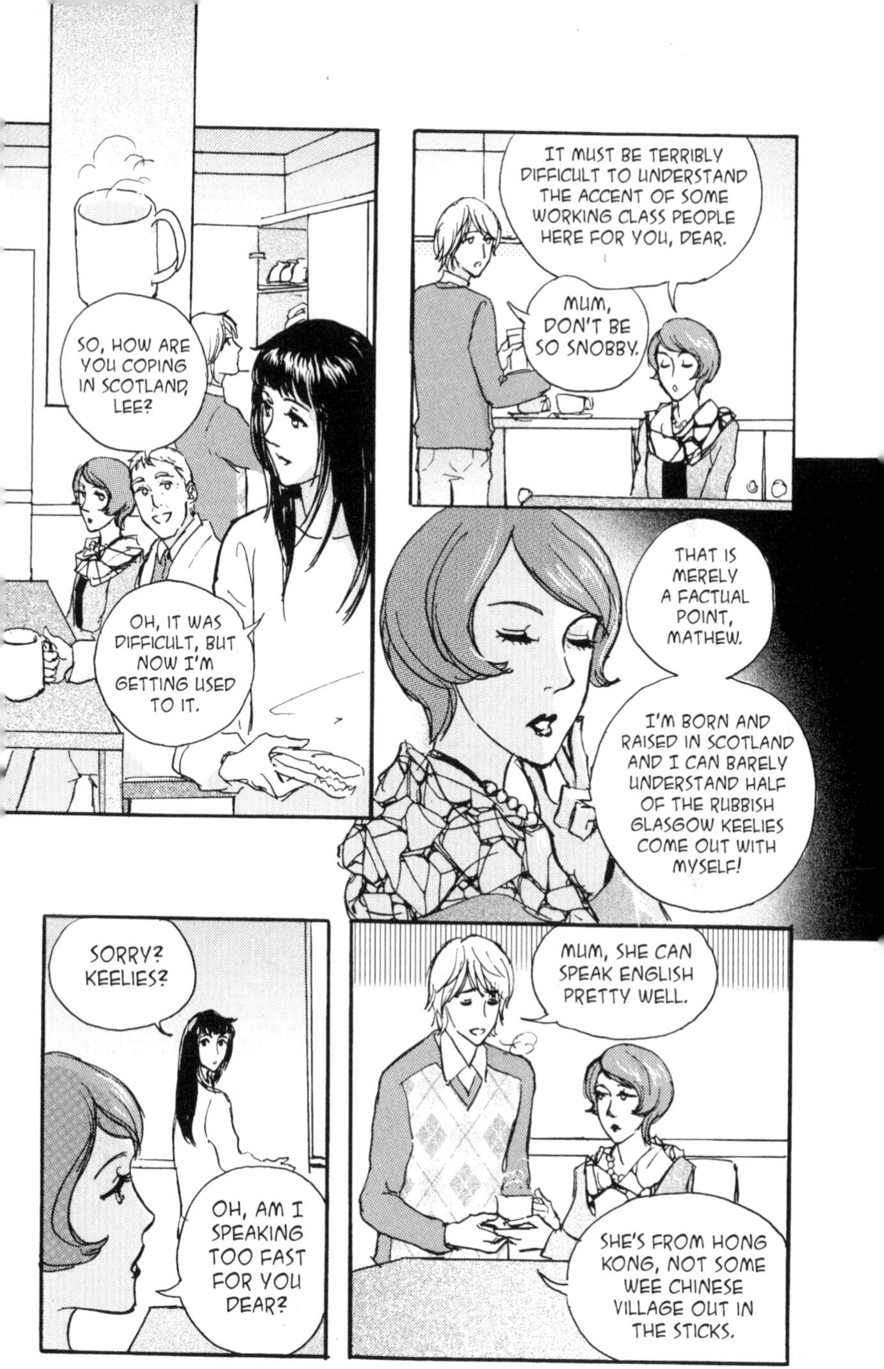

SO, HOW ARE YOU COPING IN SCOTLAND, LEE?
OH, IT WAS DIFFICULT, BUT NOW I'M GETTING USED TO IT.
IT MUST BE TERRIBLY DIFFICULT TO UNDERSTAND THE ACCENT OF SOME WORKING CLASS PEOPLE HERE FOR YOU, DEAR.
MUM, DON'T BE SO SNOBBY.
THAT IS MERELY A FACTUAL POINT, MATHEW.
I'M BORN AND RAISED IN SCOTLAND AND I CAN BARELY UNDERSTAND HALF OF THE RUBBISH GLASGOW KEELIES COME OUT WITH MYSELF!
SORRY? KEELIES?
OH, AM I SPEAKING TOO FAST FOR YOU DEAR?
MUM, SHE CAN SPEAK ENGLISH PRETTY WELL.
SHE'S FROM HONG KONG, NOT SOME WEE CHINESE VILLAGE OUT IN THE STICKS.

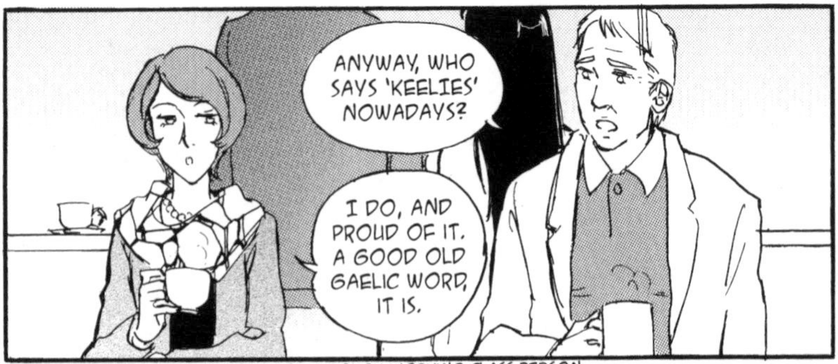
ANYWAY, WHO SAYS 'KEELIES' NOWADAYS?
I DO, AND PROUD OF IT. A GOOD OLD GAELIC WORD, IT IS.

* KEELIE IS A DEROGATORY WORD FOR A ROUGH WORKING CLASS PERSON.

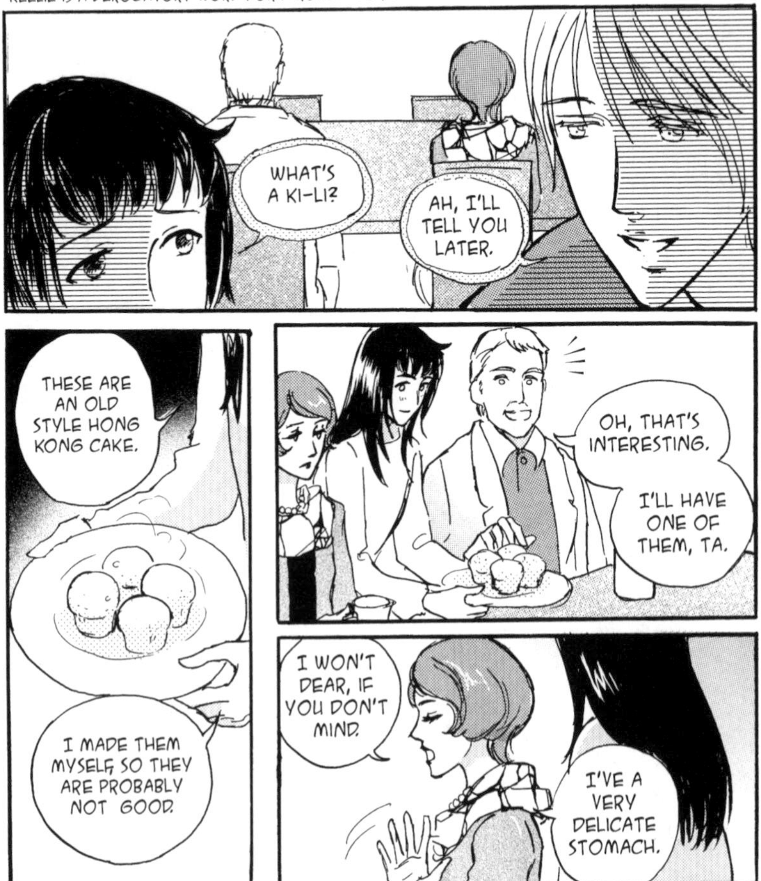
WHAT'S A KI-LI?
AH, I'LL TELL YOU LATER.
THESE ARE AN OLD STYLE HONG KONG CAKE.
I MADE THEM MYSELF, SO THEY ARE PROBABLY NOT GOOD.
OH, THAT'S INTERESTING.
I'LL HAVE ONE OF THEM, TA.
I WON'T DEAR, IF YOU DON'T MIND.
I'VE A VERY DELICATE STOMACH.

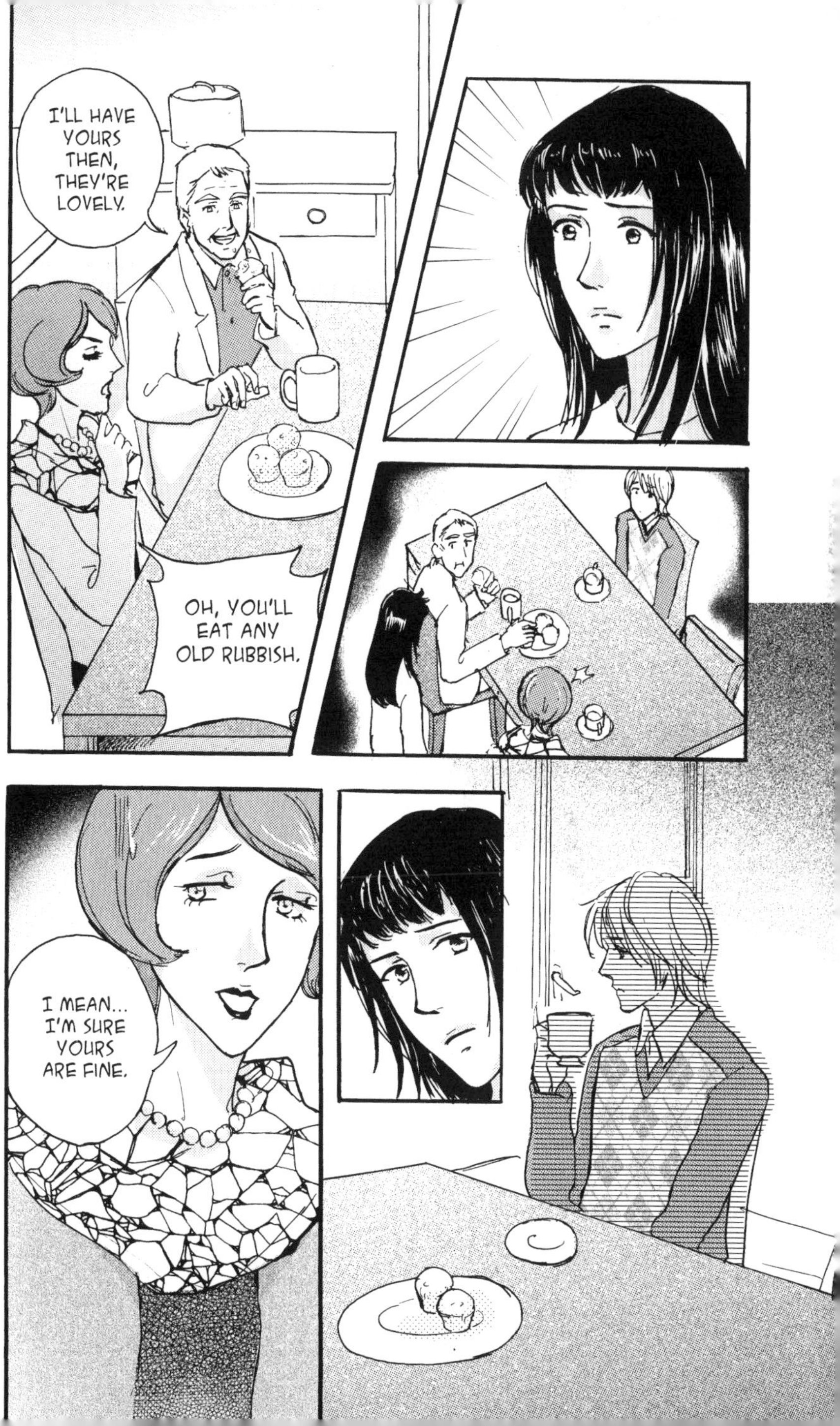
I'LL HAVE YOURS THEN, THEY'RE LOVELY.
OH, YOU'LL EAT ANY OLD RUBBISH.
I MEAN... I'M SURE YOURS ARE FINE.

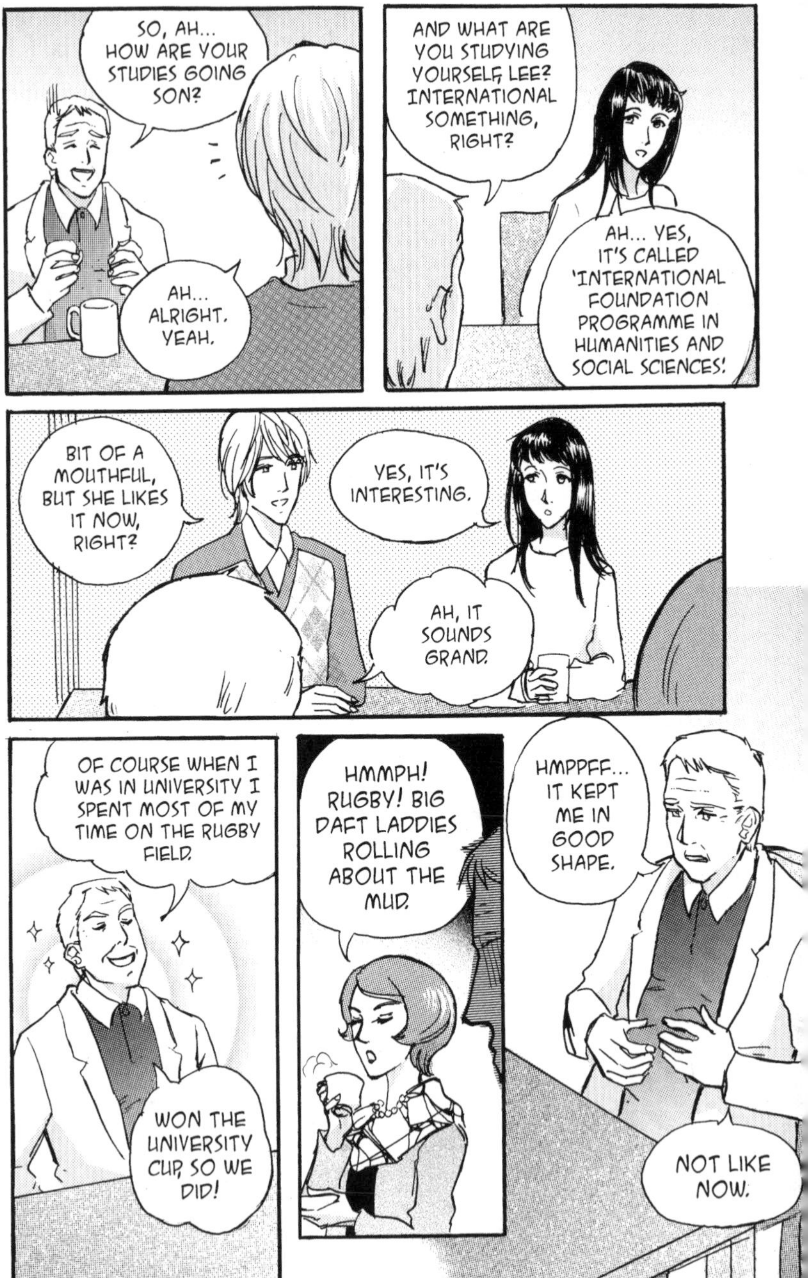
SO, AH... HOW ARE YOUR STUDIES GOING SON?
AH... ALRIGHT. YEAH.
AND WHAT ARE YOU STUDYING YOURSELF, LEE? INTERNATIONAL SOMETHING, RIGHT?
AH... YES, IT'S CALLED 'INTERNATIONAL FOUNDATION PROGRAMME IN HUMANITIES AND SOCIAL SCIENCES.'
BIT OF A MOUTHFUL, BUT SHE LIKES IT NOW, RIGHT?
YES, IT'S INTERESTING.
AH, IT SOUNDS GRAND.
OF COURSE WHEN I WAS IN UNIVERSITY I SPENT MOST OF MY TIME ON THE RUGBY FIELD.
WON THE UNIVERSITY CUP, SO WE DID!
HMMPH! RUGBY! BIG DAFT LADDIES ROLLING ABOUT THE MUD.
HMPPFF... IT KEPT ME IN GOOD SHAPE.
NOT LIKE NOW.

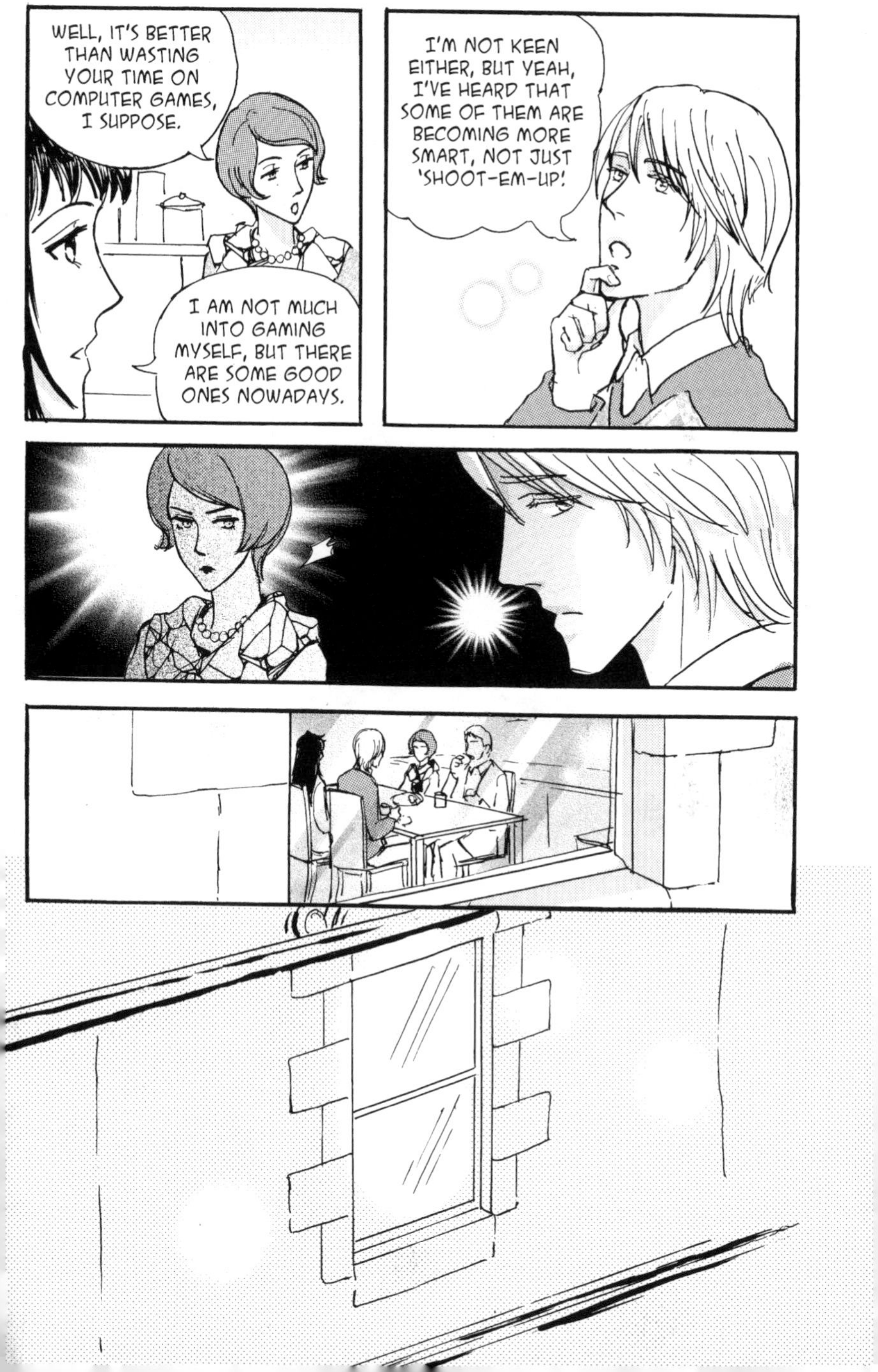
WELL, IT'S BETTER THAN WASTING YOUR TIME ON COMPUTER GAMES, I SUPPOSE.
I AM NOT MUCH INTO GAMING MYSELF, BUT THERE ARE SOME GOOD ONES NOWADAYS.
I'M NOT KEEN EITHER, BUT YEAH, I'VE HEARD THAT SOME OF THEM ARE BECOMING MORE SMART, NOT JUST 'SHOOT-EM-UP'.

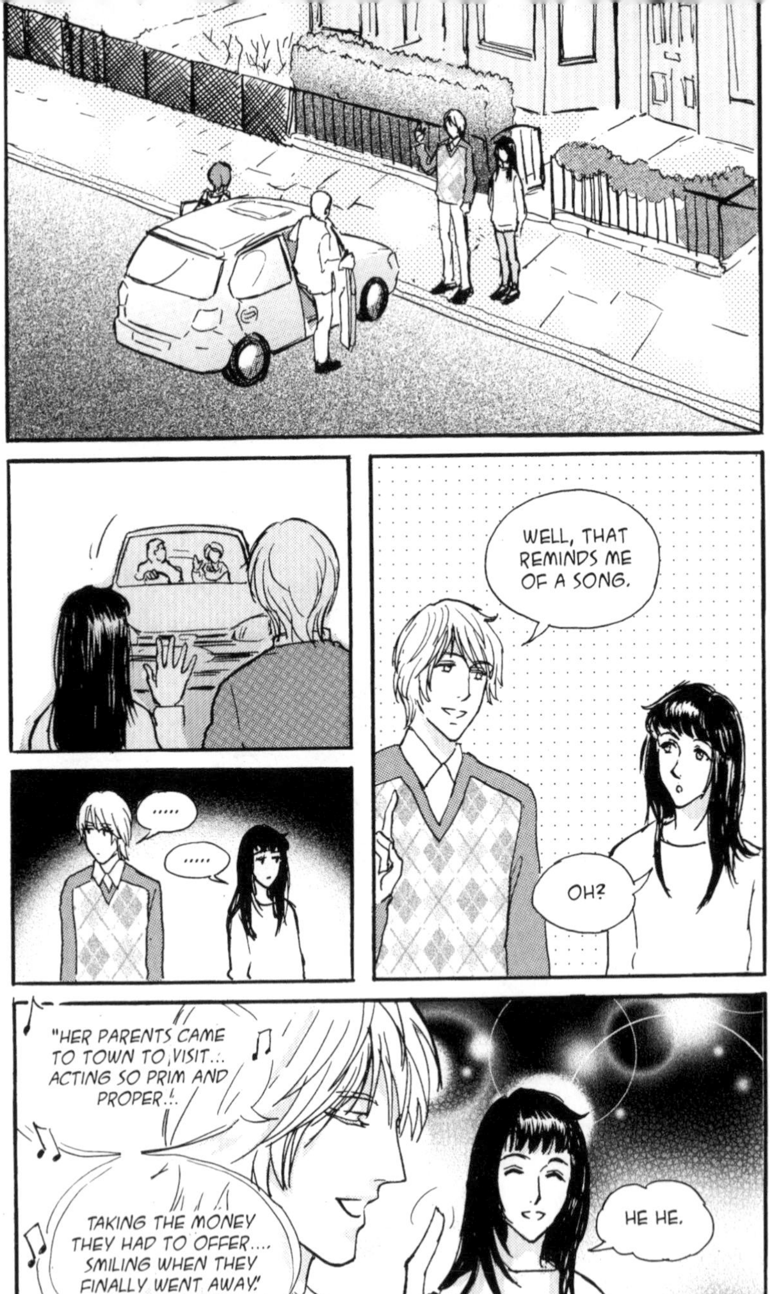

......
......
WELL, THAT REMINDS ME OF A SONG.
OH?
"HER PARENTS CAME TO TOWN TO VISIT... ACTING SO PRIM AND PROPER...
TAKING THE MONEY THEY HAD TO OFFER.... SMILING WHEN THEY FINALLY WENT AWAY."
HE HE.

'TRACY HAD A HARD DAY SUNDAY.' BY THE WEST COAST POP ART EXPERIMENTAL BAND, 1967.

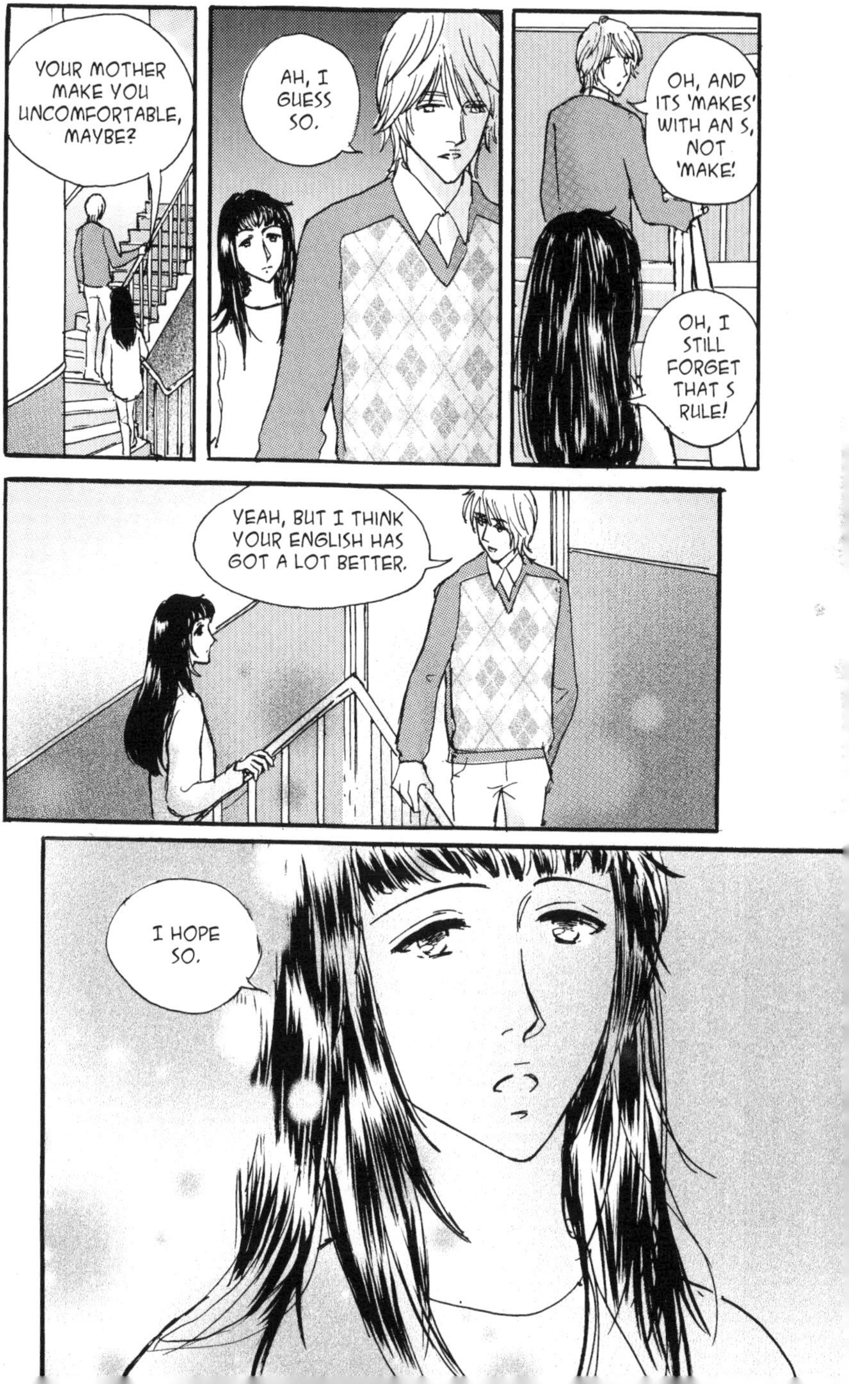
YOUR MOTHER MAKE YOU UNCOMFORTABLE, MAYBE?
AH, I GUESS SO.
OH, AND ITS 'MAKES' WITH AN S, NOT 'MAKE'.
OH, I STILL FORGET THAT S RULE!
YEAH, BUT I THINK YOUR ENGLISH HAS GOT A LOT BETTER.
I HOPE SO.

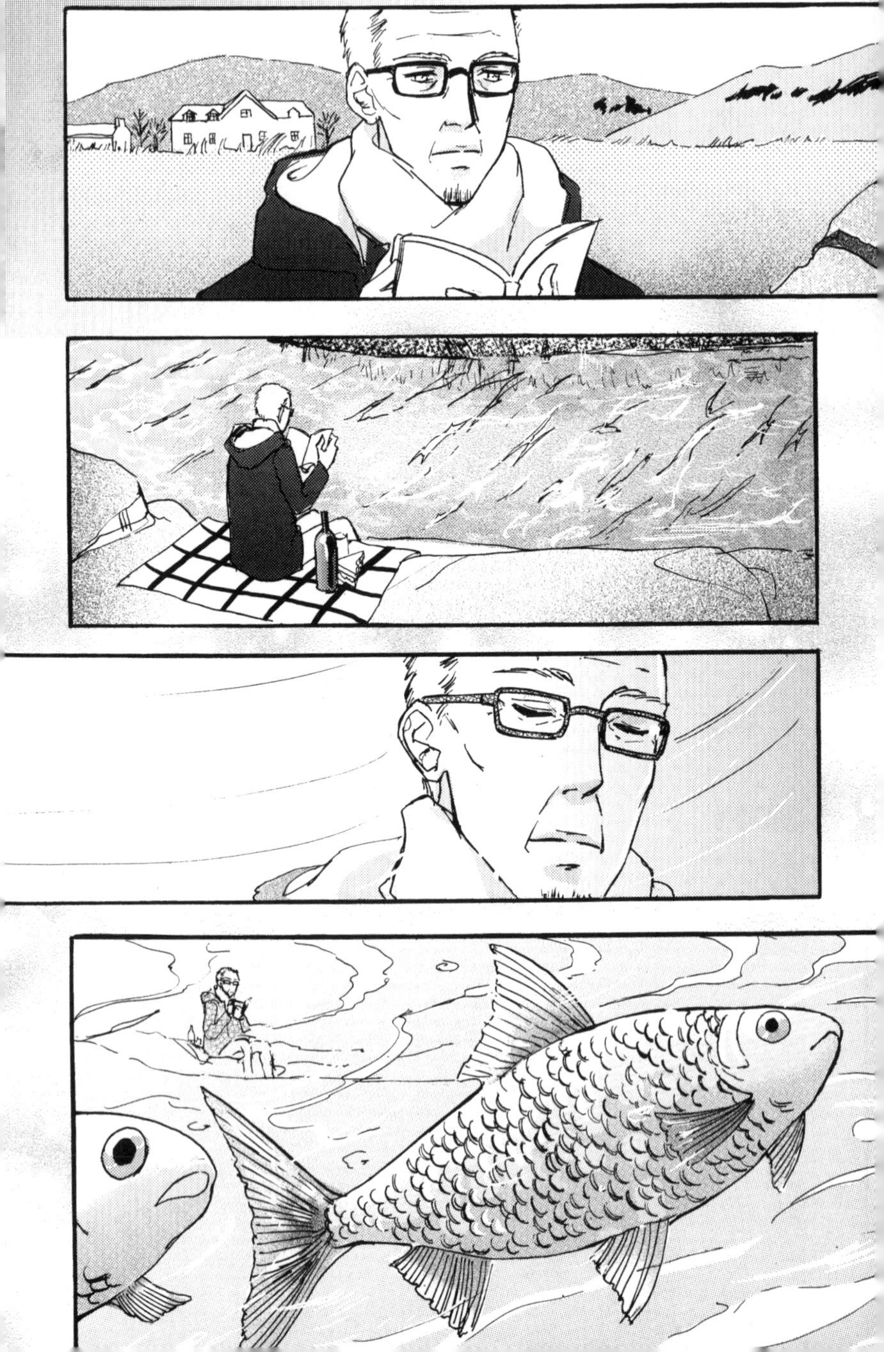

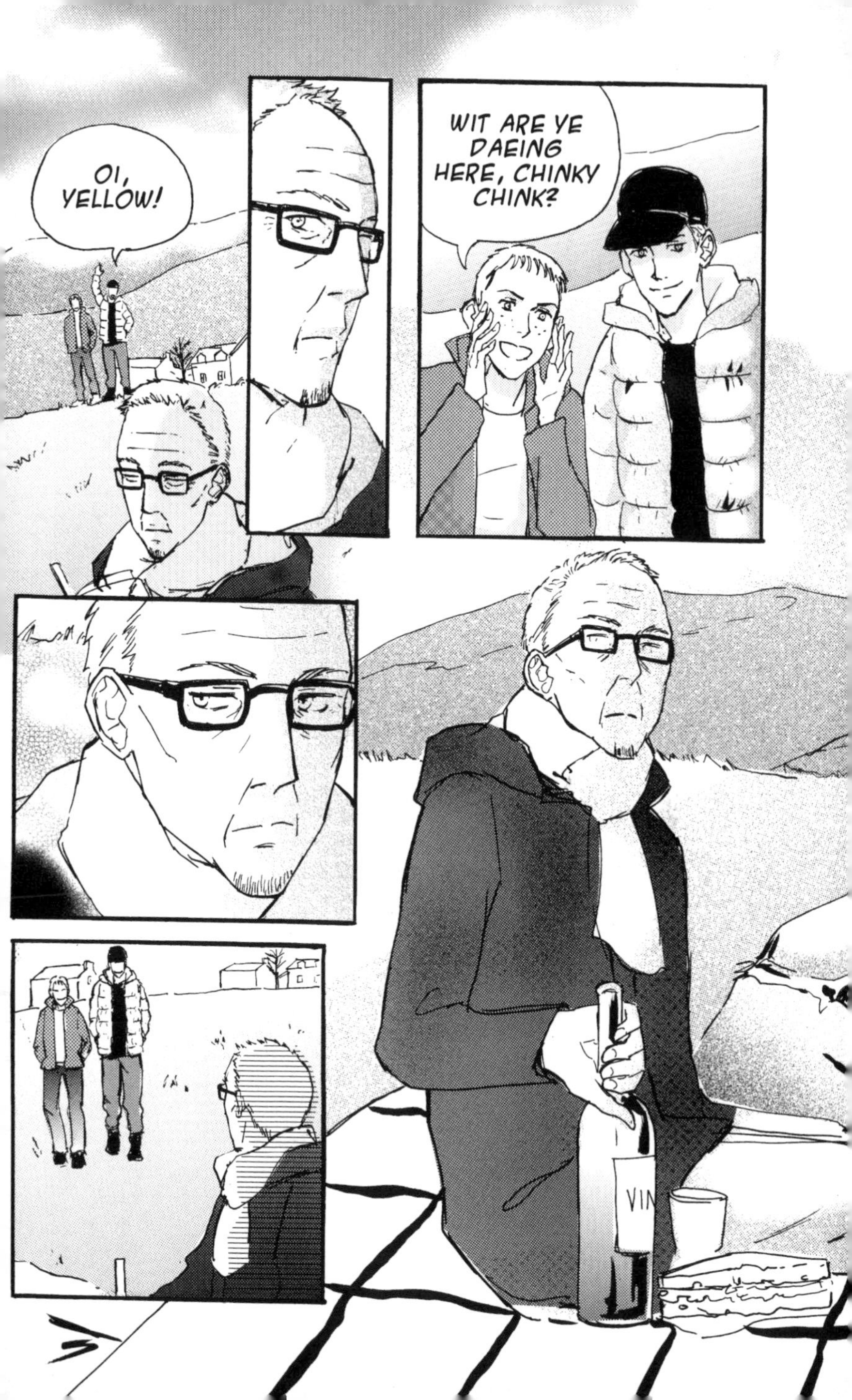
OI, YELLOW!
WIT ARE YE DAEING HERE, CHINKY CHINK?
VIN

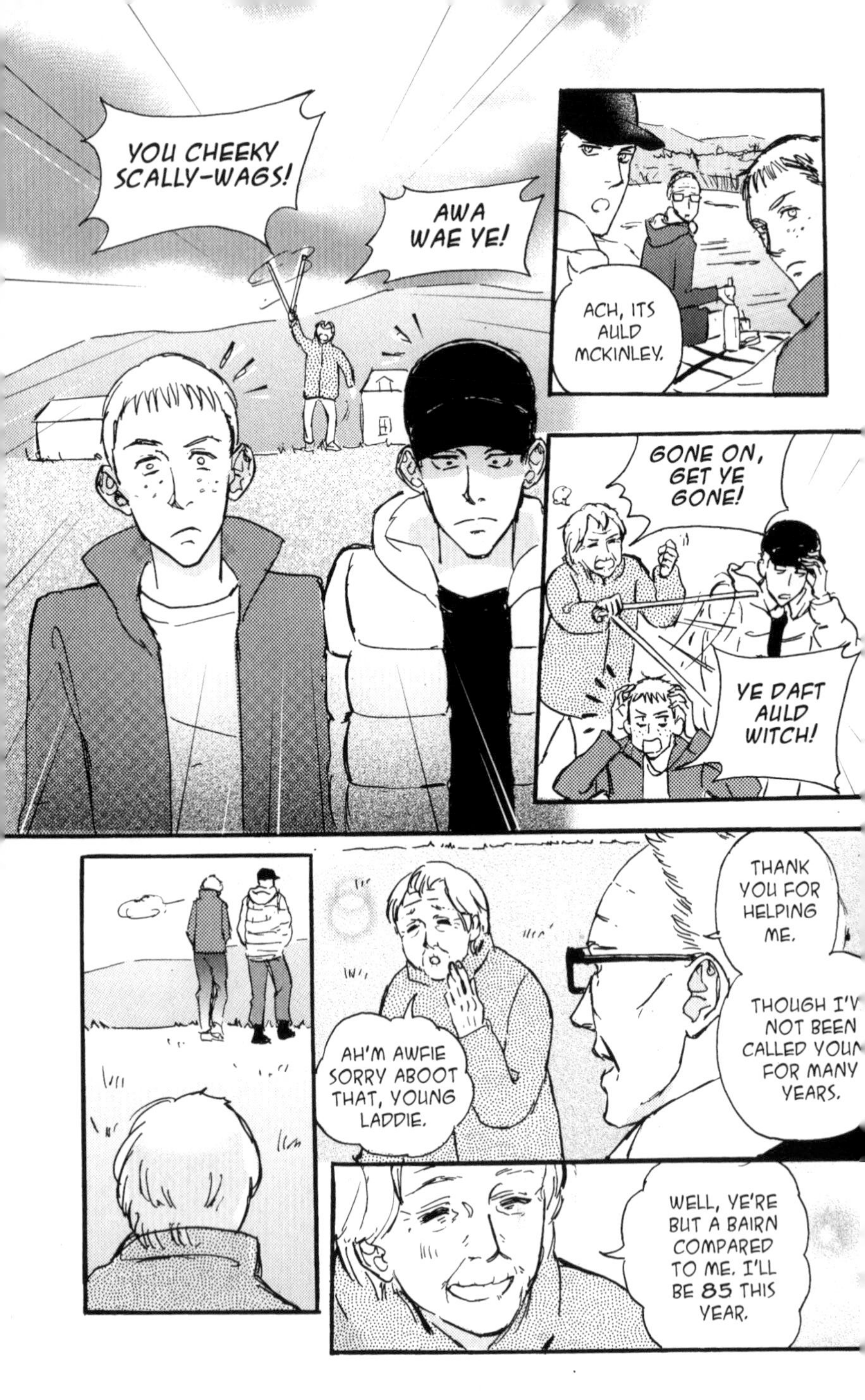
YOU CHEEKY SCALLY-WAGS!
AWA WAE YE!
ACH, ITS AULD MCKINLEY.
GONE ON, GET YE GONE!
YE DAFT AULD WITCH!
THANK YOU FOR HELPING ME.
THOUGH I'VE NOT BEEN CALLED YOUNG FOR MANY YEARS.
AH'M AWFIE SORRY ABOOT THAT, YOUNG LADDIE.
WELL, YE'RE BUT A BAIRN COMPARED TO ME. I'LL BE 85 THIS YEAR.

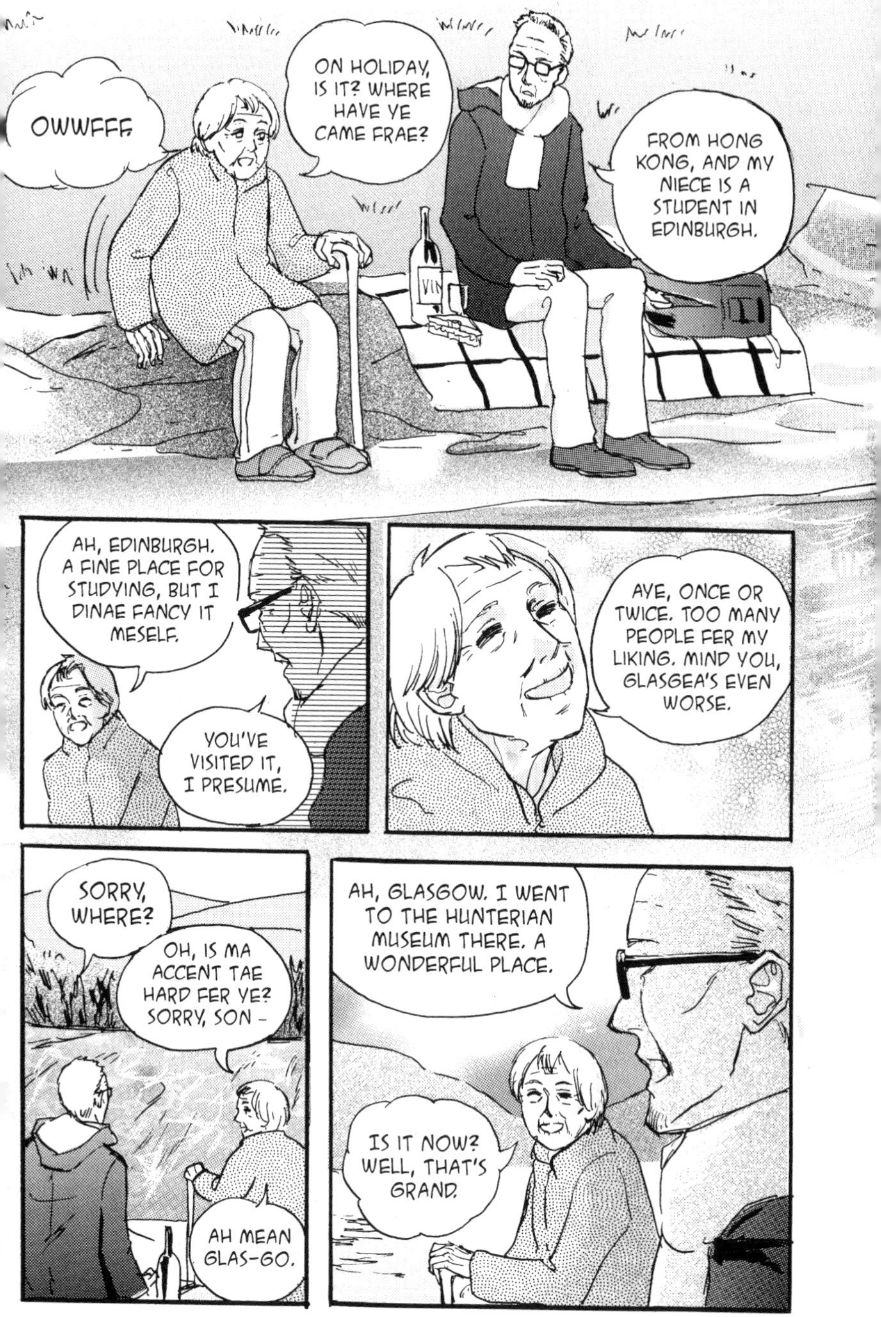
OWWFFF
ON HOLIDAY, IS IT? WHERE HAVE YE CAME FRAE?
FROM HONG KONG, AND MY NIECE IS A STUDENT IN EDINBURGH.
VIN
AH, EDINBURGH. A FINE PLACE FOR STUDYING, BUT I DINAE FANCY IT MESELF.
YOU'VE VISITED IT, I PRESUME.
AYE, ONCE OR TWICE. TOO MANY PEOPLE FER MY LIKING. MIND YOU, GLASGEA'S EVEN WORSE.
SORRY, WHERE?
OH, IS MA ACCENT TAE HARD FER YE? SORRY, SON –
AH MEAN GLAS-GO.
AH, GLASGOW. I WENT TO THE HUNTERIAN MUSEUM THERE. A WONDERFUL PLACE.
IS IT NOW? WELL, THAT'S GRAND.

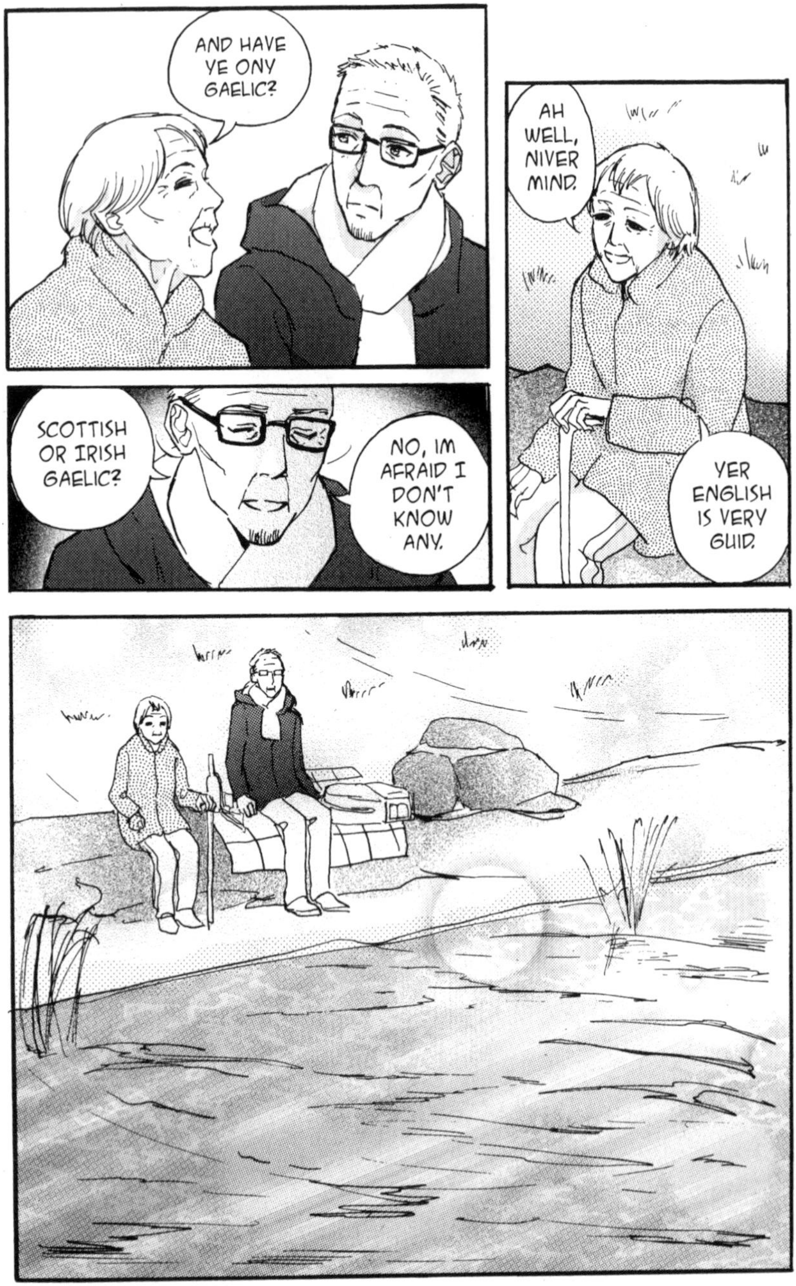
AND HAVE YE ONY GAELIC?
SCOTTISH OR IRISH GAELIC?
NO, IM AFRAID I DON'T KNOW ANY.
AH WELL, NIVER MIND.
YER ENGLISH IS VERY GUID.

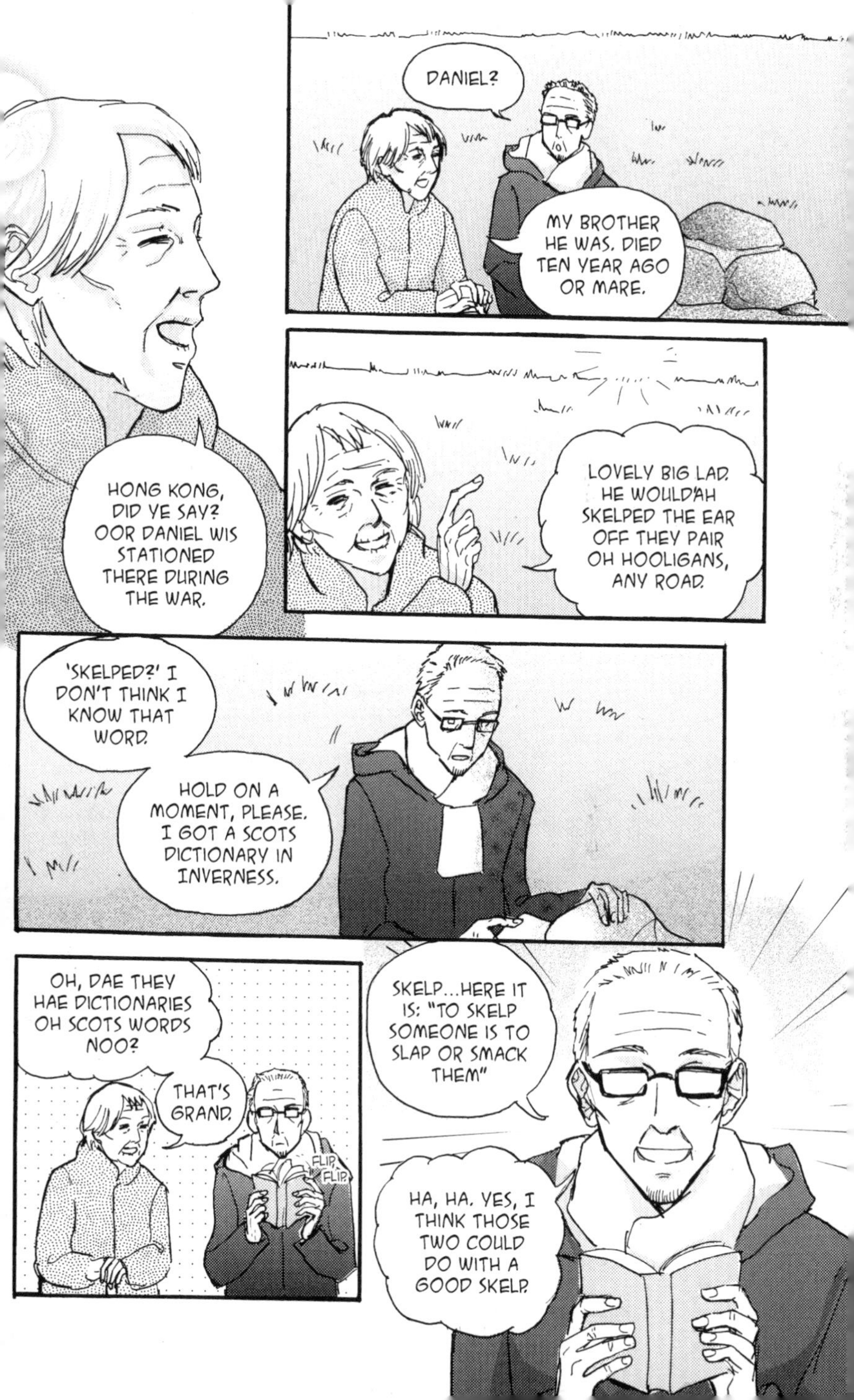
HONG KONG, DID YE SAY? OOR DANIEL WIS STATIONED THERE DURING THE WAR.
DANIEL?
MY BROTHER HE WAS. DIED TEN YEAR AGO OR MARE.
LOVELY BIG LAD. HE WOULD'AH SKELPED THE EAR OFF THEY PAIR OH HOOLIGANS, ANY ROAD.
'SKELPED?' I DON'T THINK I KNOW THAT WORD.
HOLD ON A MOMENT, PLEASE. I GOT A SCOTS DICTIONARY IN INVERNESS.
OH, DAE THEY HAE DICTIONARIES OH SCOTS WORDS NOO?
THAT'S GRAND.
FLIP
FLIP
SKELP...HERE IT IS: "TO SKELP SOMEONE IS TO SLAP OR SMACK THEM"
HA, HA. YES, I THINK THOSE TWO COULD DO WITH A GOOD SKELP.

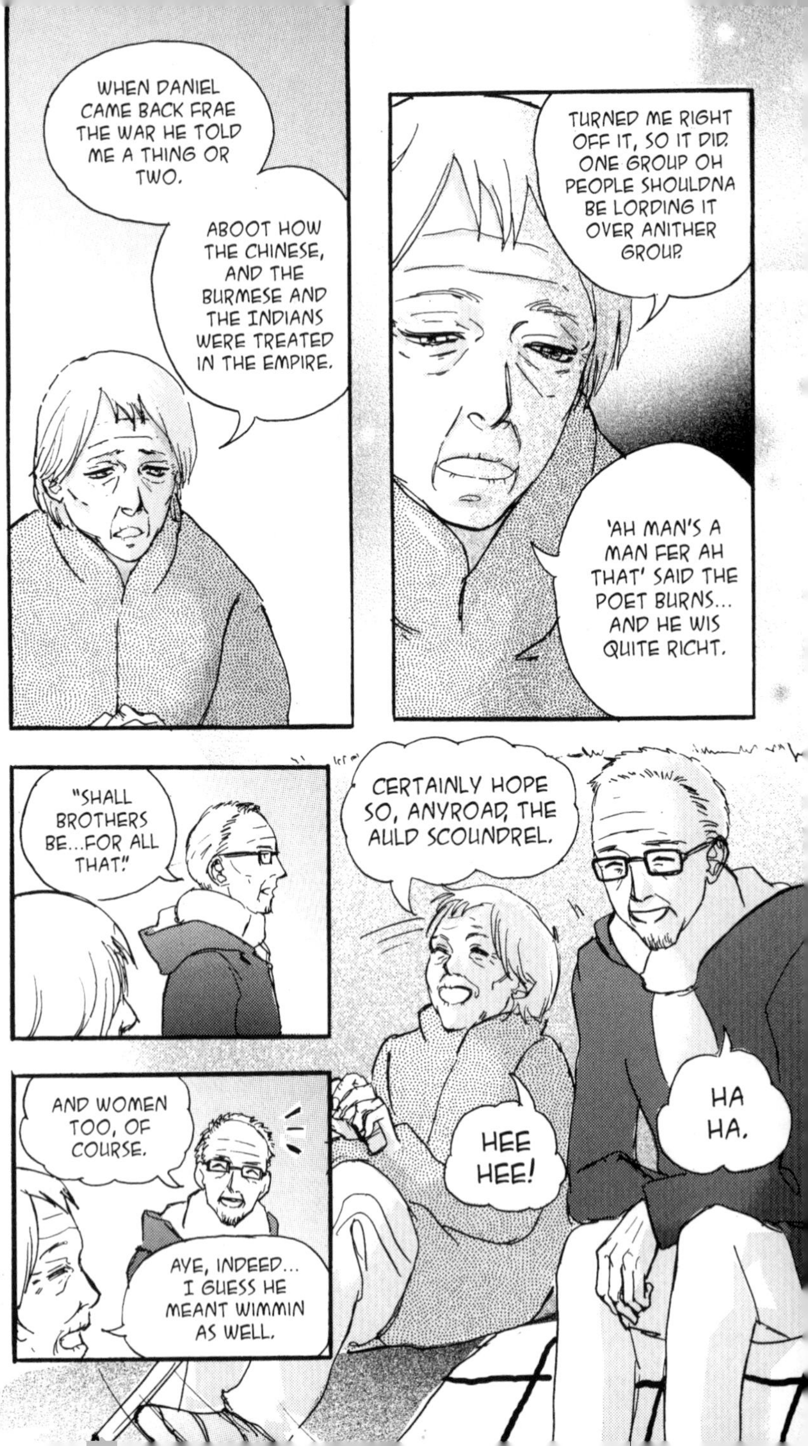
WHEN DANIEL CAME BACK FRAE THE WAR HE TOLD ME A THING OR TWO.
ABOOT HOW THE CHINESE, AND THE BURMESE AND THE INDIANS WERE TREATED IN THE EMPIRE.
TURNED ME RIGHT OFF IT, SO IT DID. ONE GROUP OH PEOPLE SHOULDNA BE LORDING IT OVER ANITHER GROUP.
'AH MAN'S A MAN FER AH THAT' SAID THE POET BURNS... AND HE WIS QUITE RICHT.
"SHALL BROTHERS BE...FOR ALL THAT."
AND WOMEN TOO, OF COURSE.
AYE, INDEED... I GUESS HE MEANT WIMMIN AS WELL.
CERTAINLY HOPE SO, ANYROAD, THE AULD SCOUNDREL.
HEE HEE!
HA HA.

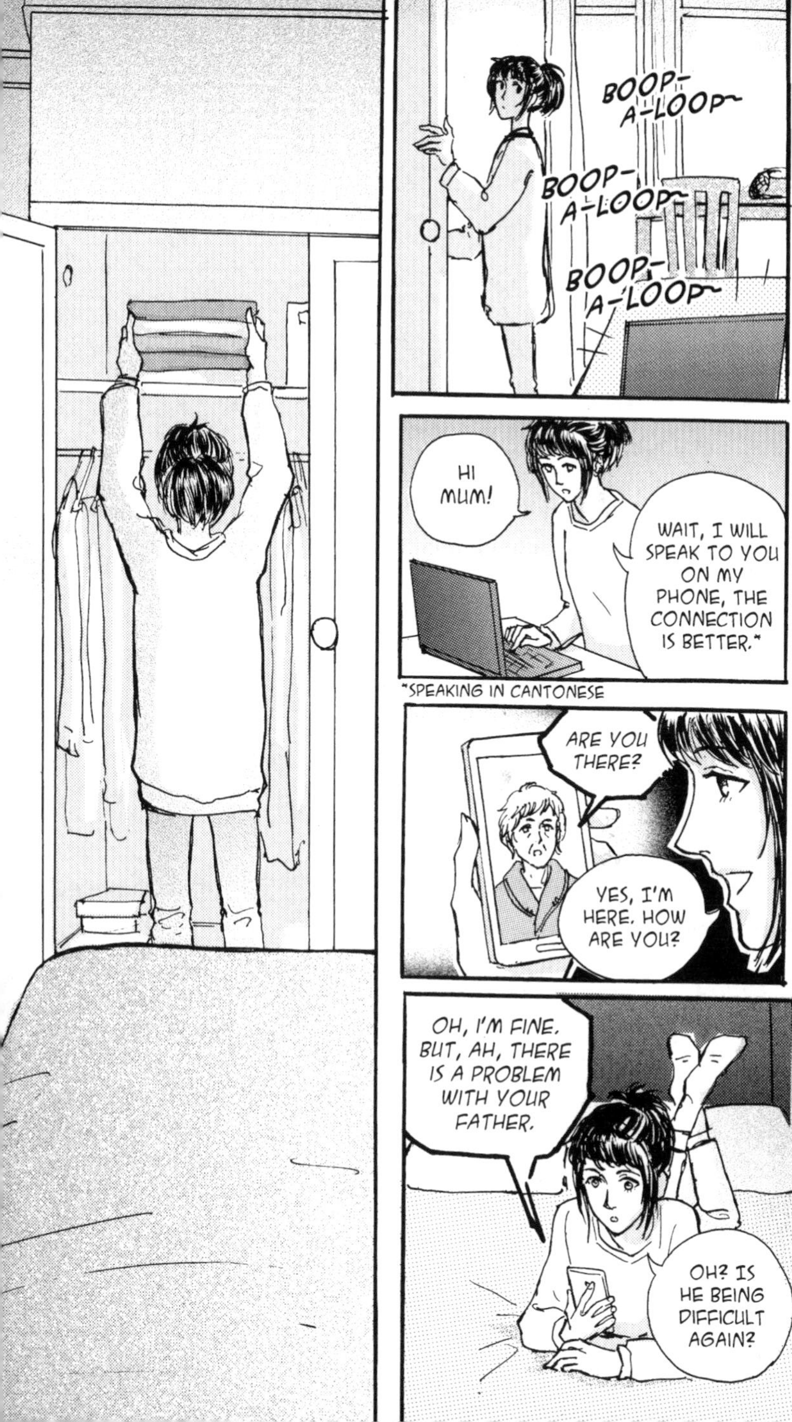
BOOP-A-LOOP~
BOOP-A-LOOP~
BOOP-A-LOOP~
HI MUM!
WAIT, I WILL SPEAK TO YOU ON MY PHONE, THE CONNECTION IS BETTER.*
ARE YOU THERE?
YES, I'M HERE. HOW ARE YOU?
OH, I'M FINE. BUT, AH, THERE IS A PROBLEM WITH YOUR FATHER.
OH? IS HE BEING DIFFICULT AGAIN?

*SPEAKING IN CANTONESE

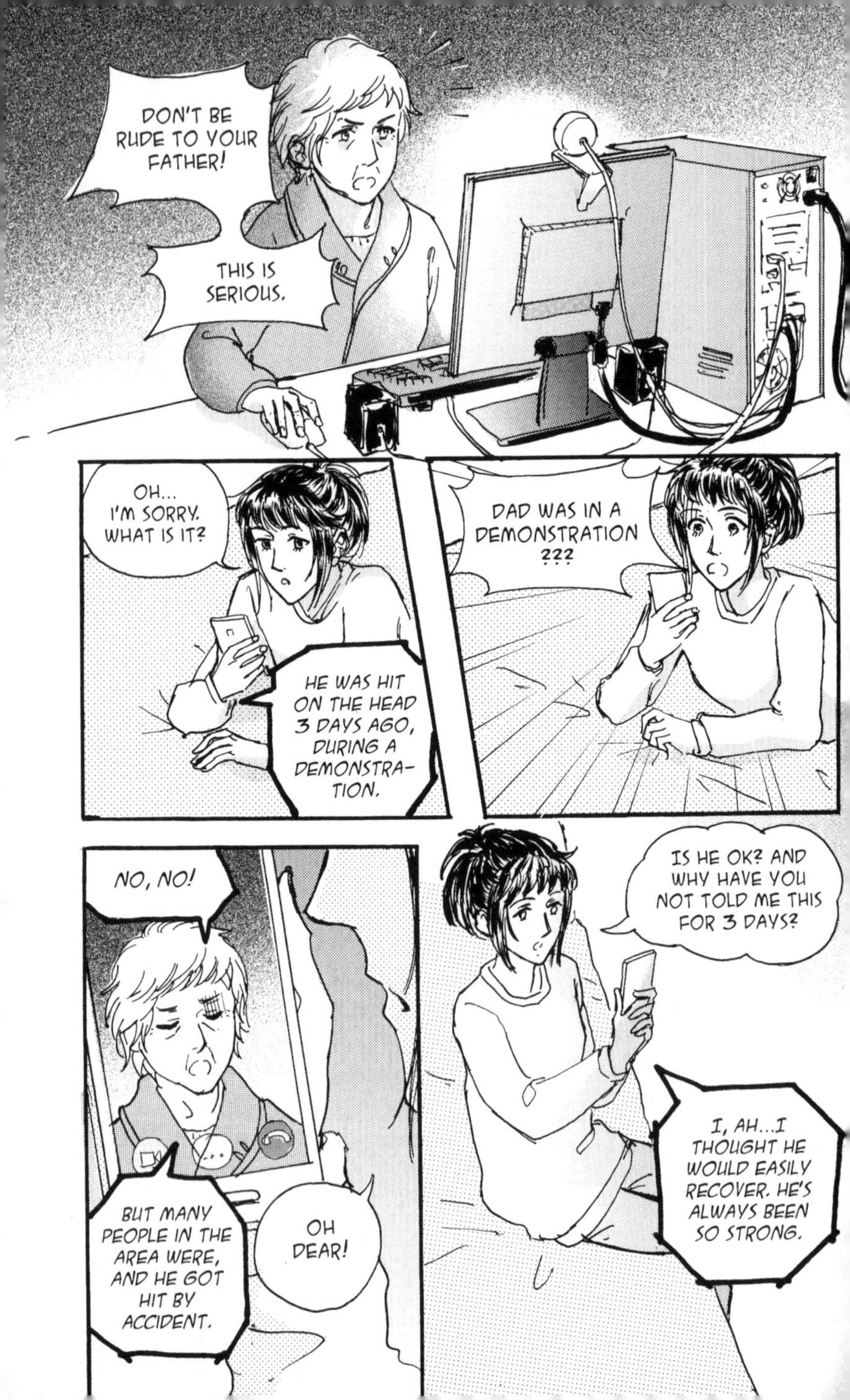
DON'T BE RUDE TO YOUR FATHER!
THIS IS SERIOUS.
OH... I'M SORRY. WHAT IS IT?
HE WAS HIT ON THE HEAD 3 DAYS AGO, DURING A DEMONSTRA-TION.
DAD WAS IN A DEMONSTRATION ???
NO, NO!
BUT MANY PEOPLE IN THE AREA WERE, AND HE GOT HIT BY ACCIDENT.
OH DEAR!
IS HE OK? AND WHY HAVE YOU NOT TOLD ME THIS FOR 3 DAYS?
I, AH...I THOUGHT HE WOULD EASILY RECOVER. HE'S ALWAYS BEEN SO STRONG.

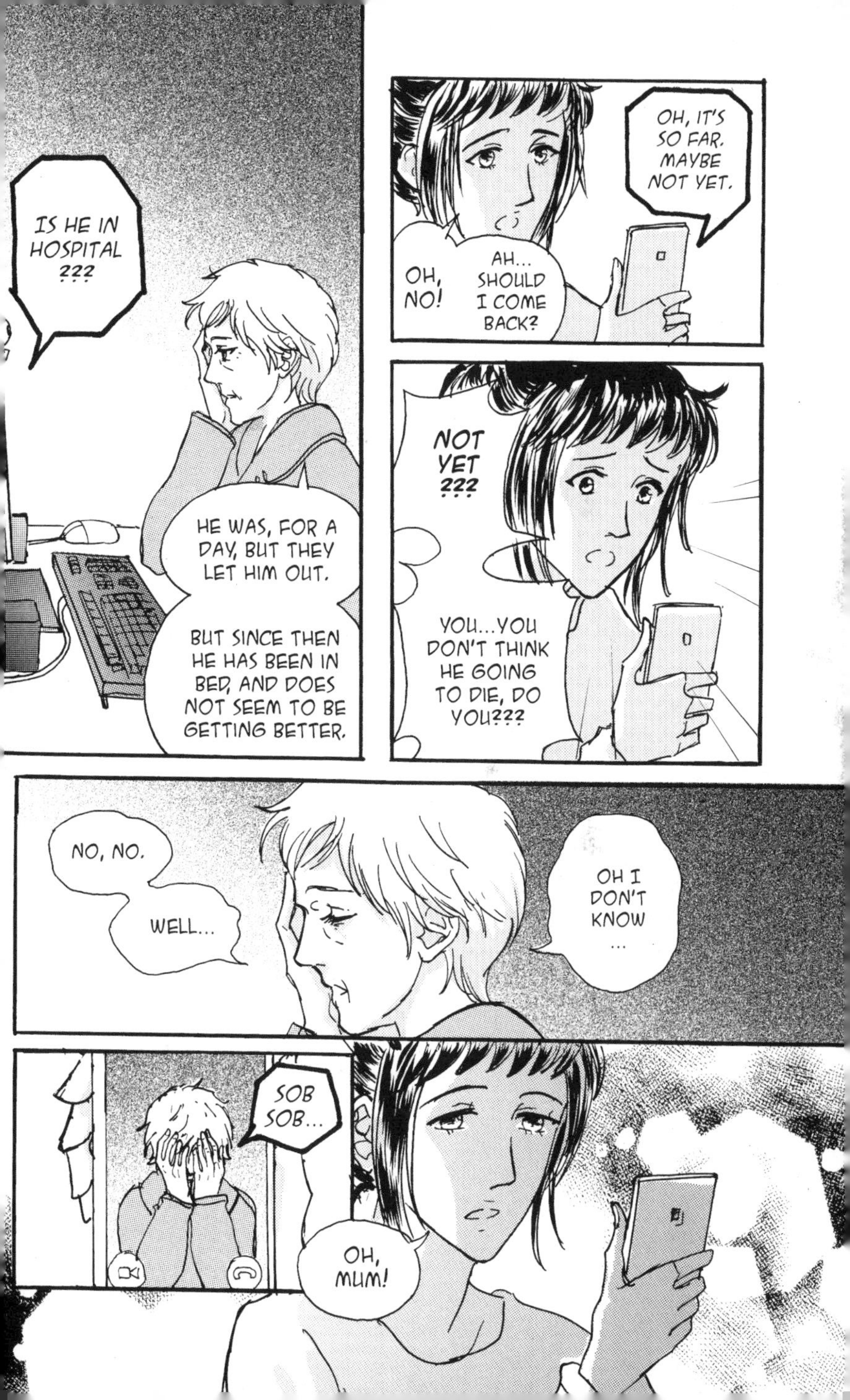
IS HE IN HOSPITAL ???
OH, IT'S SO FAR. MAYBE NOT YET.
OH, NO!
AH... SHOULD I COME BACK?
HE WAS, FOR A DAY, BUT THEY LET HIM OUT.
BUT SINCE THEN HE HAS BEEN IN BED, AND DOES NOT SEEM TO BE GETTING BETTER.
NOT YET ???
YOU...YOU DON'T THINK HE GOING TO DIE, DO YOU???
NO, NO.
WELL...
OH I DON'T KNOW ...
SOB SOB...
OH, MUM!

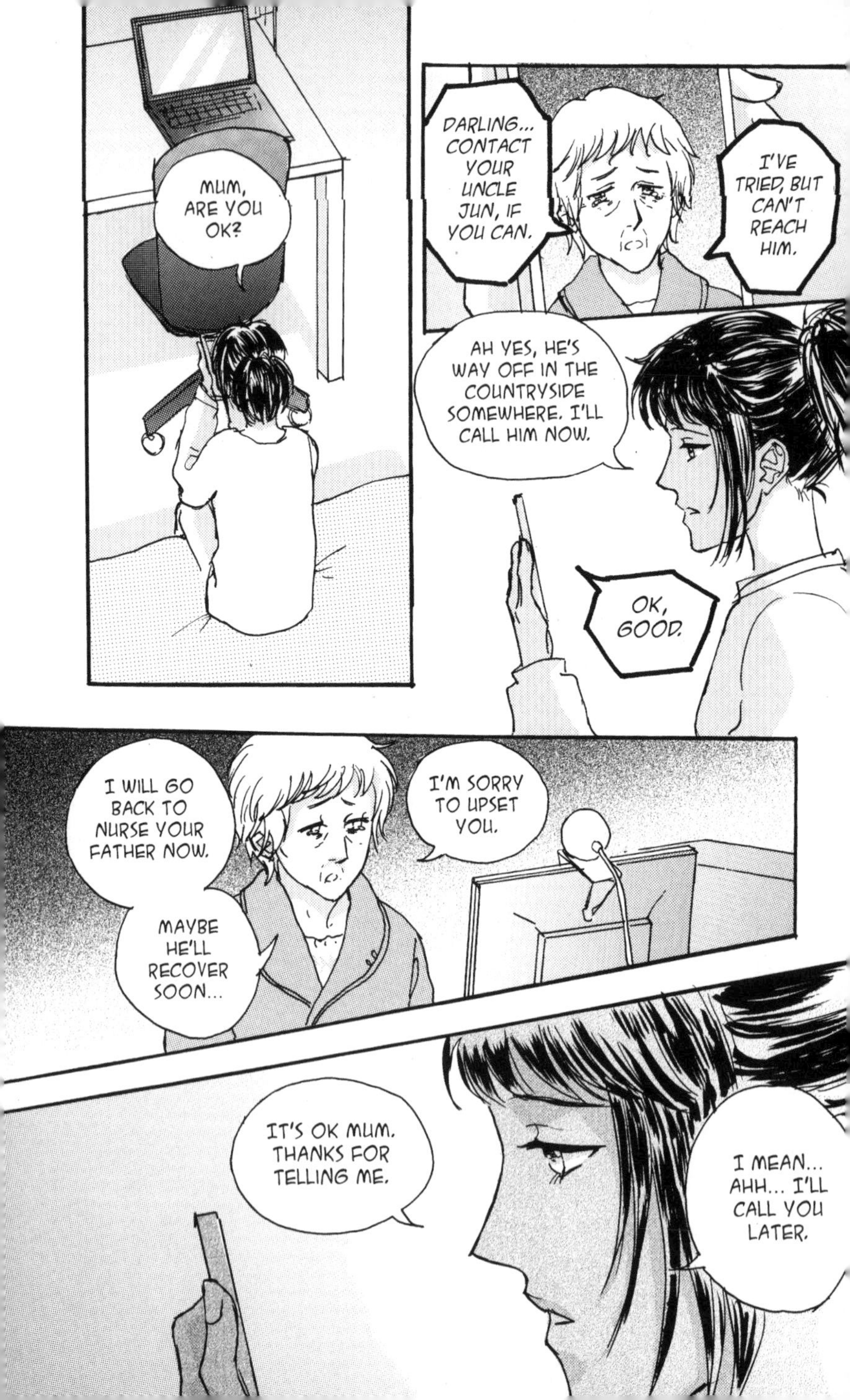
MUM, ARE YOU OK?
DARLING... CONTACT YOUR UNCLE JUN, IF YOU CAN.
I'VE TRIED, BUT CAN'T REACH HIM.
AH YES, HE'S WAY OFF IN THE COUNTRYSIDE SOMEWHERE. I'LL CALL HIM NOW.
OK, GOOD.
I WILL GO BACK TO NURSE YOUR FATHER NOW.
MAYBE HE'LL RECOVER SOON...
I'M SORRY TO UPSET YOU.
IT'S OK MUM. THANKS FOR TELLING ME.
I MEAN... AHH... I'LL CALL YOU LATER.

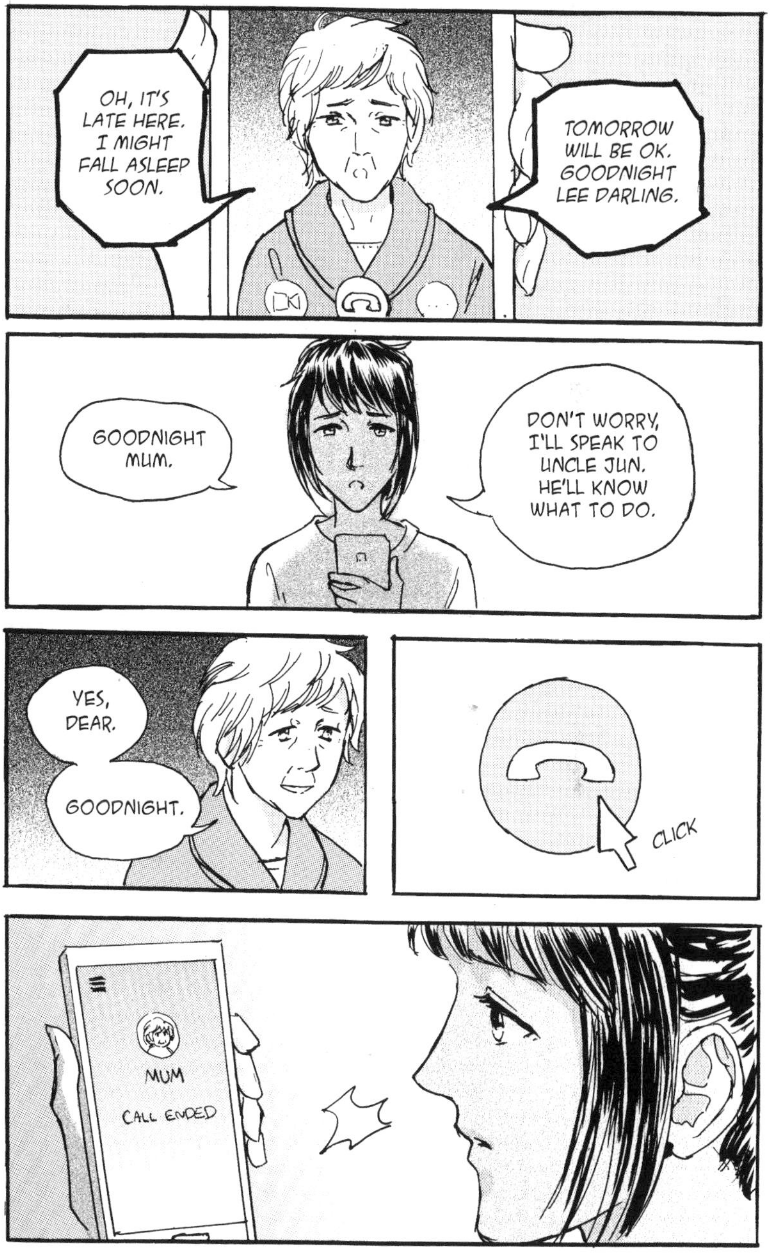
OH, IT'S LATE HERE. I MIGHT FALL ASLEEP SOON.
TOMORROW WILL BE OK. GOODNIGHT LEE DARLING.
GOODNIGHT MUM.
DON'T WORRY, I'LL SPEAK TO UNCLE JUN. HE'LL KNOW WHAT TO DO.
YES, DEAR.
GOODNIGHT.
CLICK
MUM
CALL ENDED

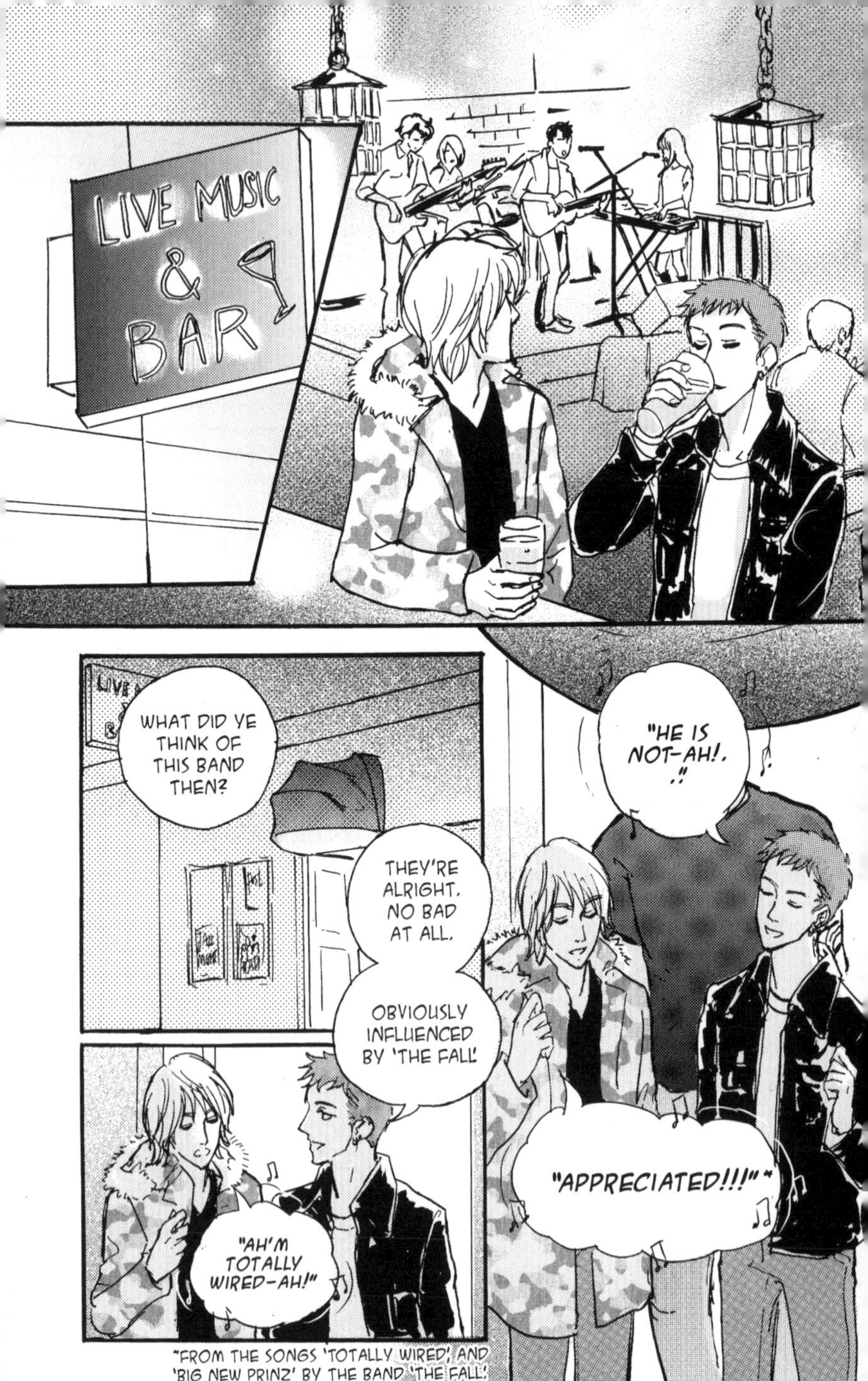
LIVE MUSIC & BAR
WHAT DID YE THINK OF THIS BAND THEN?
THEY'RE ALRIGHT. NO BAD AT ALL.
OBVIOUSLY INFLUENCED BY 'THE FALL'
"AH'M TOTALLY WIRED-AH!"
"HE IS NOT-AH!..."
"APPRECIATED!!!"*

*FROM THE SONGS 'TOTALLY WIRED' AND 'BIG NEW PRINZ' BY THE BAND 'THE FALL'.

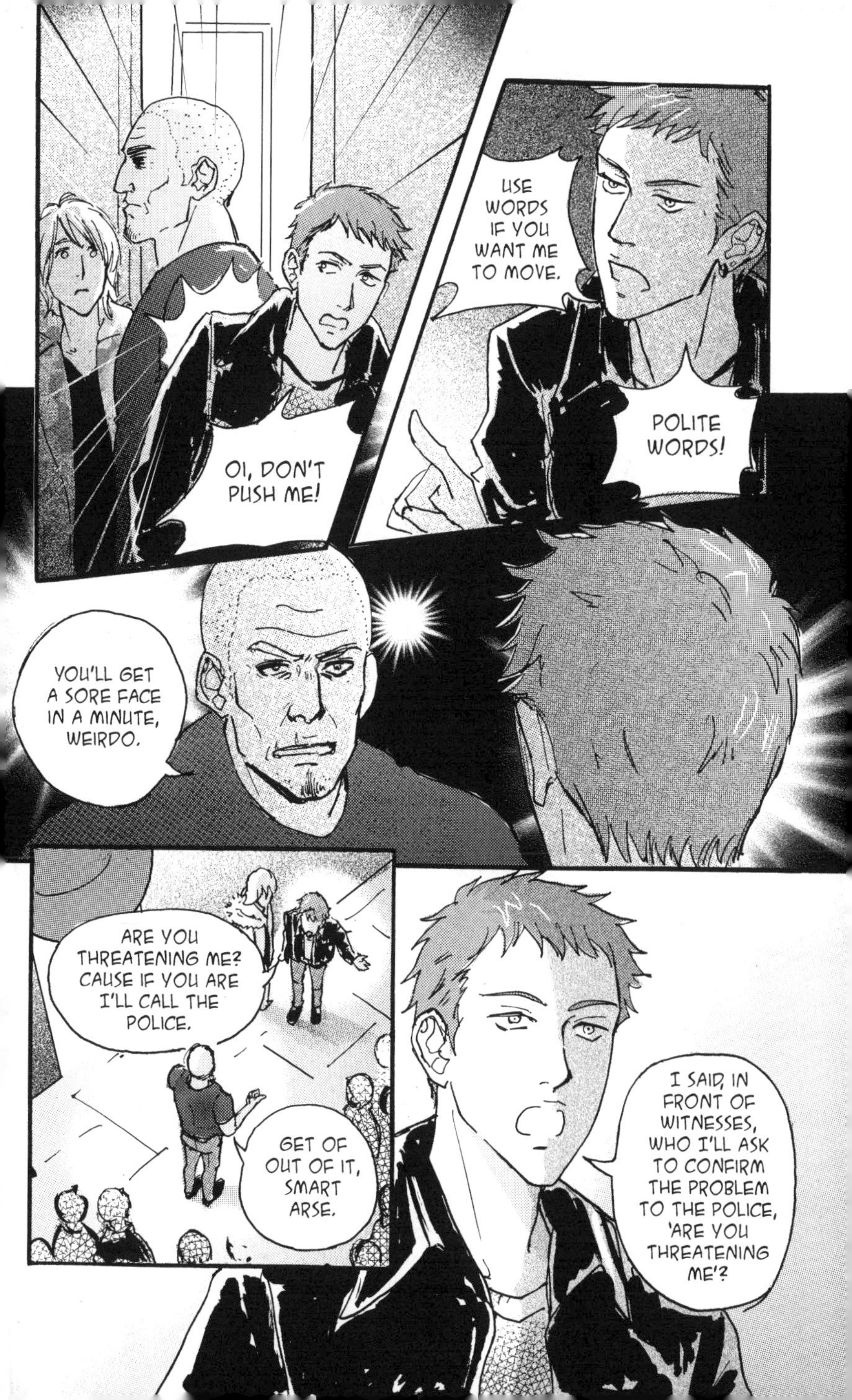
OI, DON'T PUSH ME!
USE WORDS IF YOU WANT ME TO MOVE.
POLITE WORDS!
YOU'LL GET A SORE FACE IN A MINUTE, WEIRDO.
ARE YOU THREATENING ME? CAUSE IF YOU ARE I'LL CALL THE POLICE.
GET OF OUT OF IT, SMART ARSE.
I SAID, IN FRONT OF WITNESSES, WHO I'LL ASK TO CONFIRM THE PROBLEM TO THE POLICE, 'ARE YOU THREATENING ME'?

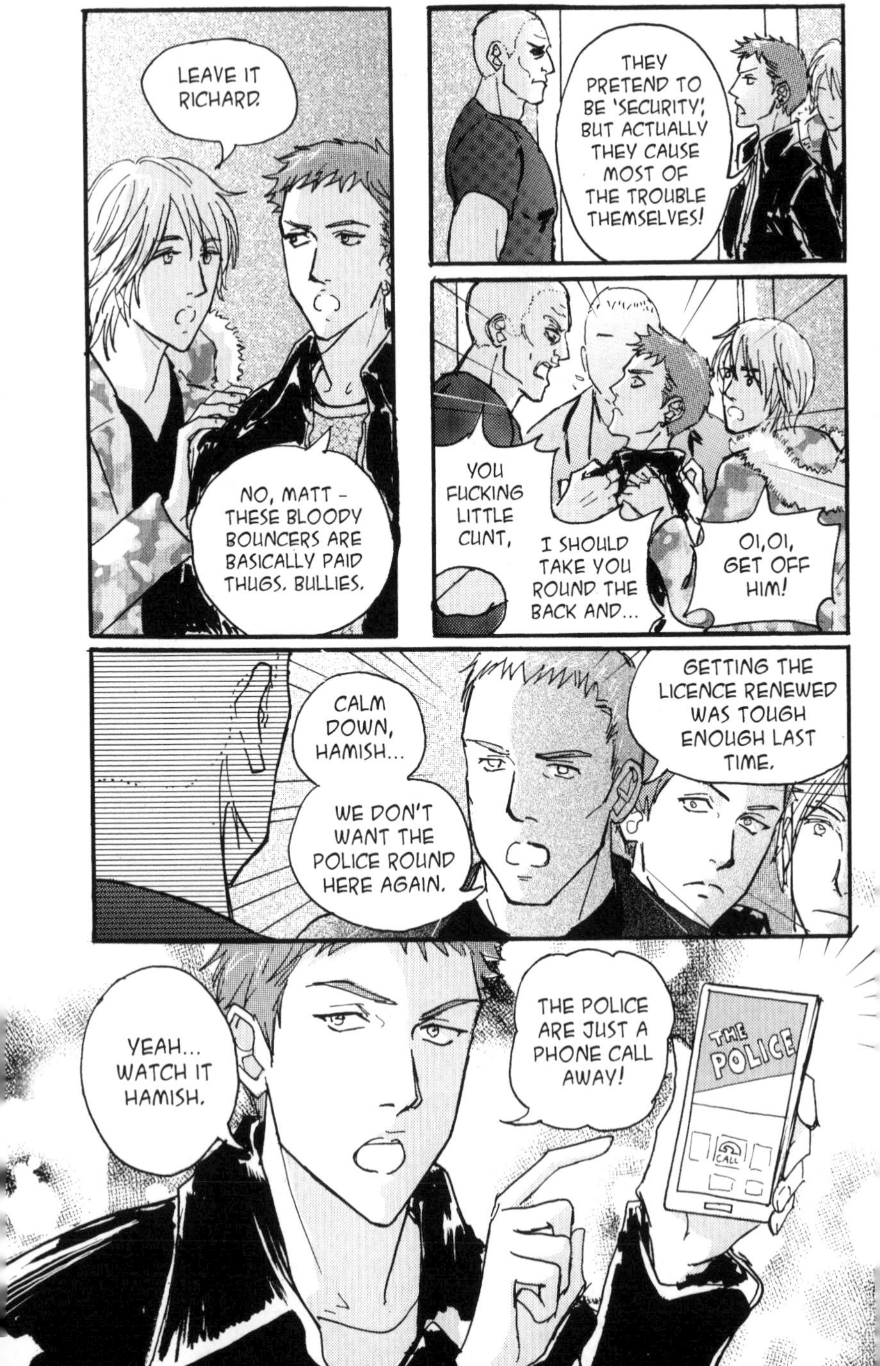
LEAVE IT RICHARD.
NO, MATT - THESE BLOODY BOUNCERS ARE BASICALLY PAID THUGS. BULLIES.
THEY PRETEND TO BE 'SECURITY', BUT ACTUALLY THEY CAUSE MOST OF THE TROUBLE THEMSELVES!
YOU FUCKING LITTLE CUNT,
I SHOULD TAKE YOU ROUND THE BACK AND...
OI, OI, GET OFF HIM!
CALM DOWN, HAMISH...
WE DON'T WANT THE POLICE ROUND HERE AGAIN.
GETTING THE LICENCE RENEWED WAS TOUGH ENOUGH LAST TIME.
YEAH... WATCH IT HAMISH.
THE POLICE ARE JUST A PHONE CALL AWAY!
THE POLICE
CALL

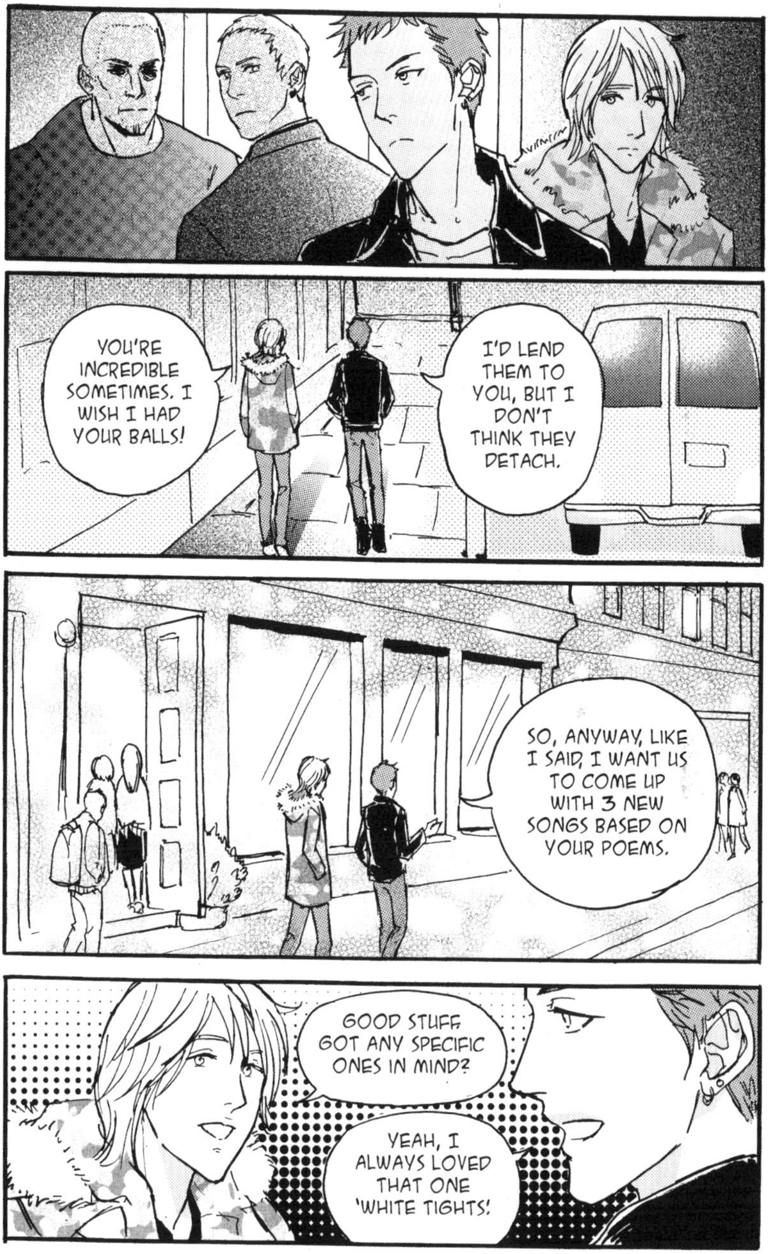
YOU'RE INCREDIBLE SOMETIMES. I WISH I HAD YOUR BALLS!
I'D LEND THEM TO YOU, BUT I DON'T THINK THEY DETACH.
SO, ANYWAY, LIKE I SAID, I WANT US TO COME UP WITH 3 NEW SONGS BASED ON YOUR POEMS.
GOOD STUFF. GOT ANY SPECIFIC ONES IN MIND?
YEAH, I ALWAYS LOVED THAT ONE 'WHITE TIGHTS.'

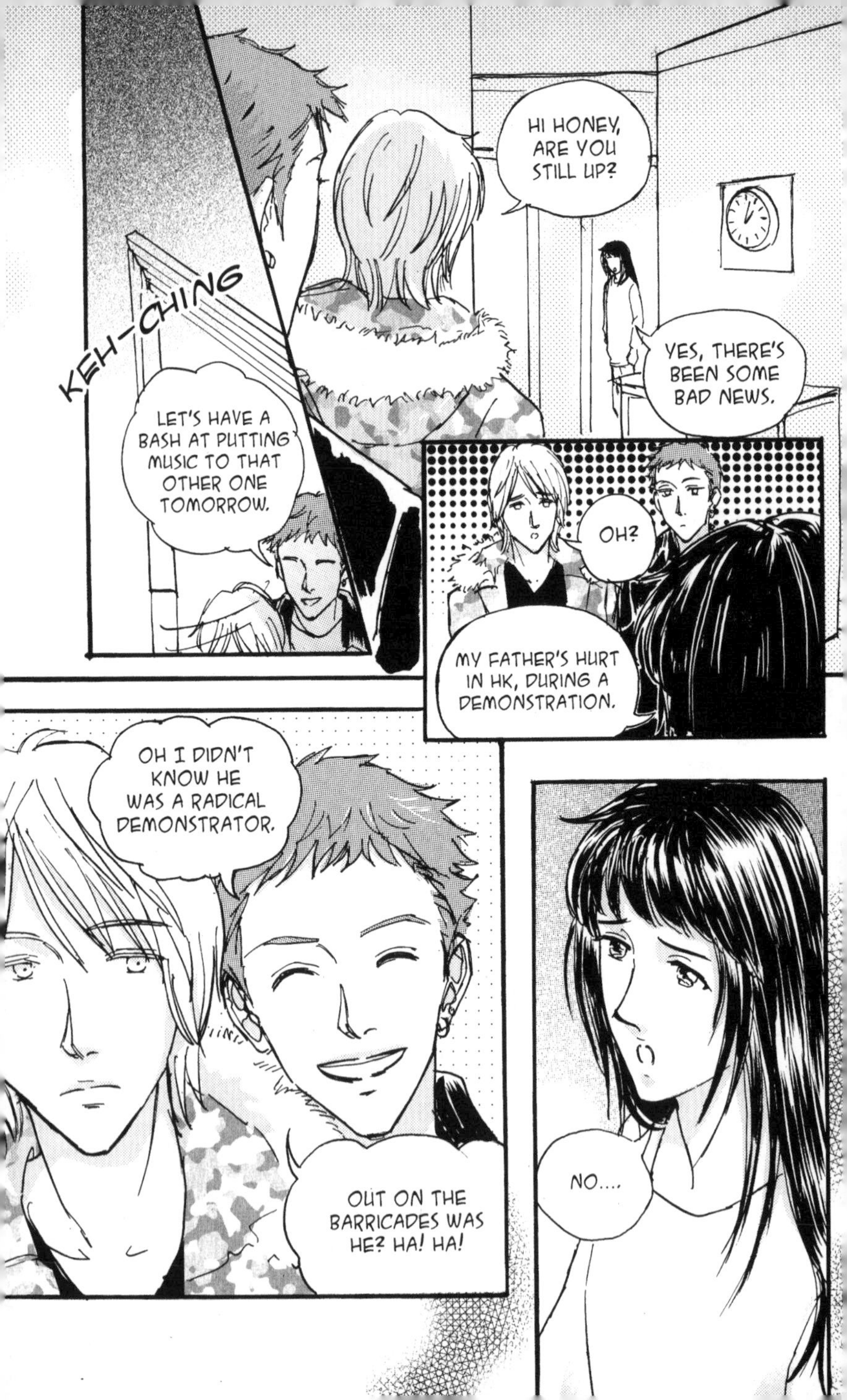
KEH-CHING
LET'S HAVE A BASH AT PUTTING MUSIC TO THAT OTHER ONE TOMORROW.
HI HONEY, ARE YOU STILL UP?
YES, THERE'S BEEN SOME BAD NEWS.
OH?
MY FATHER'S HURT IN HK, DURING A DEMONSTRATION.
OH I DIDN'T KNOW HE WAS A RADICAL DEMONSTRATOR.
OUT ON THE BARRICADES WAS HE? HA! HA!
NO....

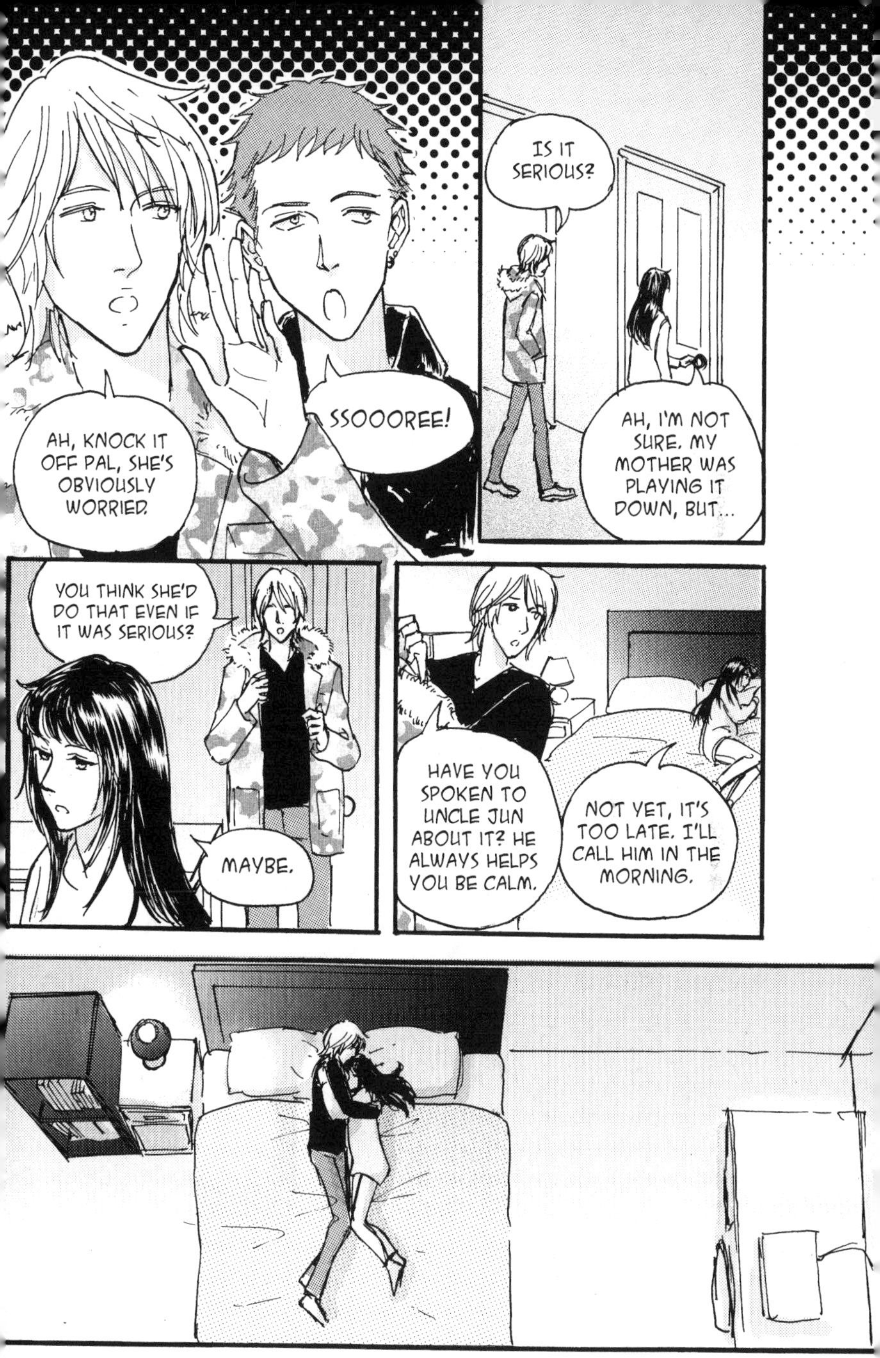
AH, KNOCK IT OFF PAL, SHE'S OBVIOUSLY WORRIED.
SSOOOREE!
IS IT SERIOUS?
AH, I'M NOT SURE. MY MOTHER WAS PLAYING IT DOWN, BUT...
YOU THINK SHE'D DO THAT EVEN IF IT WAS SERIOUS?
MAYBE.
HAVE YOU SPOKEN TO UNCLE JUN ABOUT IT? HE ALWAYS HELPS YOU BE CALM.
NOT YET, IT'S TOO LATE. I'LL CALL HIM IN THE MORNING.

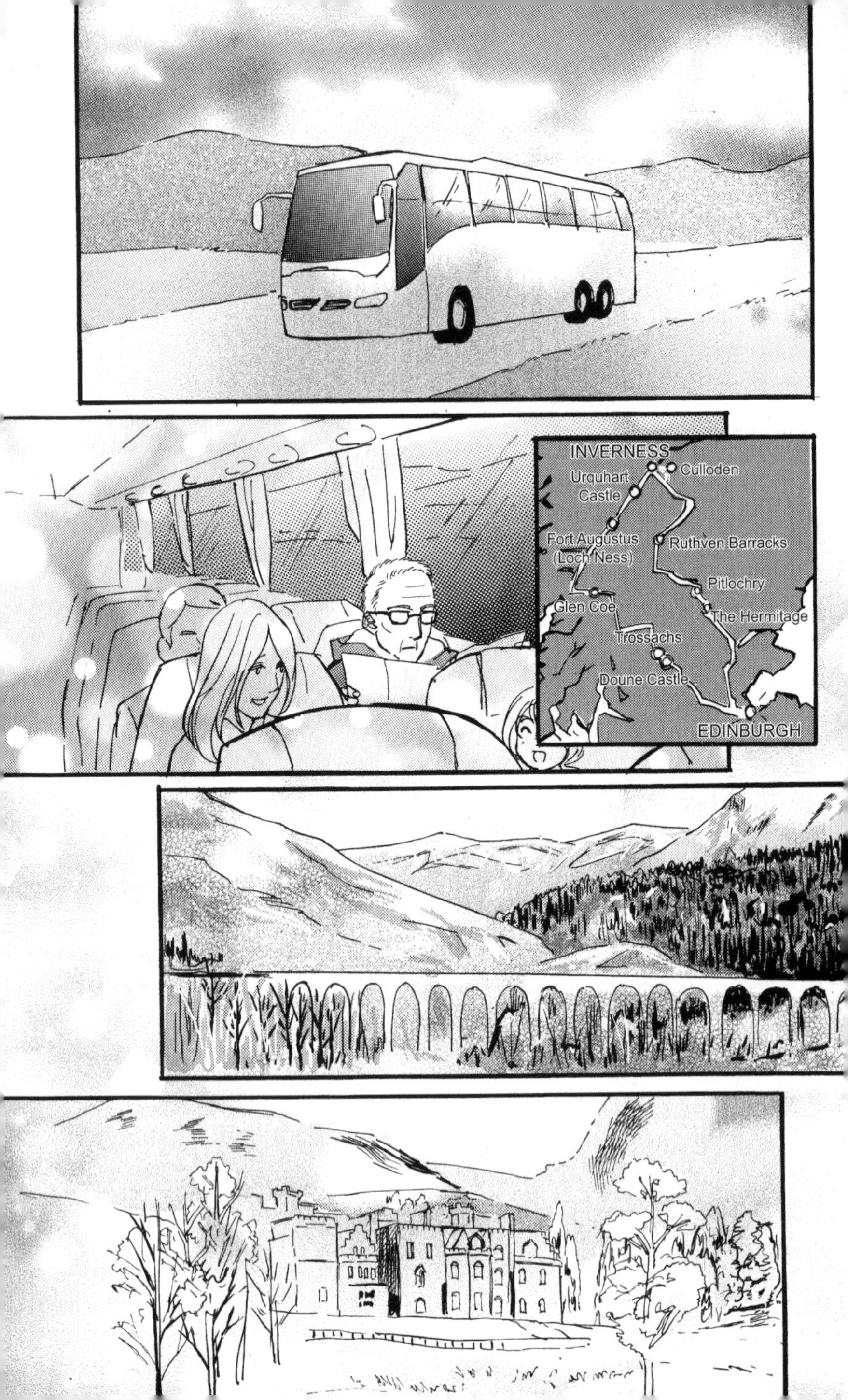
INVERNESS
Culloden
Urquhart Castle
Fort Augustus (Loch Ness)
Ruthven Barracks
Pitlochry
Glen Coe
The Hermitage
Trossachs
Doune Castle
EDINBURGH

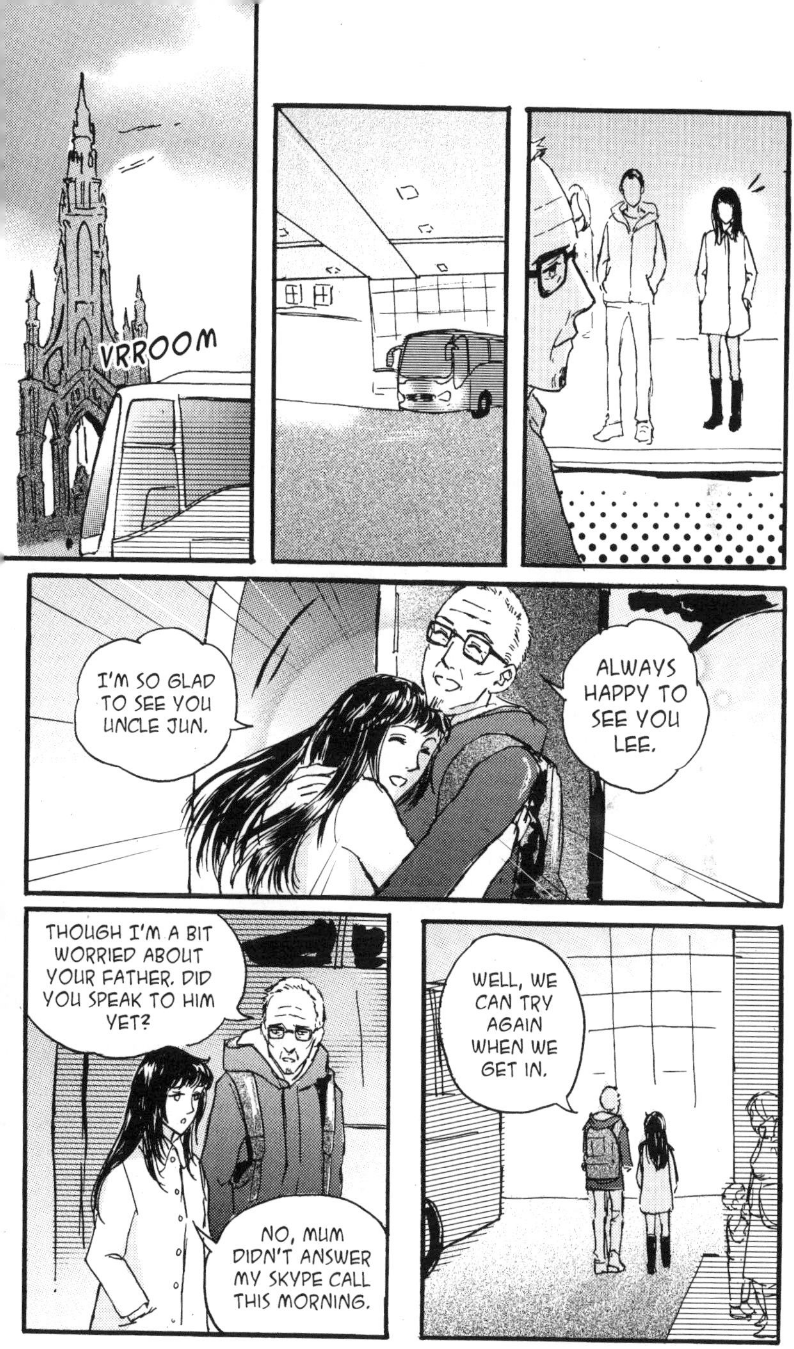
VRROOM
I'M SO GLAD TO SEE YOU UNCLE JUN.
ALWAYS HAPPY TO SEE YOU LEE.
THOUGH I'M A BIT WORRIED ABOUT YOUR FATHER. DID YOU SPEAK TO HIM YET?
NO, MUM DIDN'T ANSWER MY SKYPE CALL THIS MORNING.
WELL, WE CAN TRY AGAIN WHEN WE GET IN.

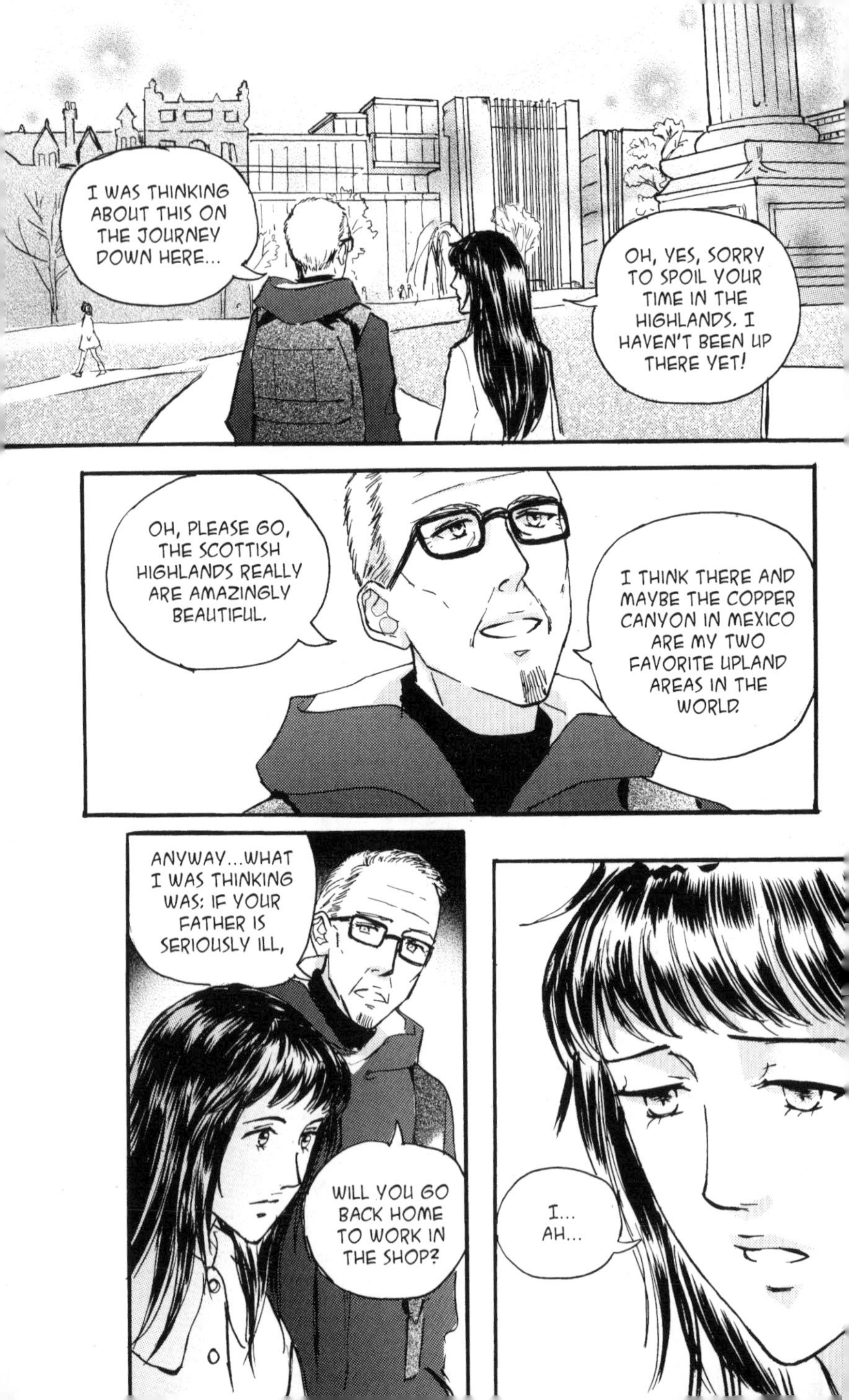
I WAS THINKING ABOUT THIS ON THE JOURNEY DOWN HERE...
OH, YES, SORRY TO SPOIL YOUR TIME IN THE HIGHLANDS. I HAVEN'T BEEN UP THERE YET!
OH, PLEASE GO, THE SCOTTISH HIGHLANDS REALLY ARE AMAZINGLY BEAUTIFUL.
I THINK THERE AND MAYBE THE COPPER CANYON IN MEXICO ARE MY TWO FAVORITE UPLAND AREAS IN THE WORLD.
ANYWAY...WHAT I WAS THINKING WAS: IF YOUR FATHER IS SERIOUSLY ILL,
WILL YOU GO BACK HOME TO WORK IN THE SHOP?
I... AH...

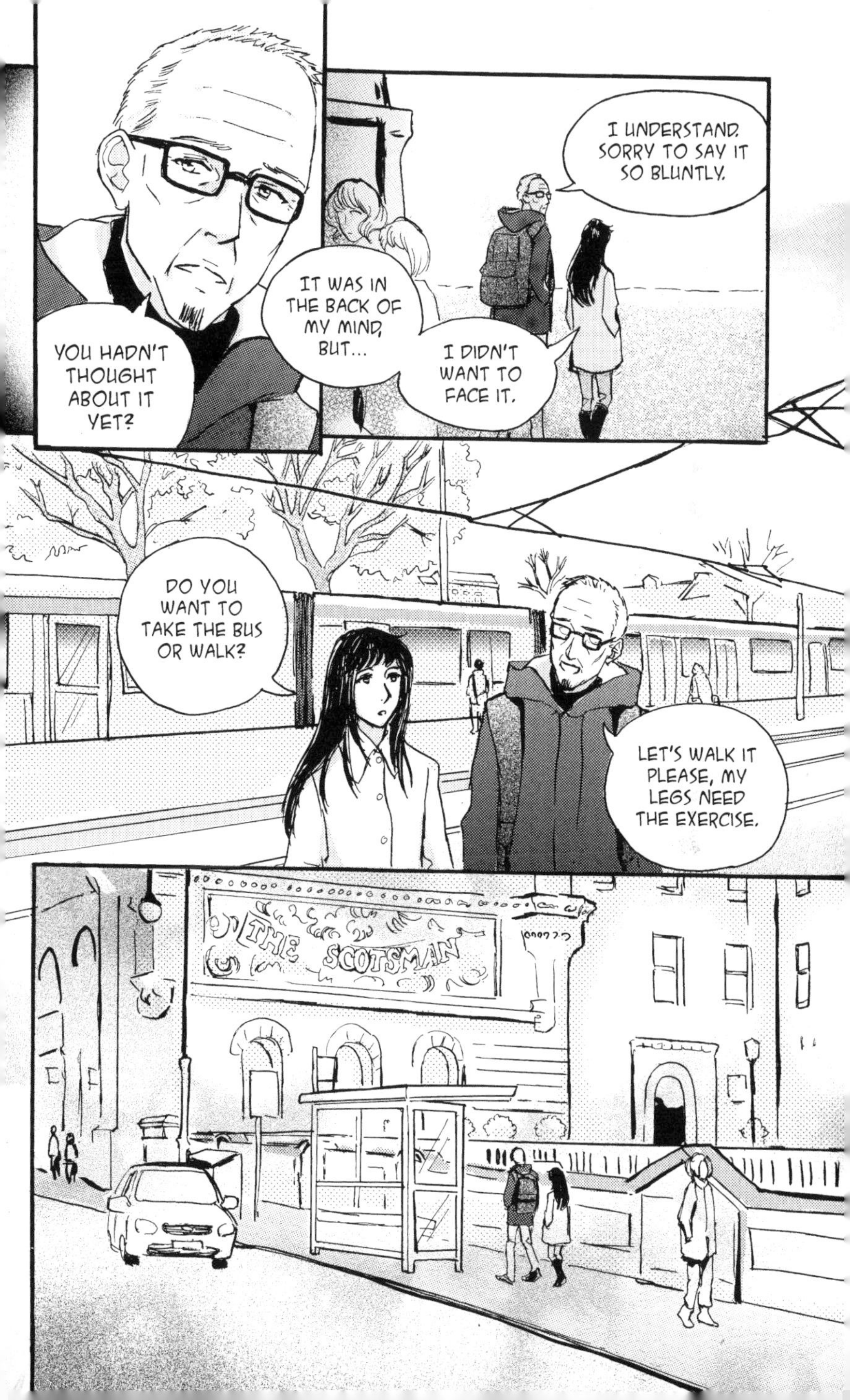
I UNDERSTAND. SORRY TO SAY IT SO BLUNTLY.
YOU HADN'T THOUGHT ABOUT IT YET?
IT WAS IN THE BACK OF MY MIND, BUT...
I DIDN'T WANT TO FACE IT.
DO YOU WANT TO TAKE THE BUS OR WALK?
LET'S WALK IT PLEASE, MY LEGS NEED THE EXERCISE.
THE SCOTSMAN

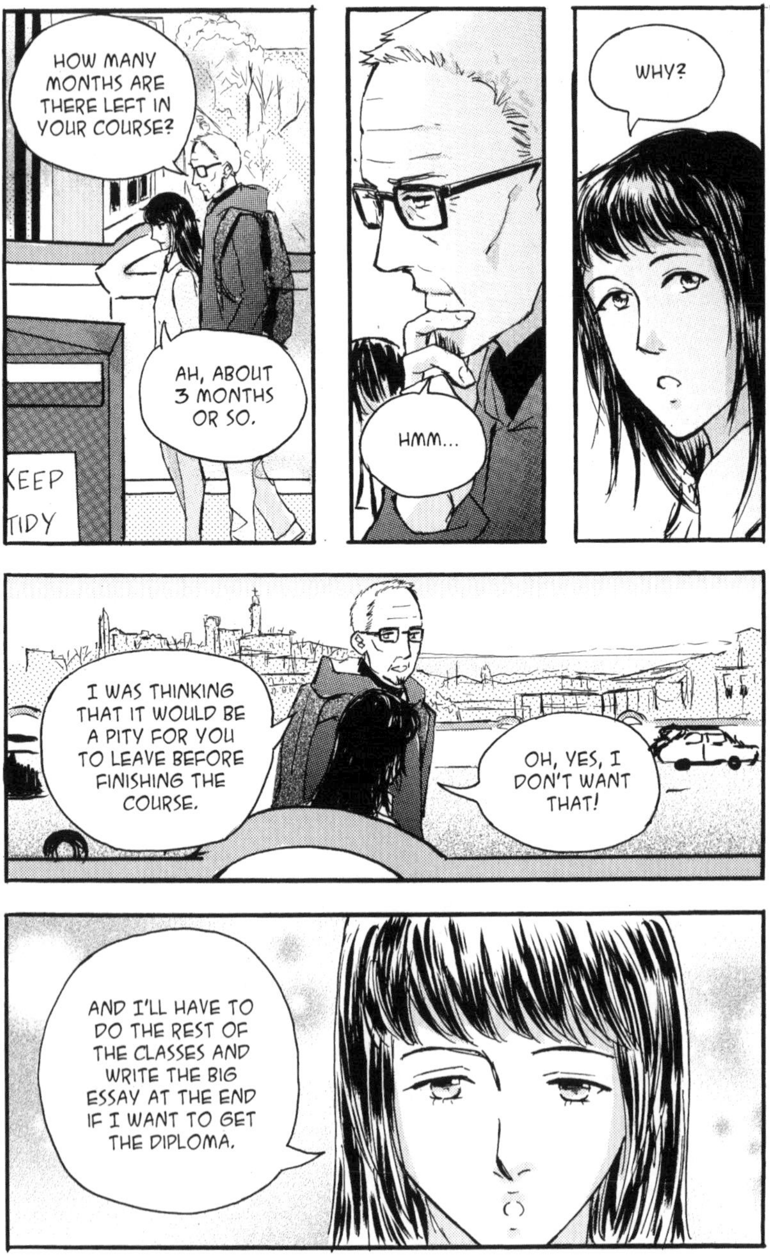
HOW MANY MONTHS ARE THERE LEFT IN YOUR COURSE?
AH, ABOUT 3 MONTHS OR SO.
KEEP TIDY
HMM...
WHY?
I WAS THINKING THAT IT WOULD BE A PITY FOR YOU TO LEAVE BEFORE FINISHING THE COURSE.
OH, YES, I DON'T WANT THAT!
AND I'LL HAVE TO DO THE REST OF THE CLASSES AND WRITE THE BIG ESSAY AT THE END IF I WANT TO GET THE DIPLOMA.

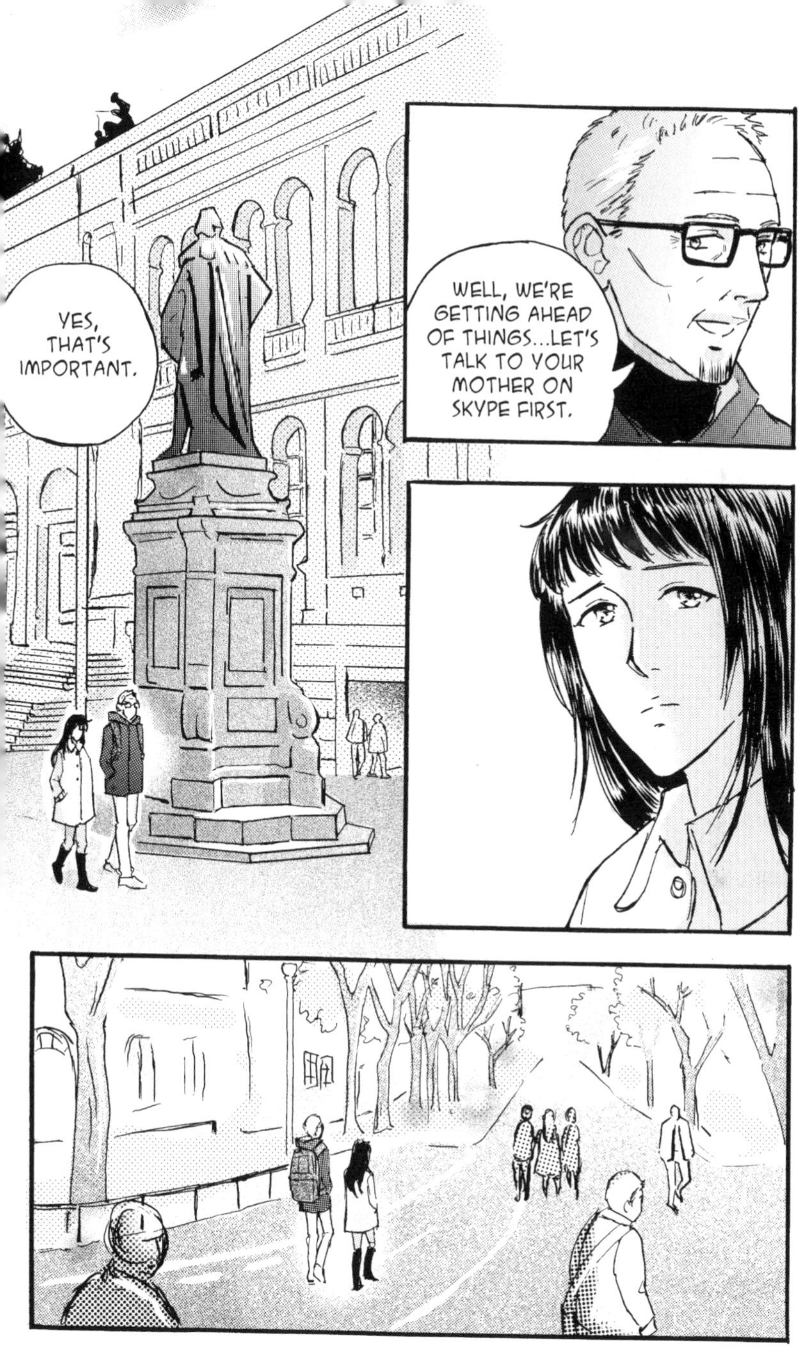
WELL, WE'RE GETTING AHEAD OF THINGS...LET'S TALK TO YOUR MOTHER ON SKYPE FIRST.
YES, THAT'S IMPORTANT.

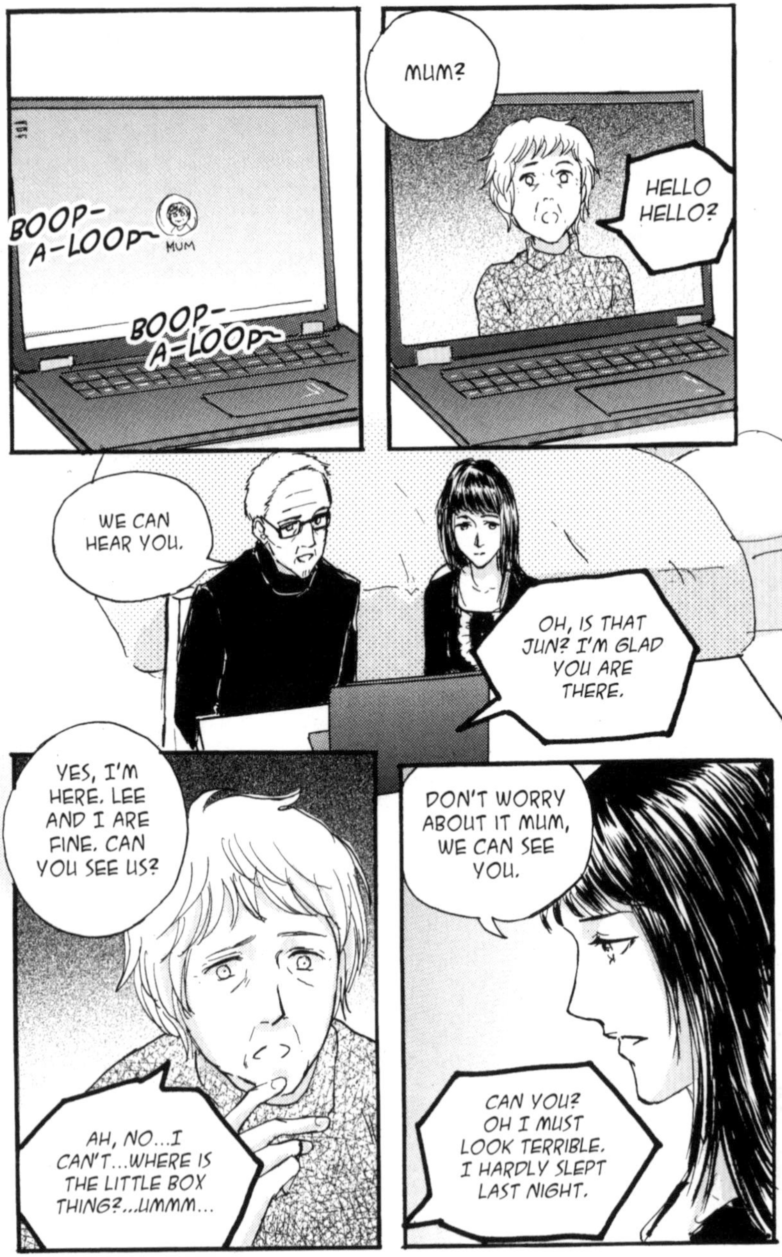
BOOP-A-LOOP
MUM
BOOP-A-LOOP
MUM?
HELLO HELLO?
WE CAN HEAR YOU.
OH, IS THAT JUN? I'M GLAD YOU ARE THERE.
YES, I'M HERE. LEE AND I ARE FINE. CAN YOU SEE US?
AH, NO...I CAN'T...WHERE IS THE LITTLE BOX THING?...UMMM...
DON'T WORRY ABOUT IT MUM, WE CAN SEE YOU.
CAN YOU? OH I MUST LOOK TERRIBLE. I HARDLY SLEPT LAST NIGHT.

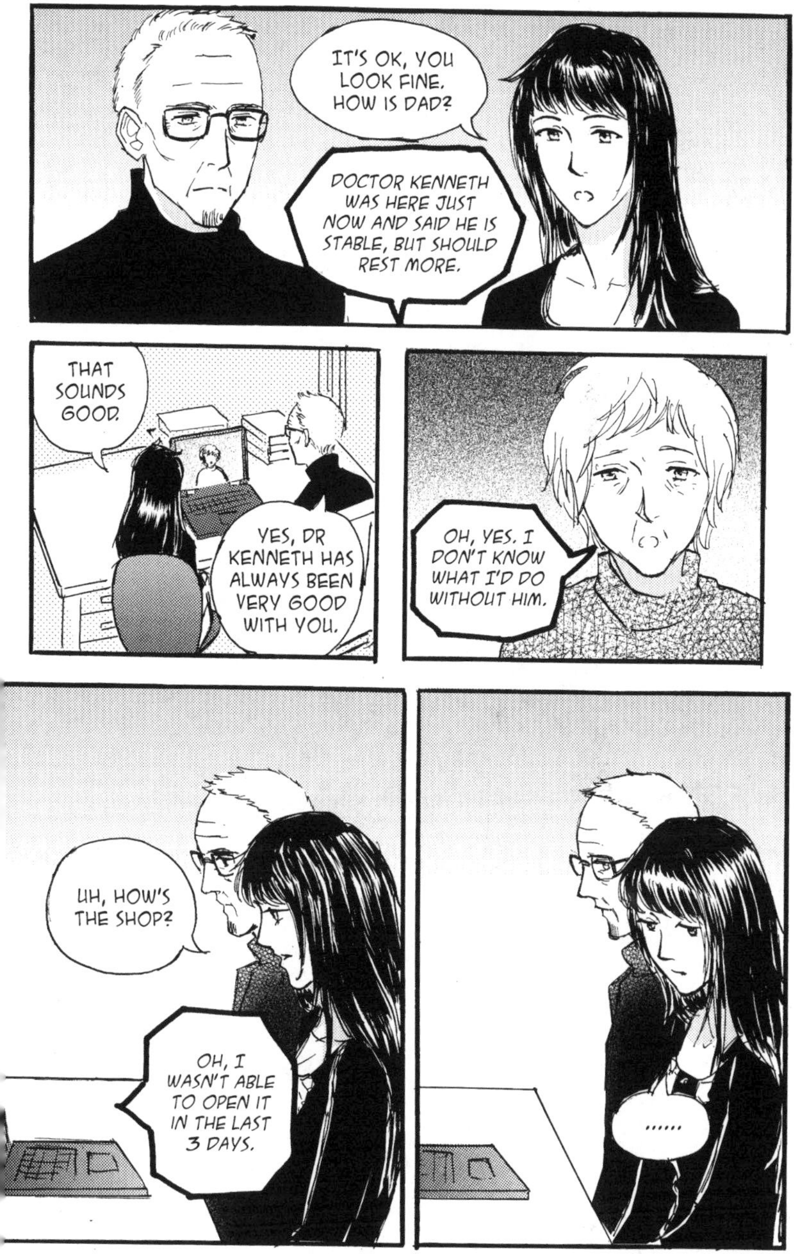
IT'S OK, YOU LOOK FINE. HOW IS DAD?
DOCTOR KENNETH WAS HERE JUST NOW AND SAID HE IS STABLE, BUT SHOULD REST MORE.
THAT SOUNDS GOOD.
YES, DR KENNETH HAS ALWAYS BEEN VERY GOOD WITH YOU.
OH, YES. I DON'T KNOW WHAT I'D DO WITHOUT HIM.
UH, HOW'S THE SHOP?
OH, I WASN'T ABLE TO OPEN IT IN THE LAST 3 DAYS.
......

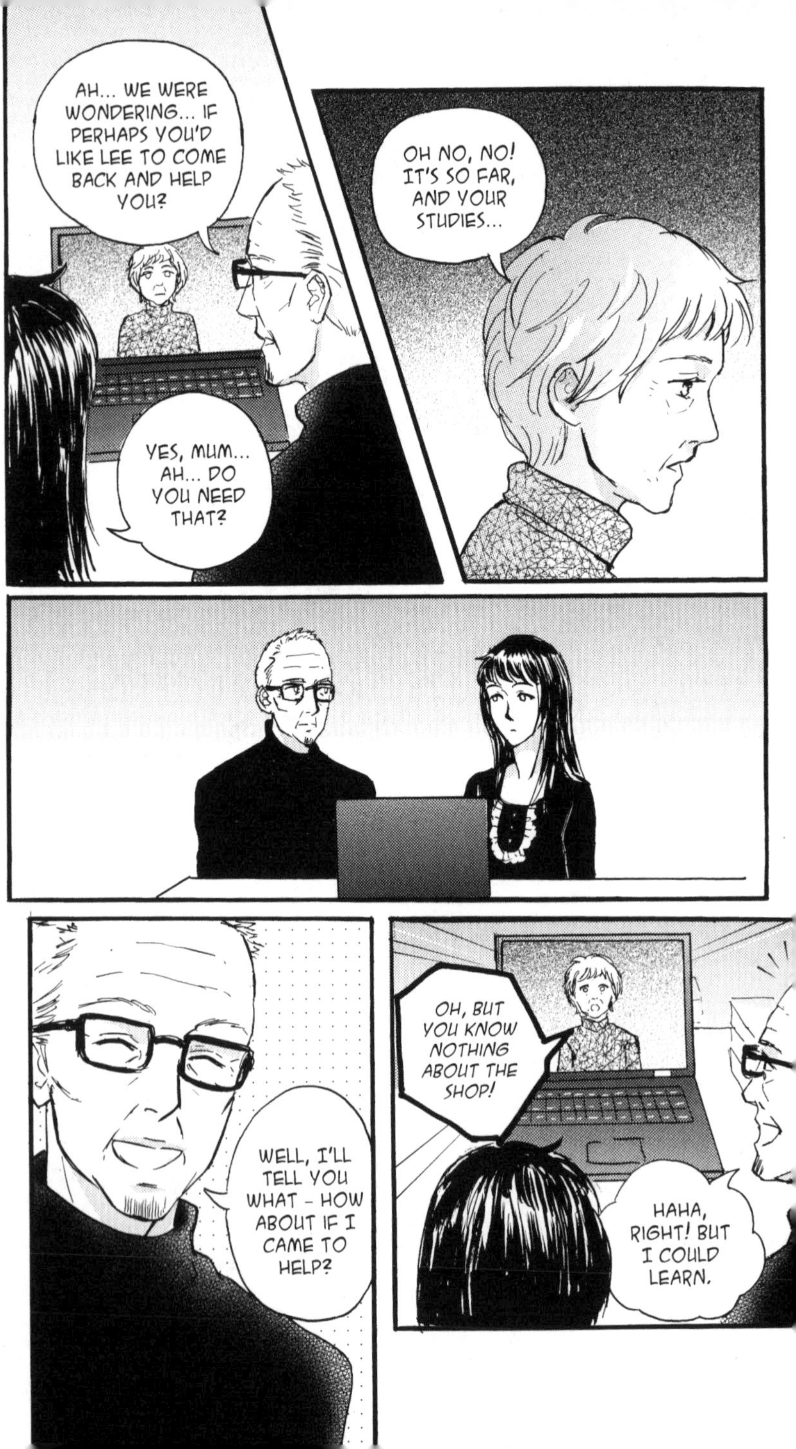
AH... WE WERE WONDERING... IF PERHAPS YOU'D LIKE LEE TO COME BACK AND HELP YOU?
YES, MUM... AH... DO YOU NEED THAT?
OH NO, NO! IT'S SO FAR, AND YOUR STUDIES...
WELL, I'LL TELL YOU WHAT - HOW ABOUT IF I CAME TO HELP?
OH, BUT YOU KNOW NOTHING ABOUT THE SHOP!
HAHA, RIGHT! BUT I COULD LEARN.

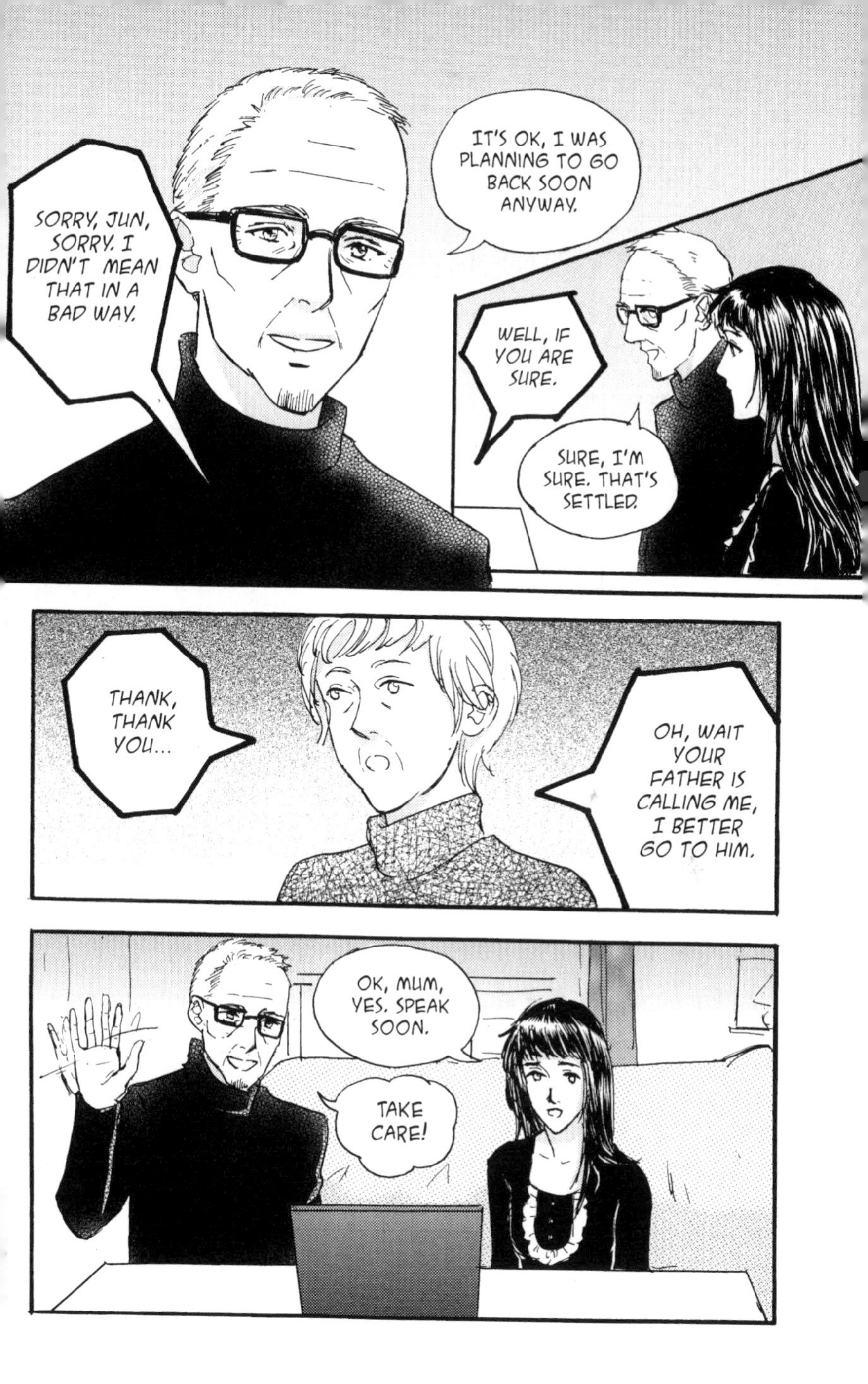
SORRY, JUN, SORRY. I DIDN'T MEAN THAT IN A BAD WAY.
IT'S OK, I WAS PLANNING TO GO BACK SOON ANYWAY.
WELL, IF YOU ARE SURE.
SURE, I'M SURE. THAT'S SETTLED.
THANK, THANK YOU...
OH, WAIT YOUR FATHER IS CALLING ME, I BETTER GO TO HIM.
OK, MUM, YES. SPEAK SOON.
TAKE CARE!

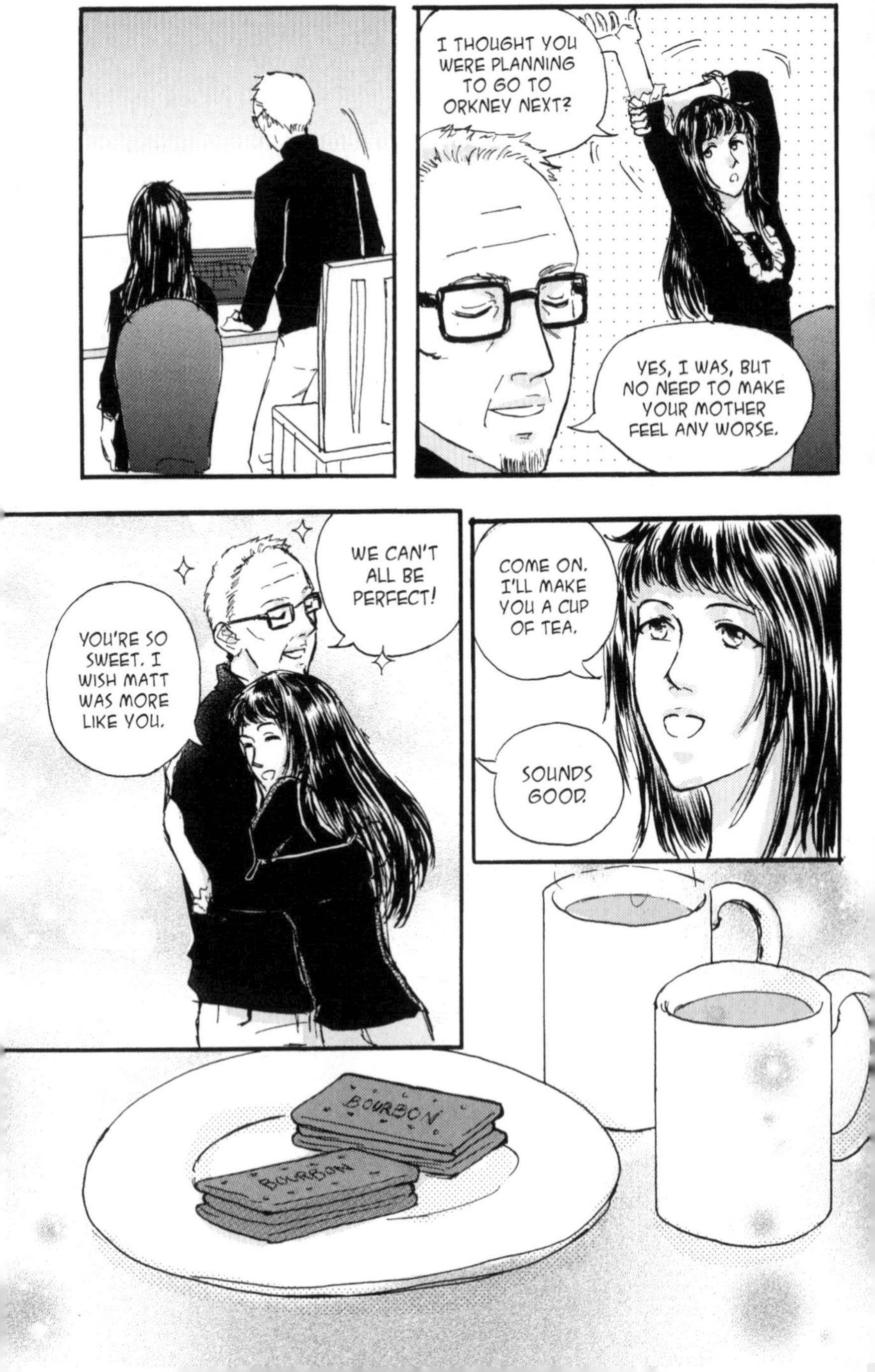
I THOUGHT YOU WERE PLANNING TO GO TO ORKNEY NEXT?
YES, I WAS, BUT NO NEED TO MAKE YOUR MOTHER FEEL ANY WORSE.
WE CAN'T ALL BE PERFECT!
YOU'RE SO SWEET. I WISH MATT WAS MORE LIKE YOU.
COME ON. I'LL MAKE YOU A CUP OF TEA.
SOUNDS GOOD.
BOURBON
BOURBON

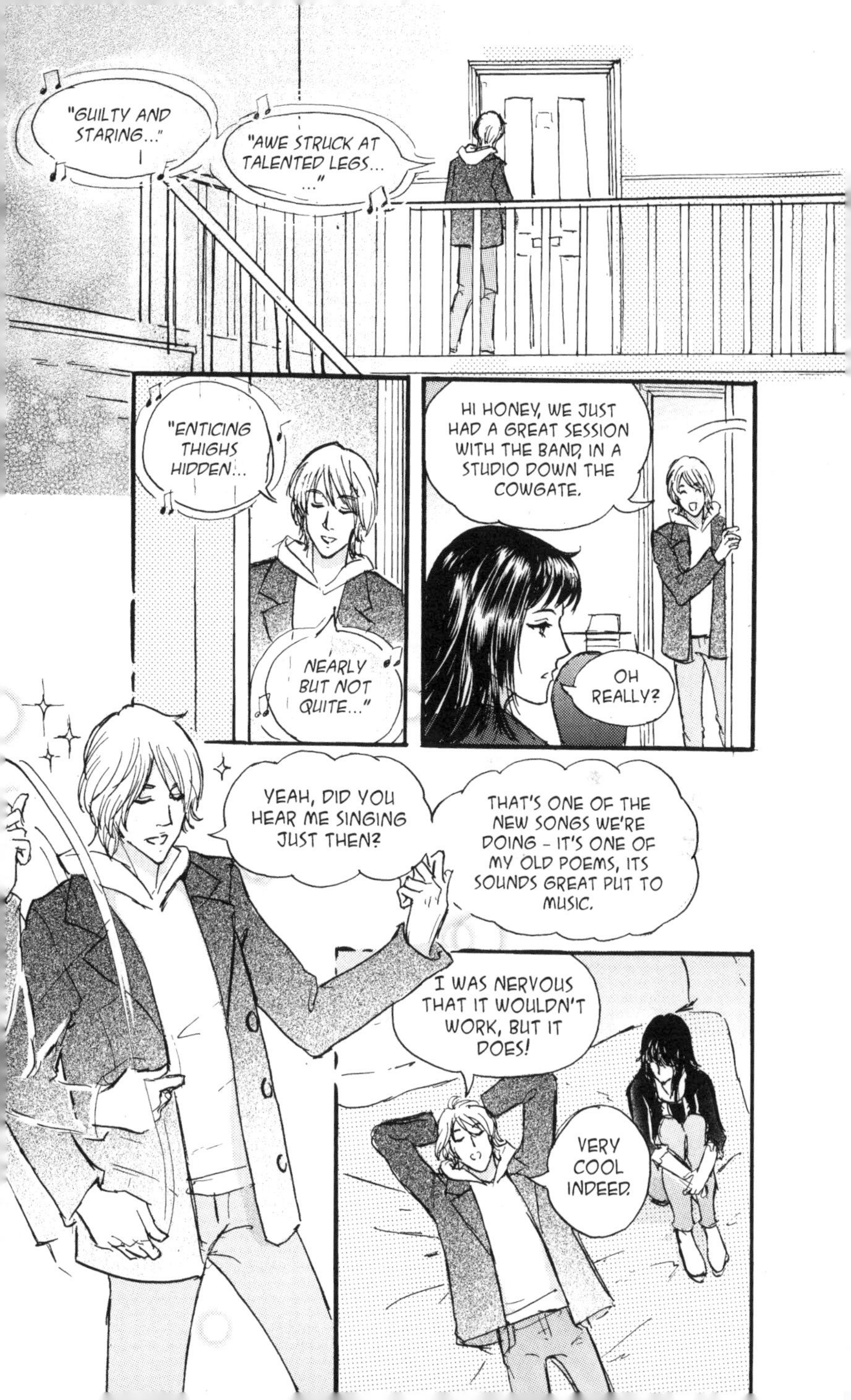
"GUILTY AND STARING..."
"AWE STRUCK AT TALENTED LEGS... ..."
"ENTICING THIGHS HIDDEN...
NEARLY BUT NOT QUITE..."
HI HONEY, WE JUST HAD A GREAT SESSION WITH THE BAND, IN A STUDIO DOWN THE COWGATE.
OH REALLY?
YEAH, DID YOU HEAR ME SINGING JUST THEN?
THAT'S ONE OF THE NEW SONGS WE'RE DOING - IT'S ONE OF MY OLD POEMS, ITS SOUNDS GREAT PUT TO MUSIC.
I WAS NERVOUS THAT IT WOULDN'T WORK, BUT IT DOES!
VERY COOL INDEED.

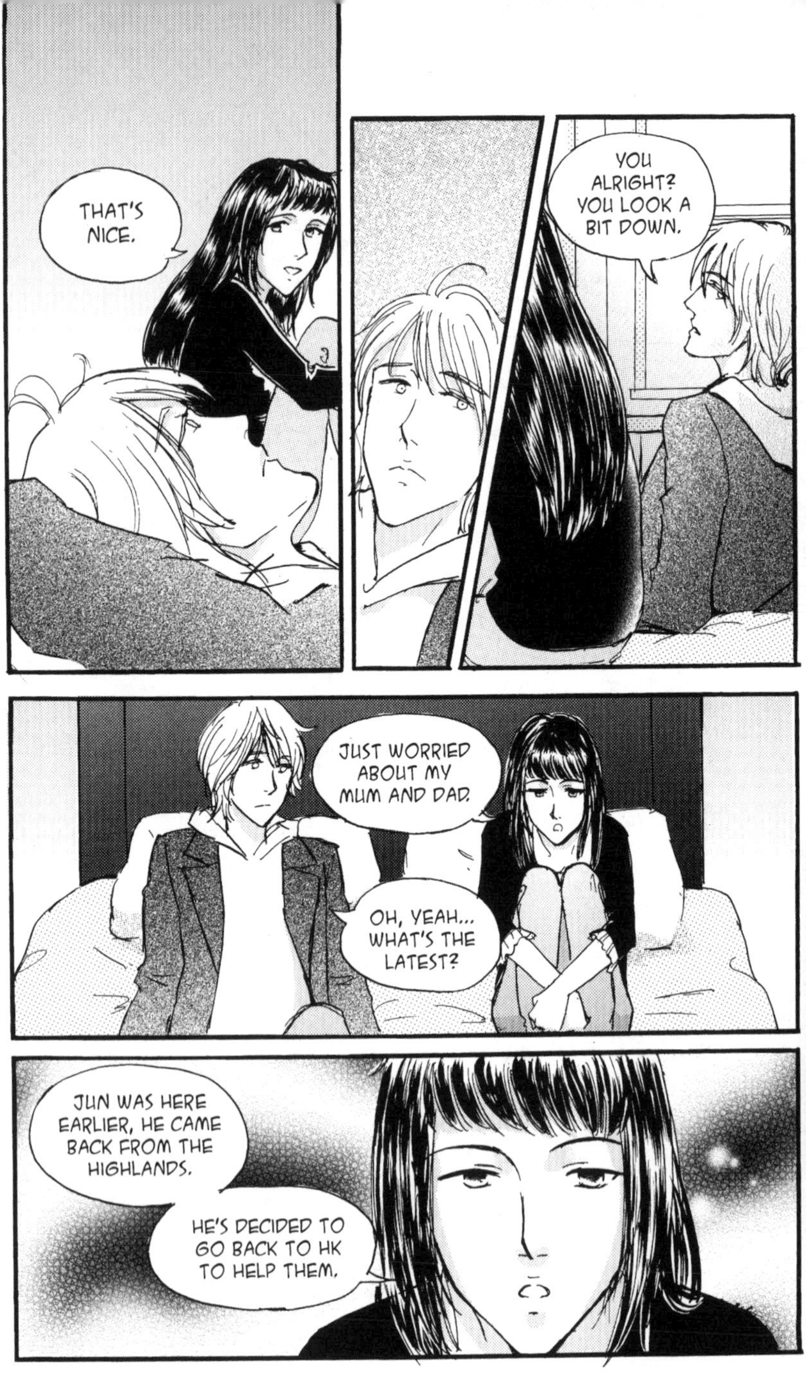
THAT'S NICE.
YOU ALRIGHT? YOU LOOK A BIT DOWN.
JUST WORRIED ABOUT MY MUM AND DAD.
OH, YEAH... WHAT'S THE LATEST?
JUN WAS HERE EARLIER, HE CAME BACK FROM THE HIGHLANDS.
HE'S DECIDED TO GO BACK TO HK TO HELP THEM.

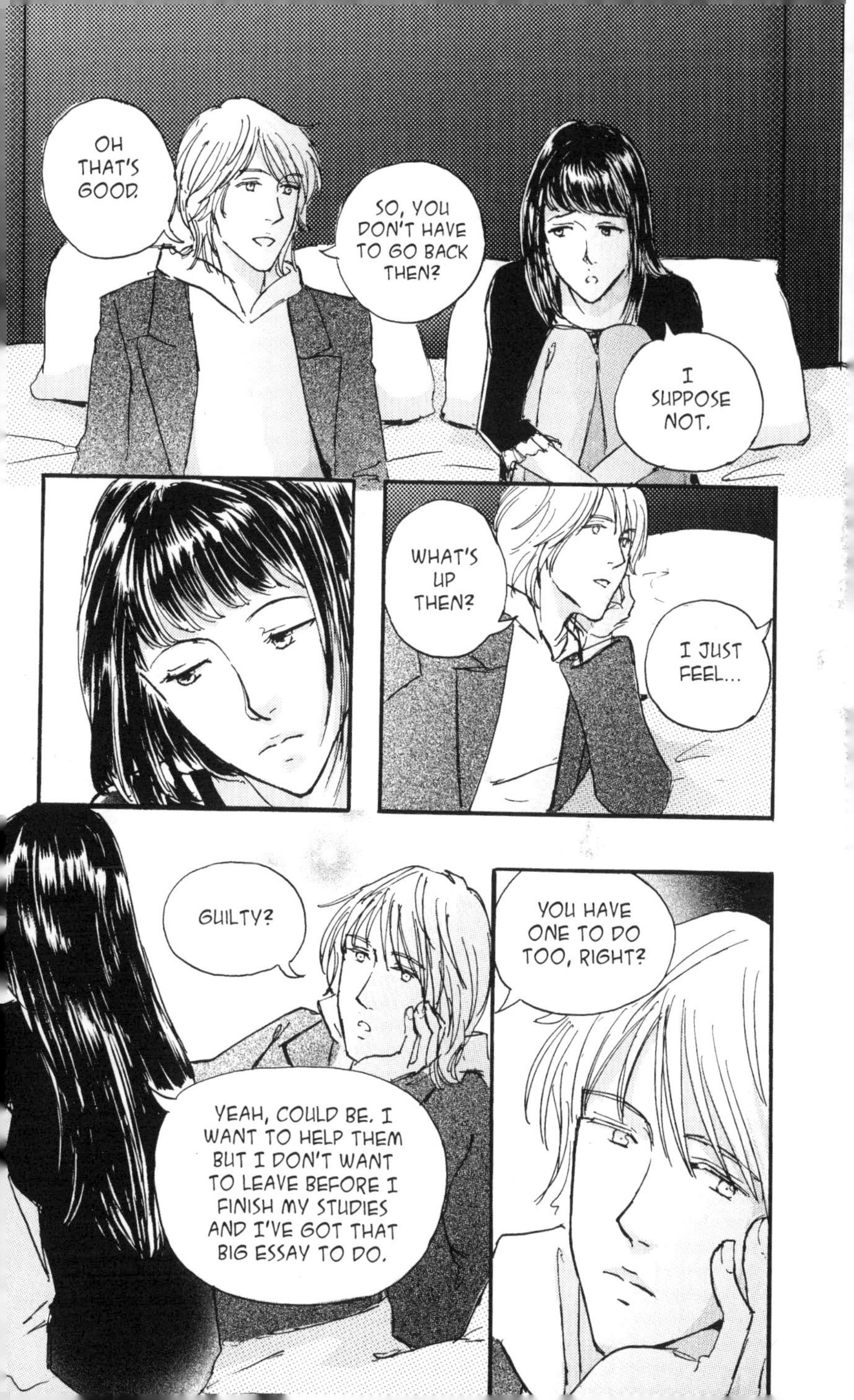
OH THAT'S GOOD.
SO, YOU DON'T HAVE TO GO BACK THEN?
I SUPPOSE NOT.
WHAT'S UP THEN?
I JUST FEEL...
GUILTY?
YEAH, COULD BE. I WANT TO HELP THEM BUT I DON'T WANT TO LEAVE BEFORE I FINISH MY STUDIES AND I'VE GOT THAT BIG ESSAY TO DO.
YOU HAVE ONE TO DO TOO, RIGHT?

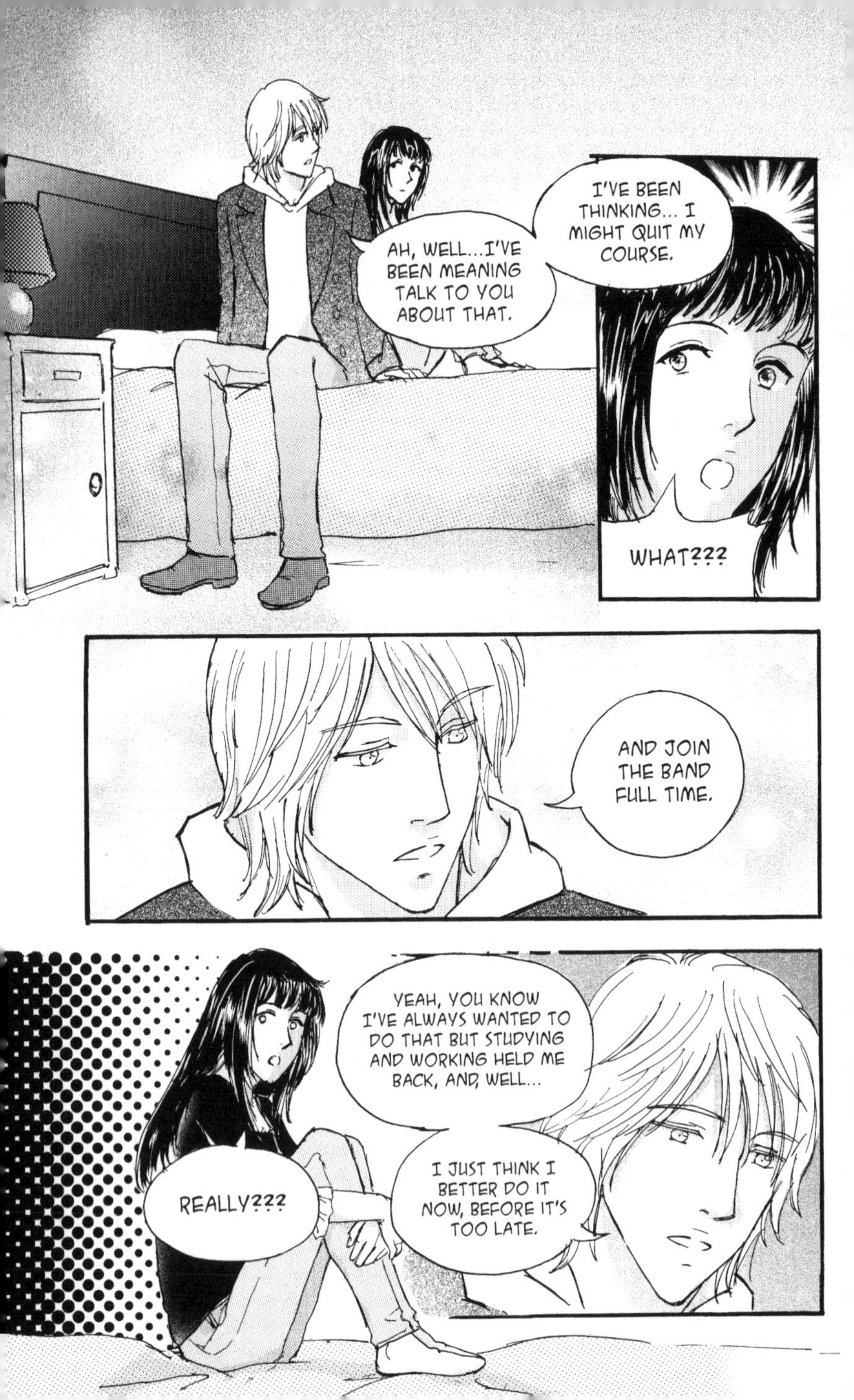
AH, WELL...I'VE BEEN MEANING TALK TO YOU ABOUT THAT.
I'VE BEEN THINKING... I MIGHT QUIT MY COURSE.
WHAT???
AND JOIN THE BAND FULL TIME.
YEAH, YOU KNOW I'VE ALWAYS WANTED TO DO THAT BUT STUDYING AND WORKING HELD ME BACK, AND, WELL...
REALLY???
I JUST THINK I BETTER DO IT NOW, BEFORE IT'S TOO LATE.

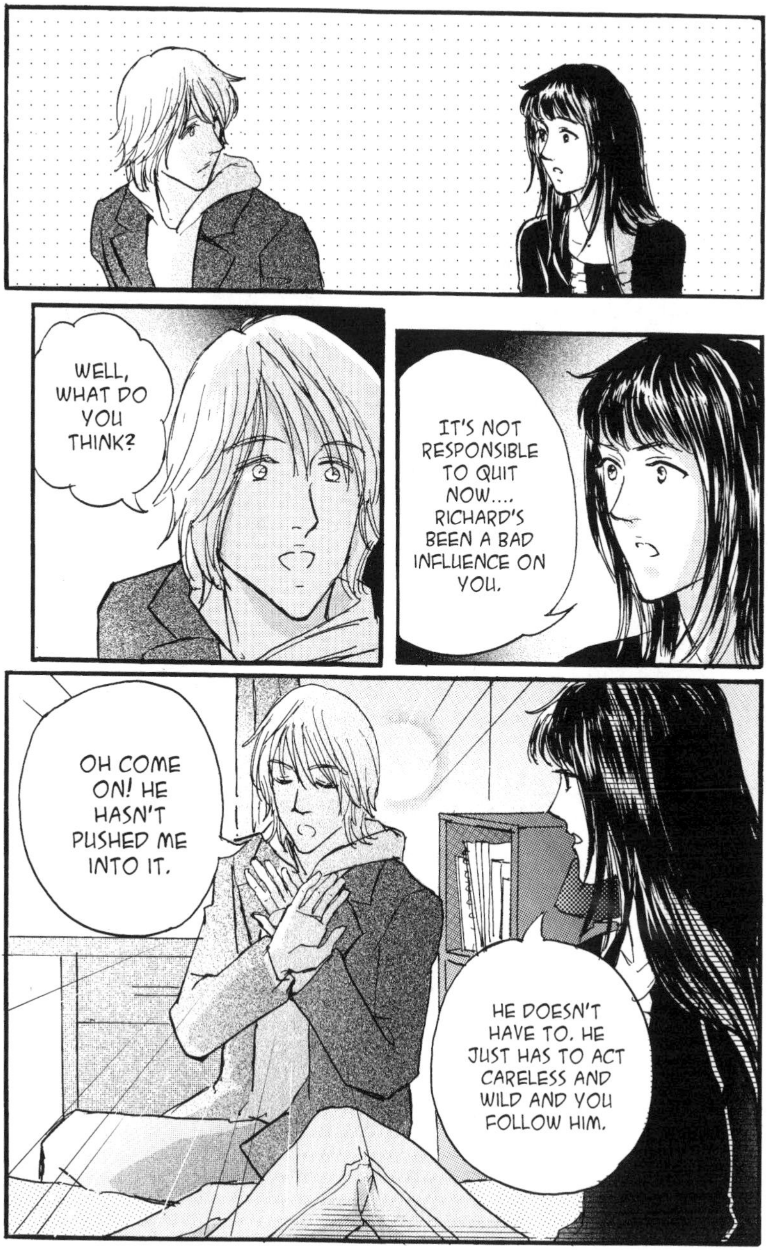
WELL, WHAT DO YOU THINK?
IT'S NOT RESPONSIBLE TO QUIT NOW.... RICHARD'S BEEN A BAD INFLUENCE ON YOU.
OH COME ON! HE HASN'T PUSHED ME INTO IT.
HE DOESN'T HAVE TO. HE JUST HAS TO ACT CARELESS AND WILD AND YOU FOLLOW HIM.

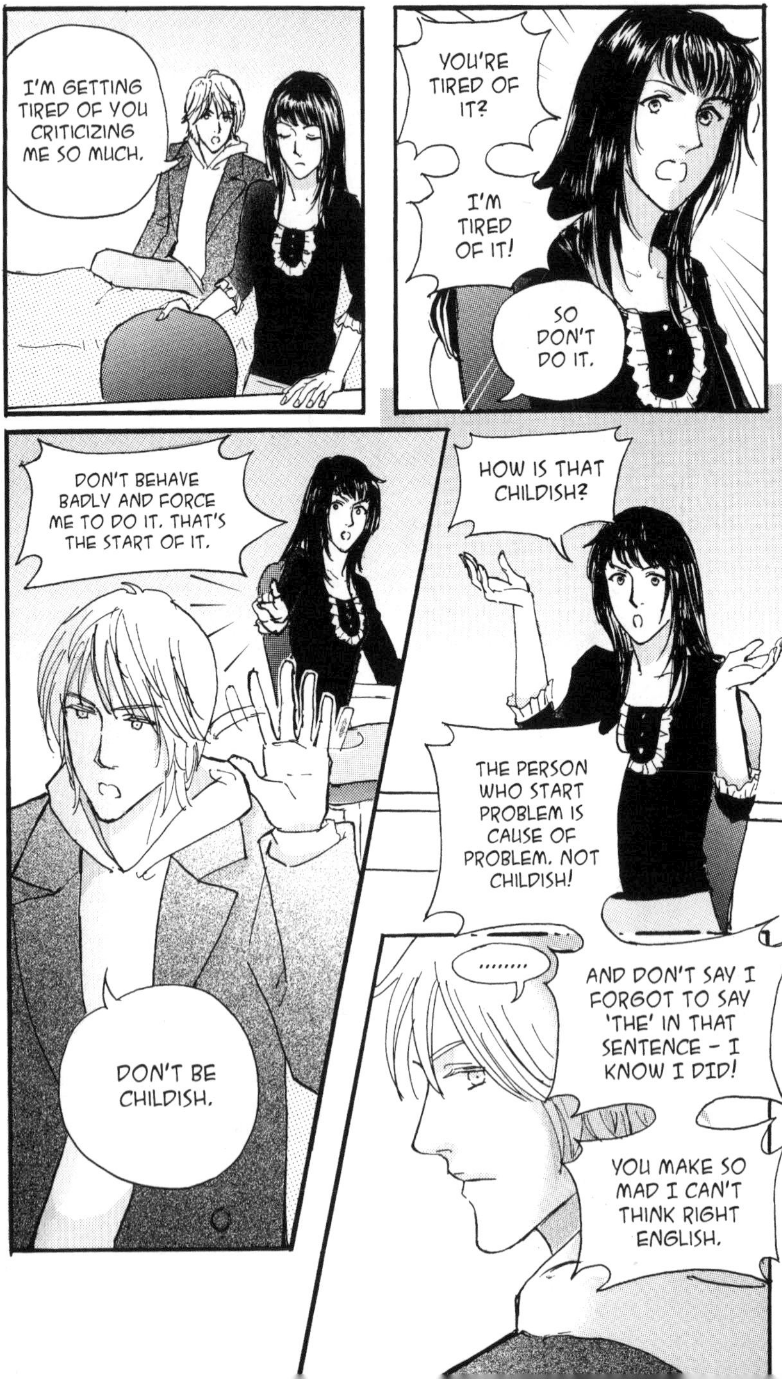
I'M GETTING TIRED OF YOU CRITICIZING ME SO MUCH.
YOU'RE TIRED OF IT?
I'M TIRED OF IT!
SO DON'T DO IT.
DON'T BEHAVE BADLY AND FORCE ME TO DO IT. THAT'S THE START OF IT.
DON'T BE CHILDISH.
HOW IS THAT CHILDISH?
THE PERSON WHO START PROBLEM IS CAUSE OF PROBLEM. NOT CHILDISH!
....
AND DON'T SAY I FORGOT TO SAY 'THE' IN THAT SENTENCE - I KNOW I DID!
YOU MAKE SO MAD I CAN'T THINK RIGHT ENGLISH.

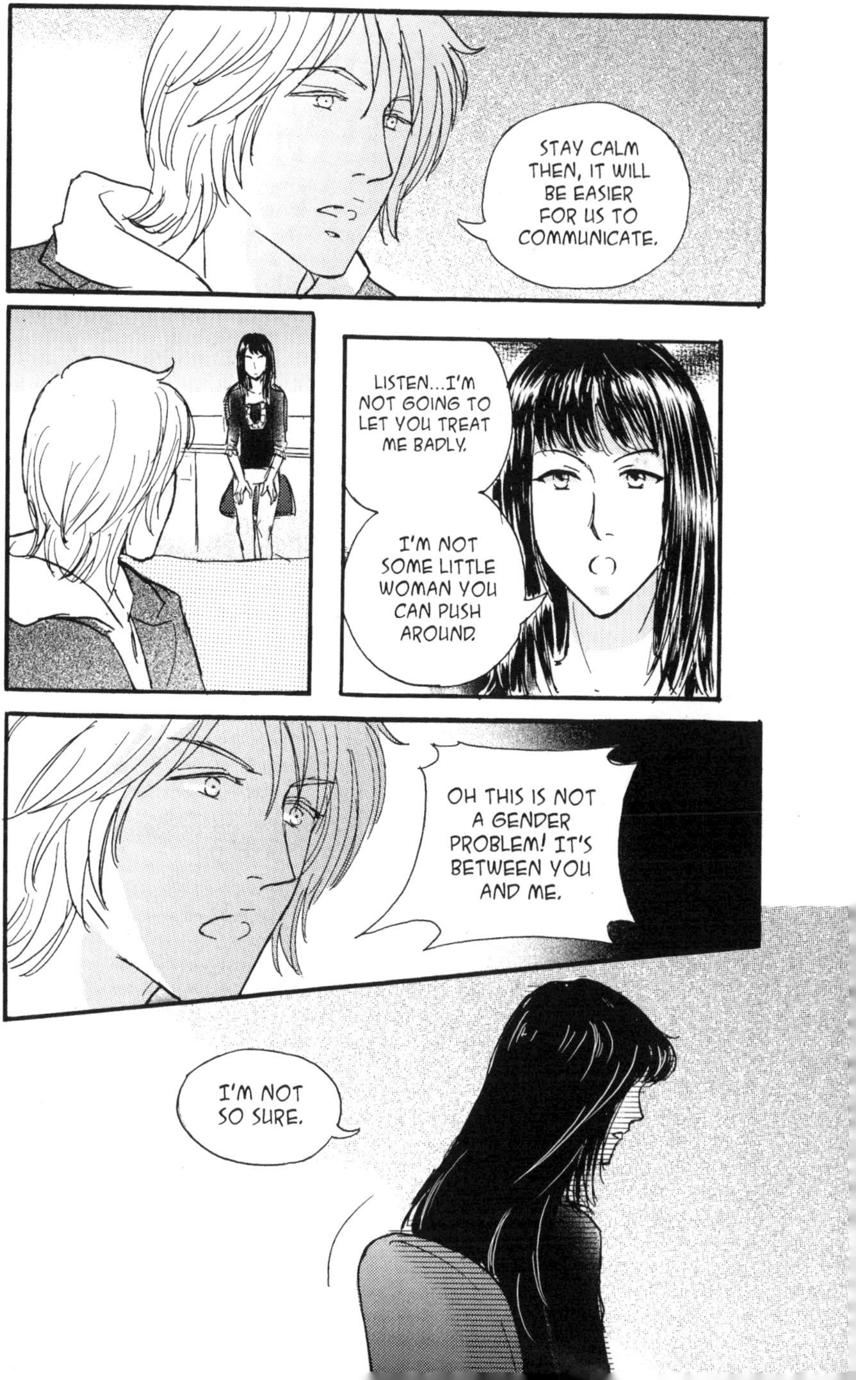
STAY CALM THEN, IT WILL BE EASIER FOR US TO COMMUNICATE.
LISTEN...I'M NOT GOING TO LET YOU TREAT ME BADLY.
I'M NOT SOME LITTLE WOMAN YOU CAN PUSH AROUND.
OH THIS IS NOT A GENDER PROBLEM! IT'S BETWEEN YOU AND ME.
I'M NOT SO SURE.

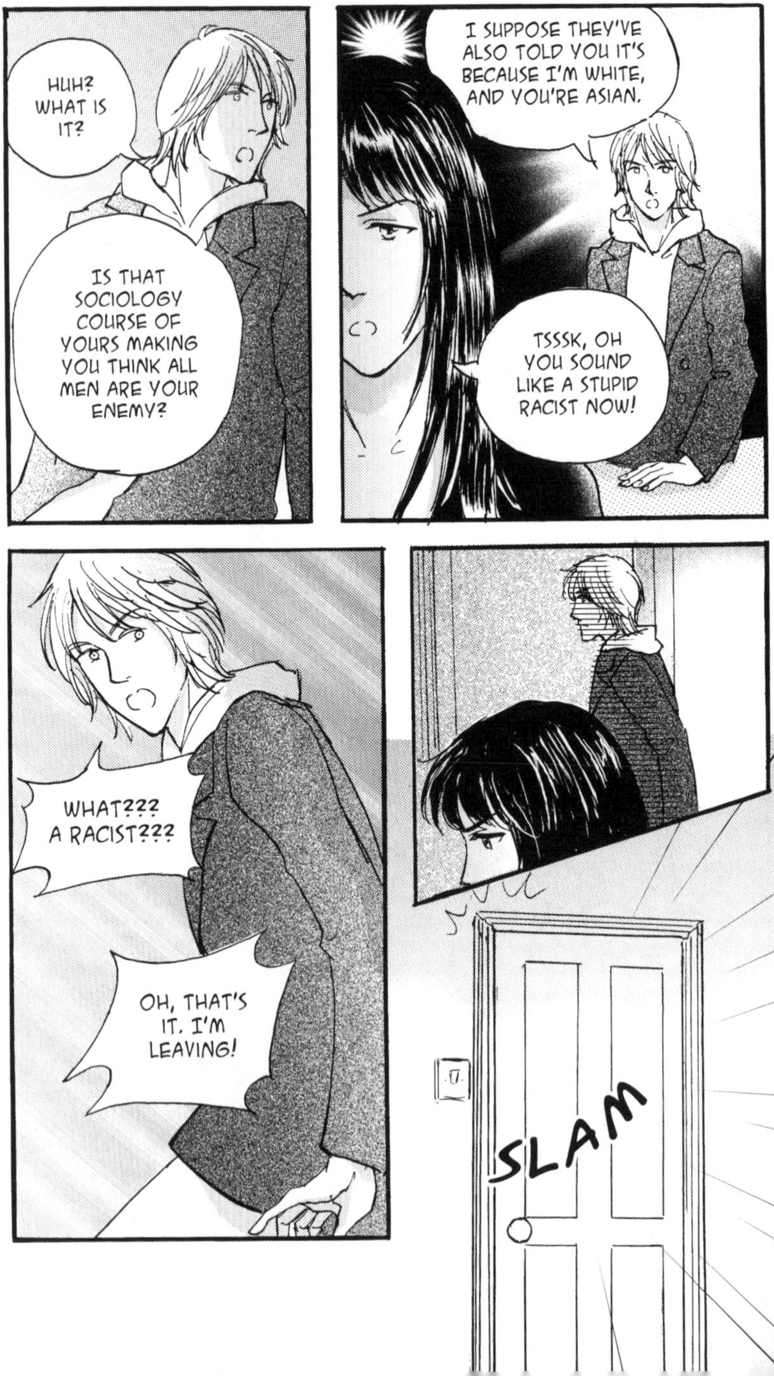
HUH? WHAT IS IT?
IS THAT SOCIOLOGY COURSE OF YOURS MAKING YOU THINK ALL MEN ARE YOUR ENEMY?
I SUPPOSE THEY'VE ALSO TOLD YOU IT'S BECAUSE I'M WHITE, AND YOU'RE ASIAN.
TSSSK, OH YOU SOUND LIKE A STUPID RACIST NOW!
WHAT??? A RACIST???
OH, THAT'S IT. I'M LEAVING!
SLAM

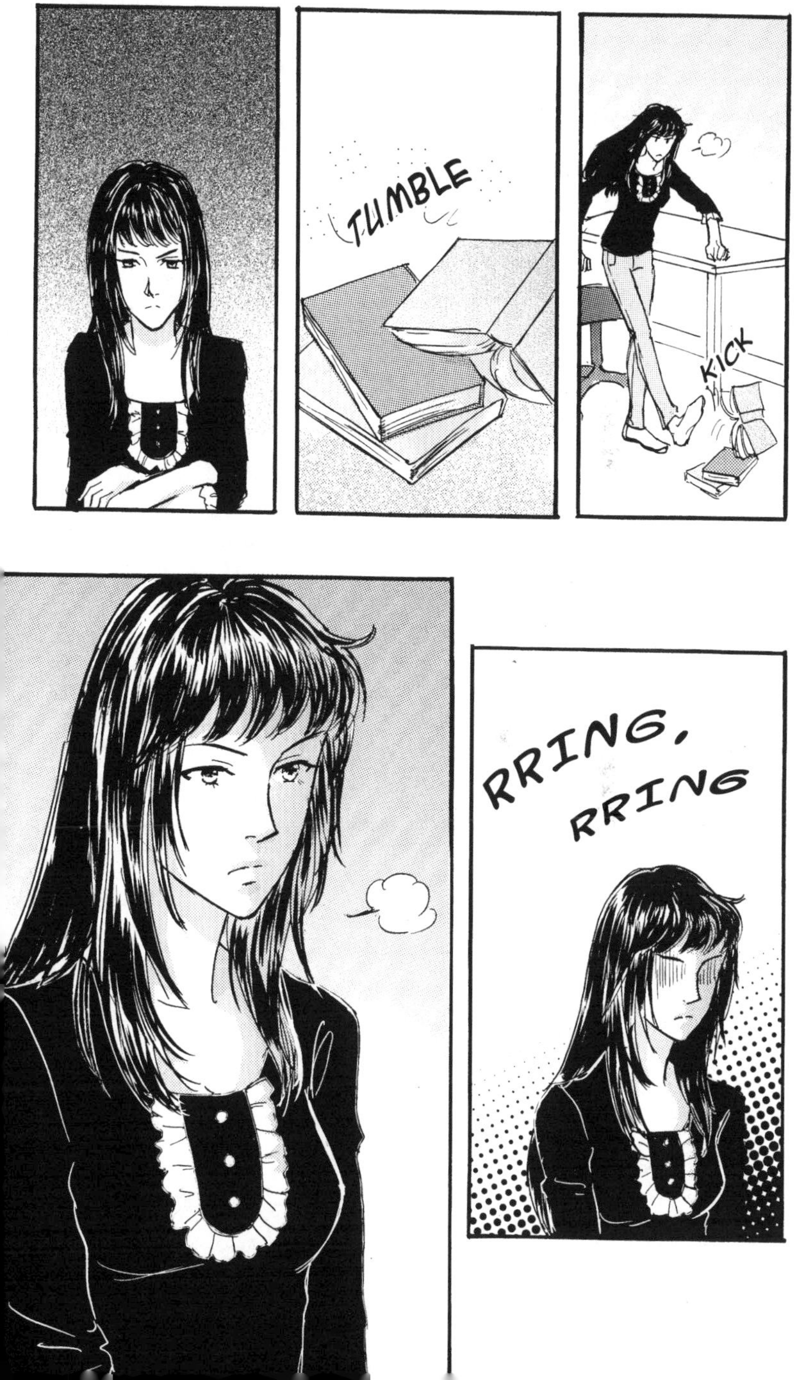
TUMBLE
KICK
RRING, RRING

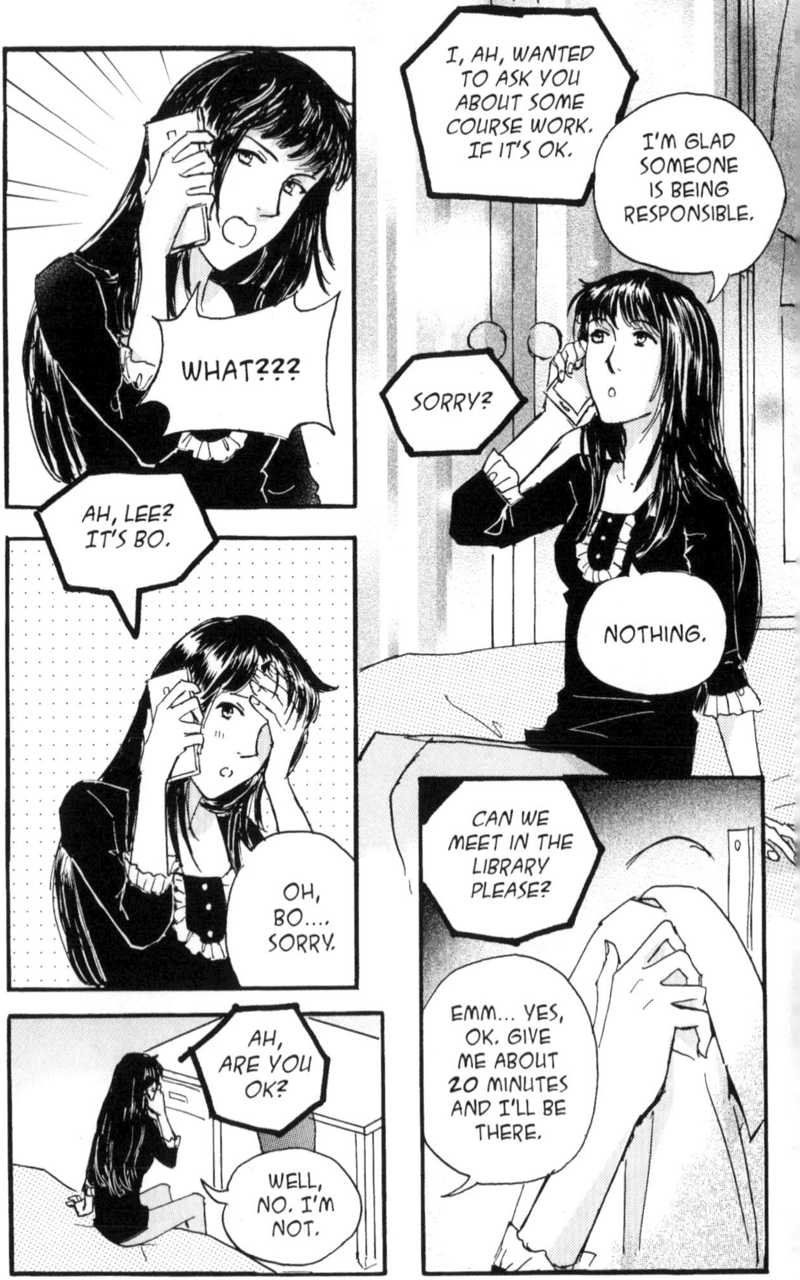
WHAT???
AH, LEE? IT'S BO.
OH, BO.... SORRY.
AH, ARE YOU OK?
WELL, NO. I'M NOT.
I, AH, WANTED TO ASK YOU ABOUT SOME COURSE WORK. IF IT'S OK.
I'M GLAD SOMEONE IS BEING RESPONSIBLE.
SORRY?
NOTHING.
CAN WE MEET IN THE LIBRARY PLEASE?
EMM... YES, OK. GIVE ME ABOUT 20 MINUTES AND I'LL BE THERE.

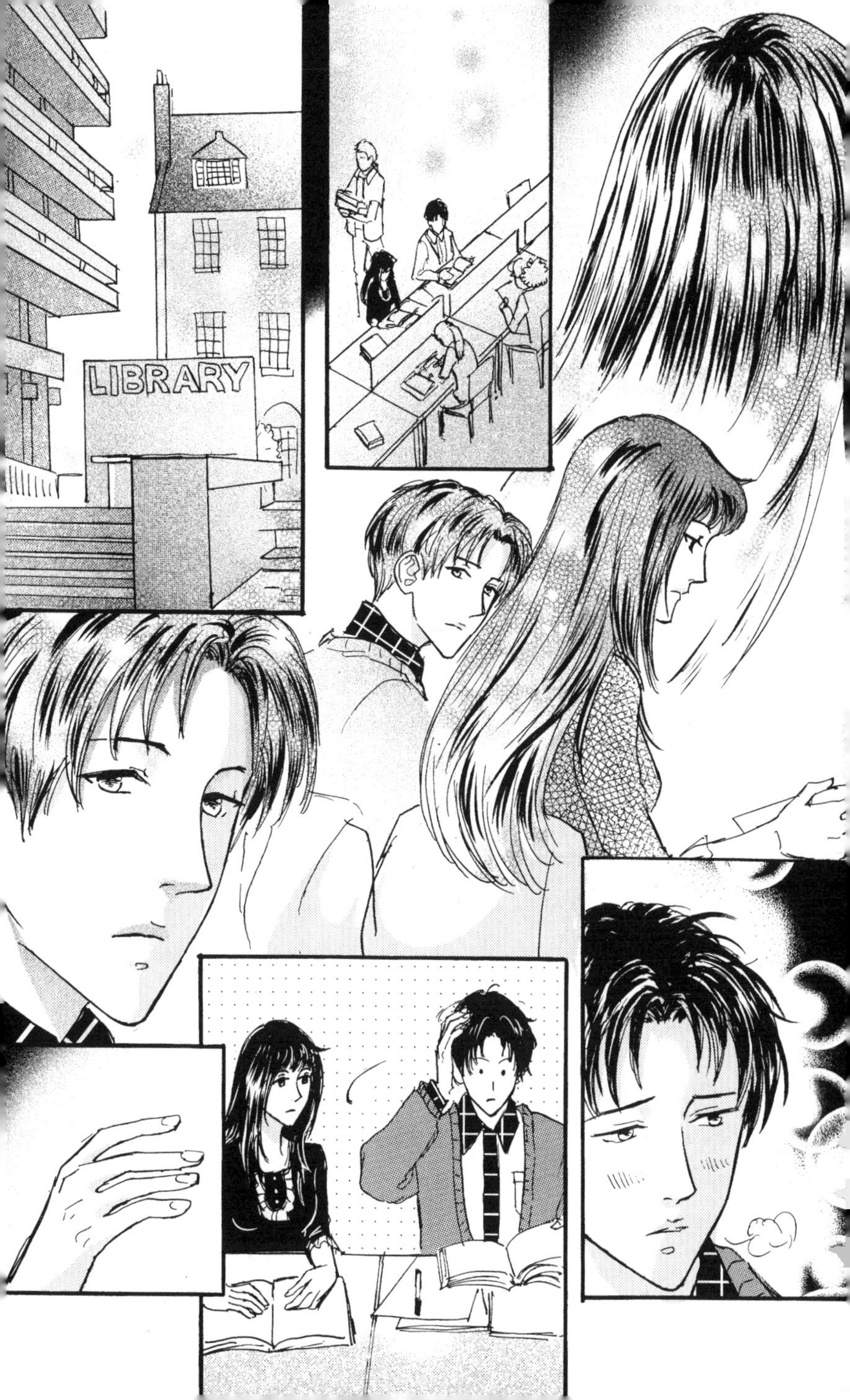
LIBRARY

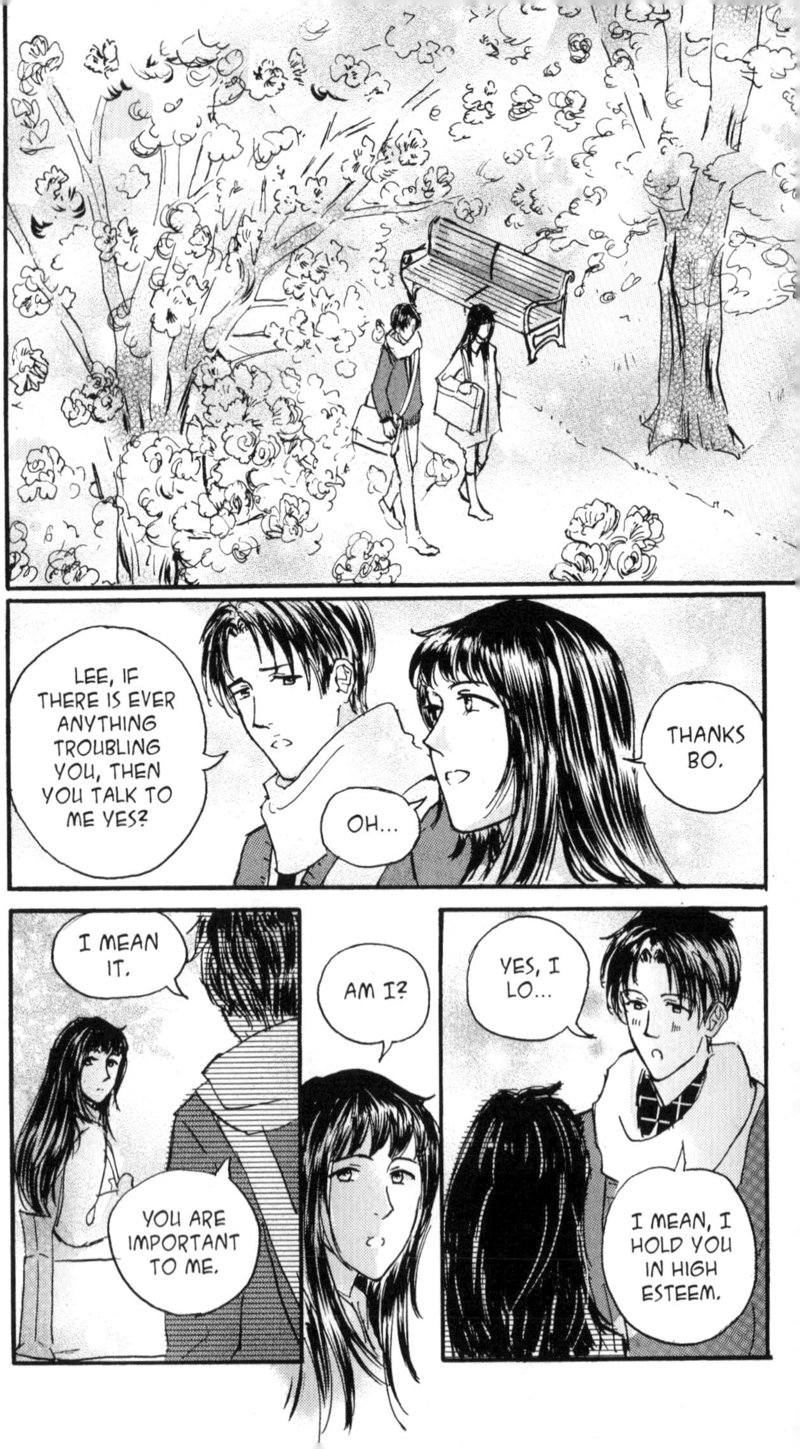
LEE, IF THERE IS EVER ANYTHING TROUBLING YOU, THEN YOU TALK TO ME YES?
OH...
THANKS BO.
I MEAN IT.
YOU ARE IMPORTANT TO ME.
AM I?
YES, I LO...
I MEAN, I HOLD YOU IN HIGH ESTEEM.

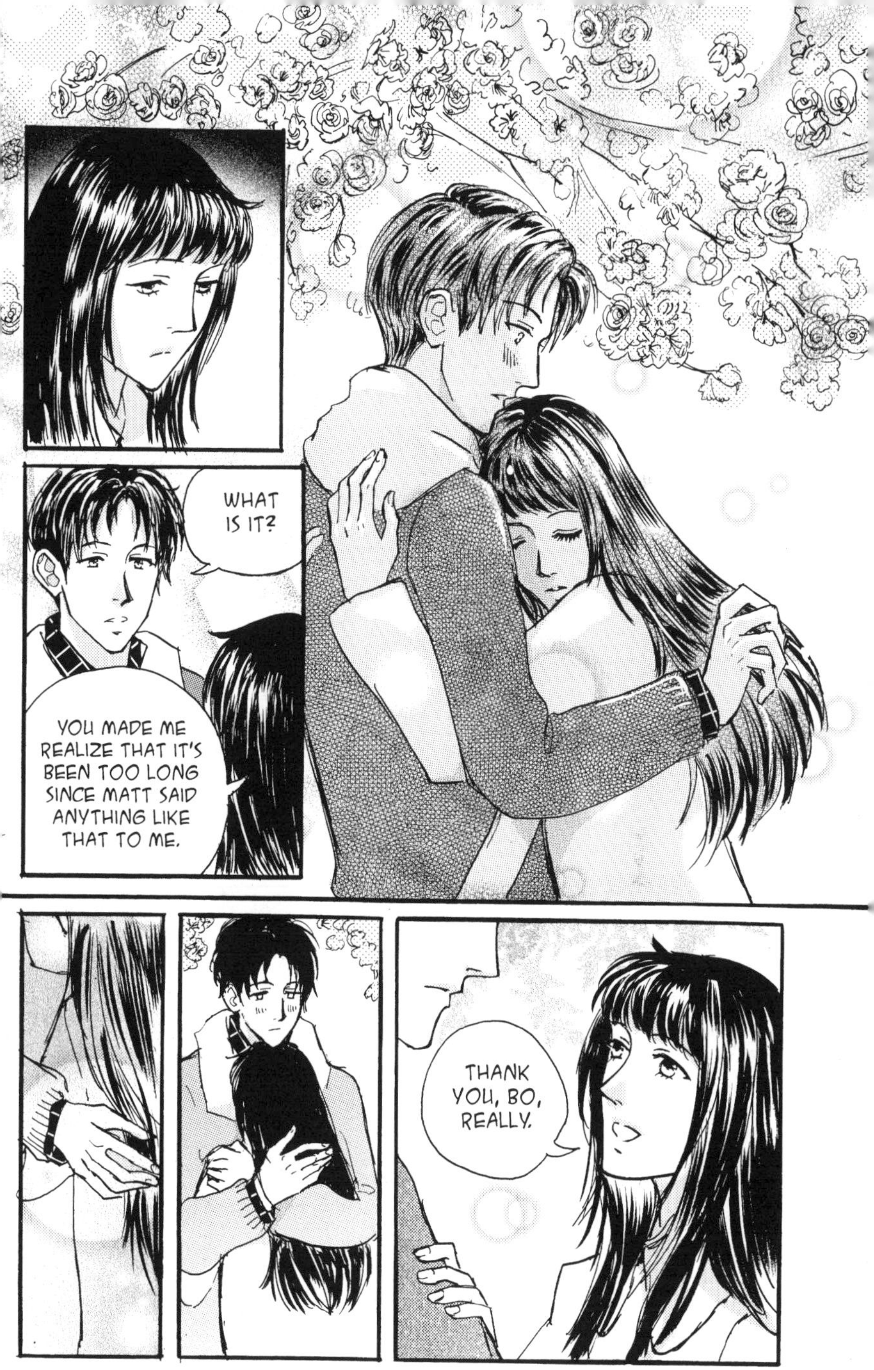
WHAT IS IT?
YOU MADE ME REALIZE THAT IT'S BEEN TOO LONG SINCE MATT SAID ANYTHING LIKE THAT TO ME.
THANK YOU, BO, REALLY.

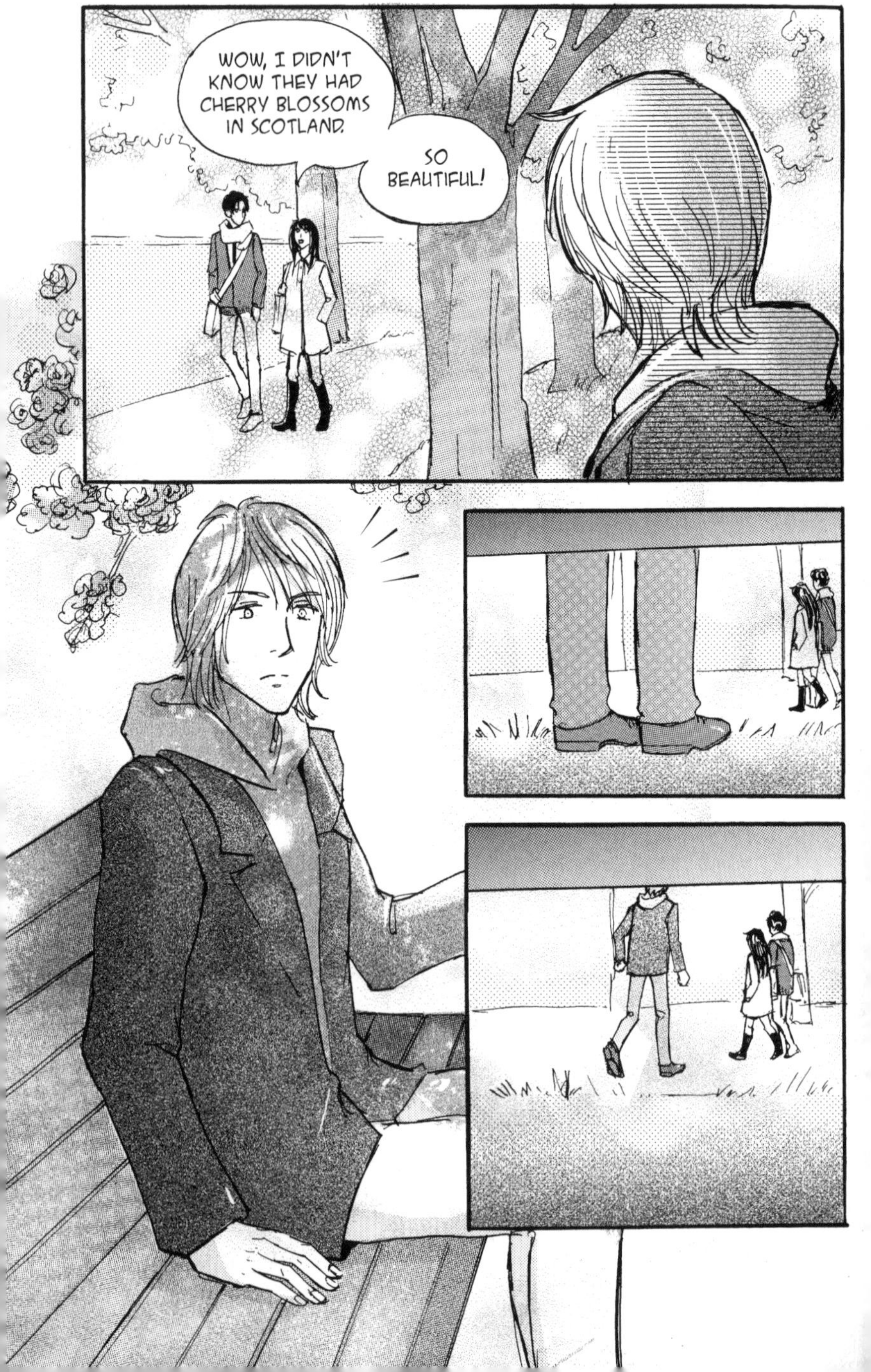
WOW, I DIDN'T KNOW THEY HAD CHERRY BLOSSOMS IN SCOTLAND.
SO BEAUTIFUL!

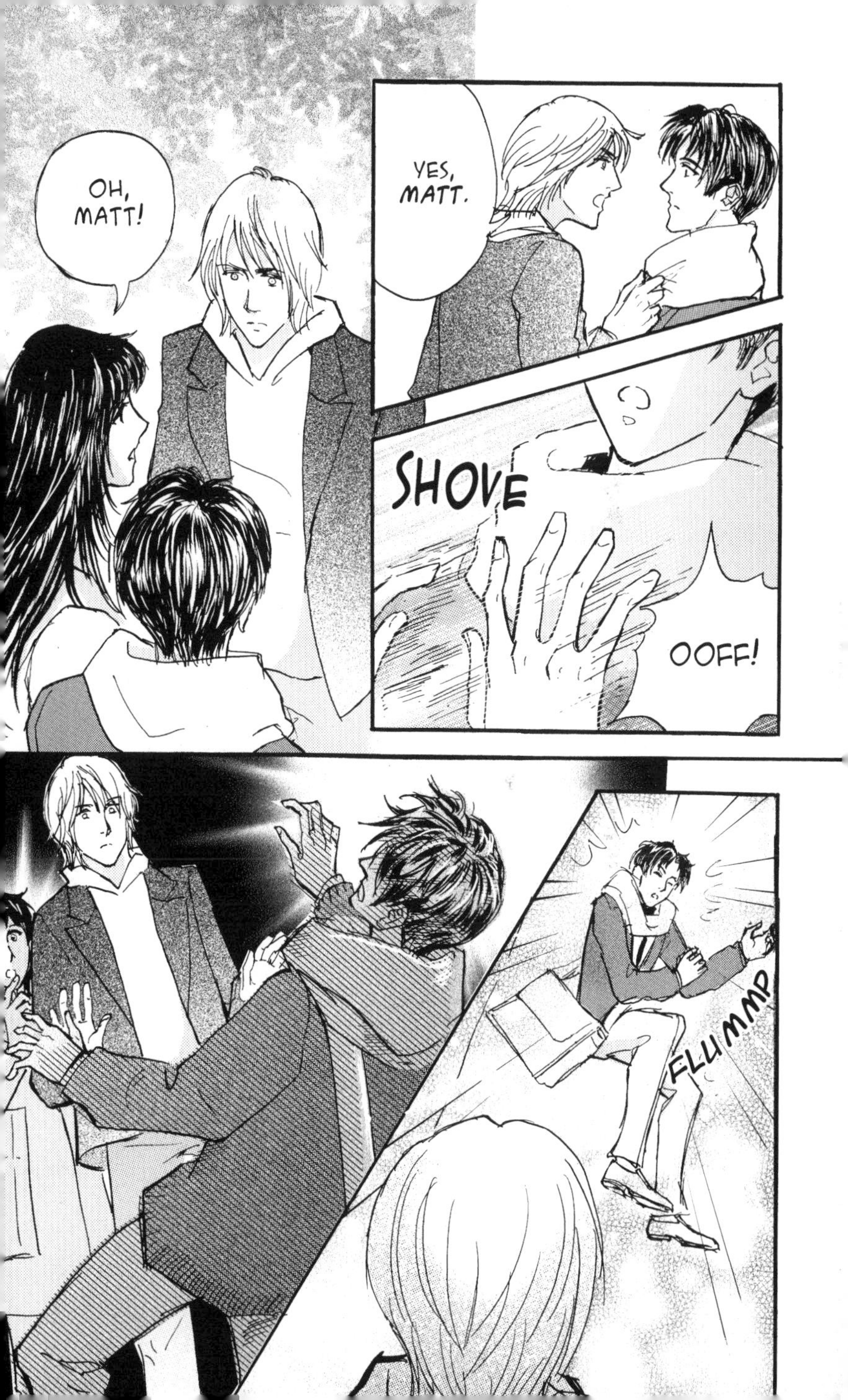
OH, MATT!
YES, MATT.
SHOVE
OOFF!
FLUMMP

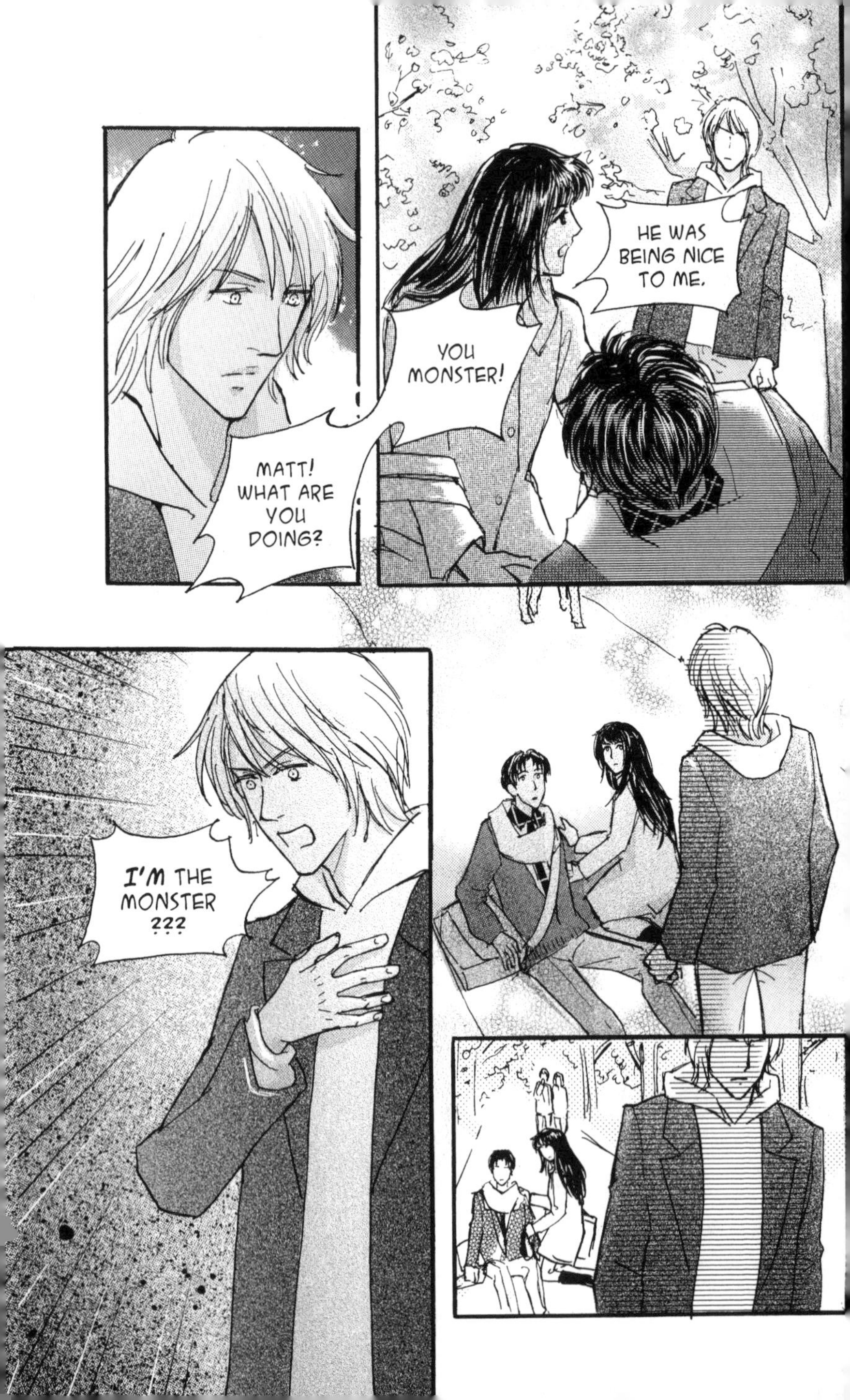
MATT! WHAT ARE YOU DOING?
YOU MONSTER!
HE WAS BEING NICE TO ME.
I'M THE MONSTER ???

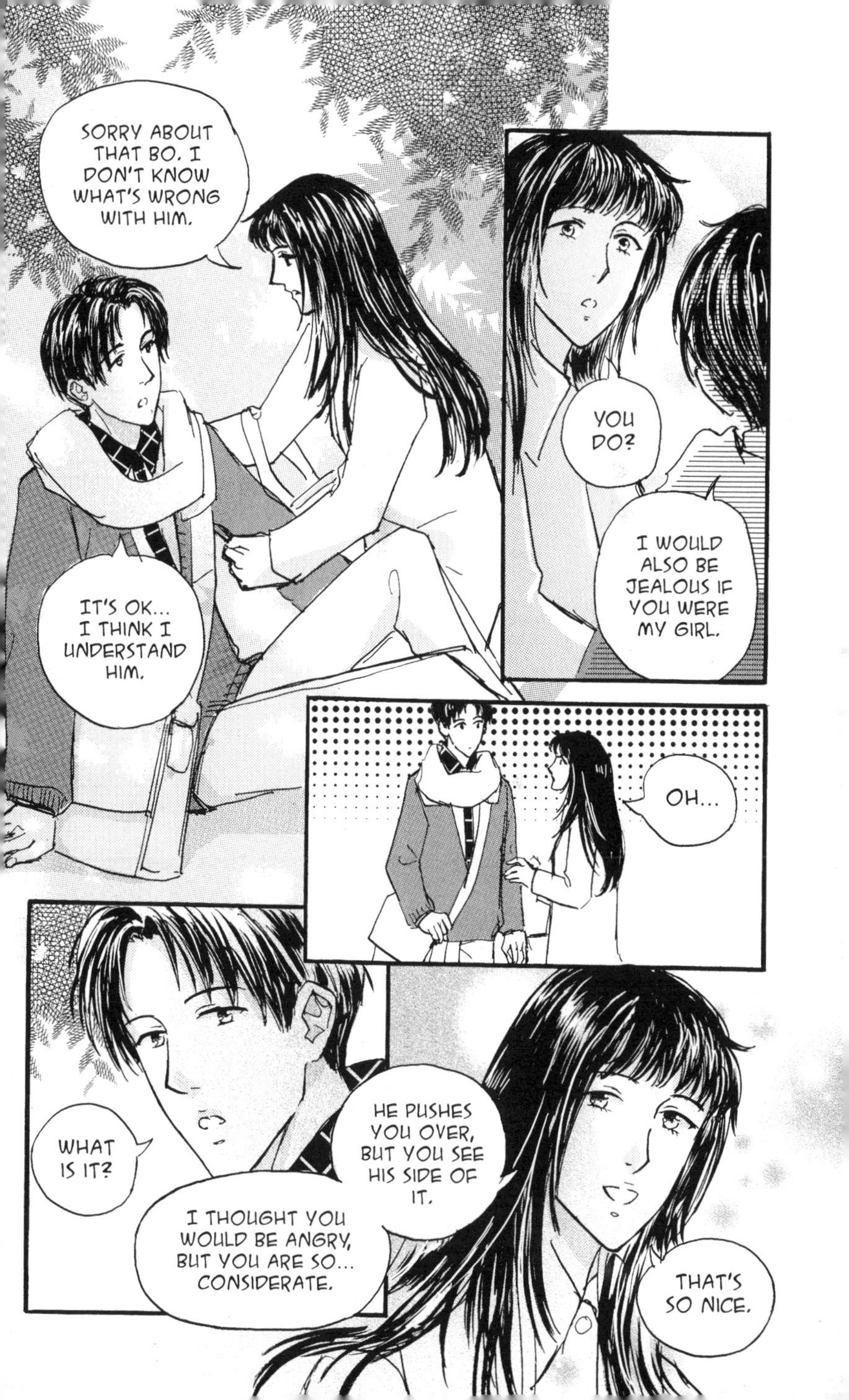
SORRY ABOUT THAT BO. I DON'T KNOW WHAT'S WRONG WITH HIM.
IT'S OK... I THINK I UNDERSTAND HIM.
YOU DO?
I WOULD ALSO BE JEALOUS IF YOU WERE MY GIRL.
OH...
WHAT IS IT?
HE PUSHES YOU OVER, BUT YOU SEE HIS SIDE OF IT.
I THOUGHT YOU WOULD BE ANGRY, BUT YOU ARE SO... CONSIDERATE.
THAT'S SO NICE.

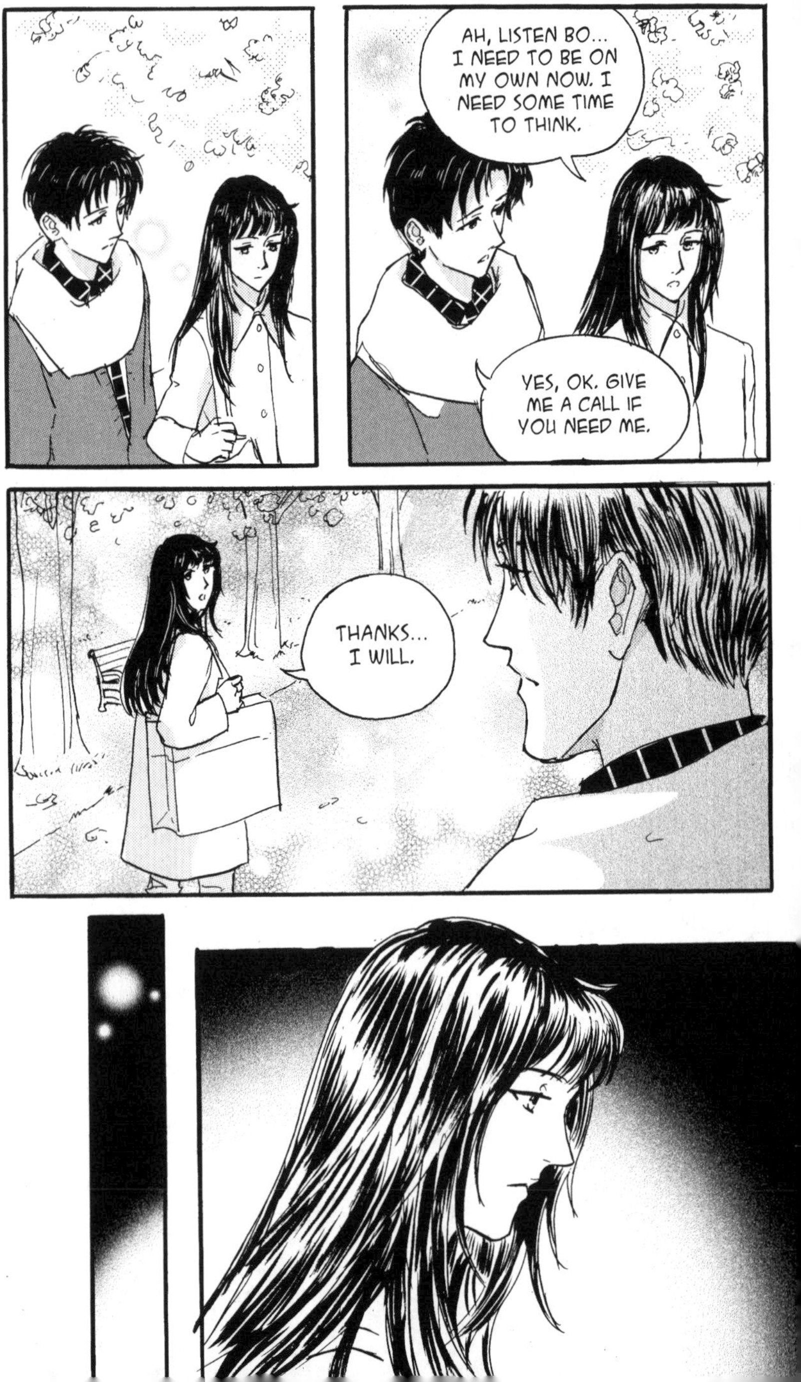
AH, LISTEN BO... I NEED TO BE ON MY OWN NOW. I NEED SOME TIME TO THINK.
YES, OK. GIVE ME A CALL IF YOU NEED ME.
THANKS... I WILL.

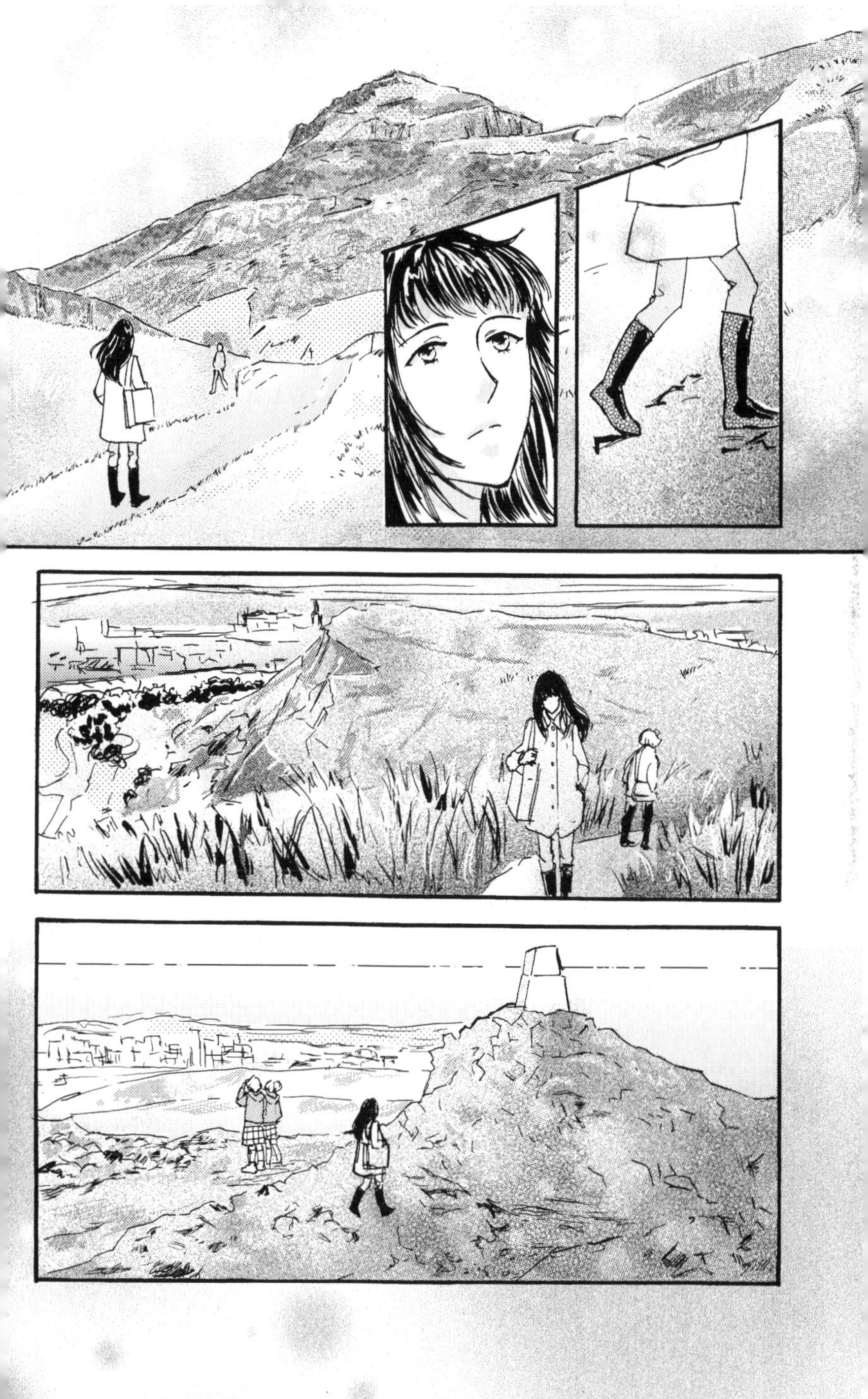

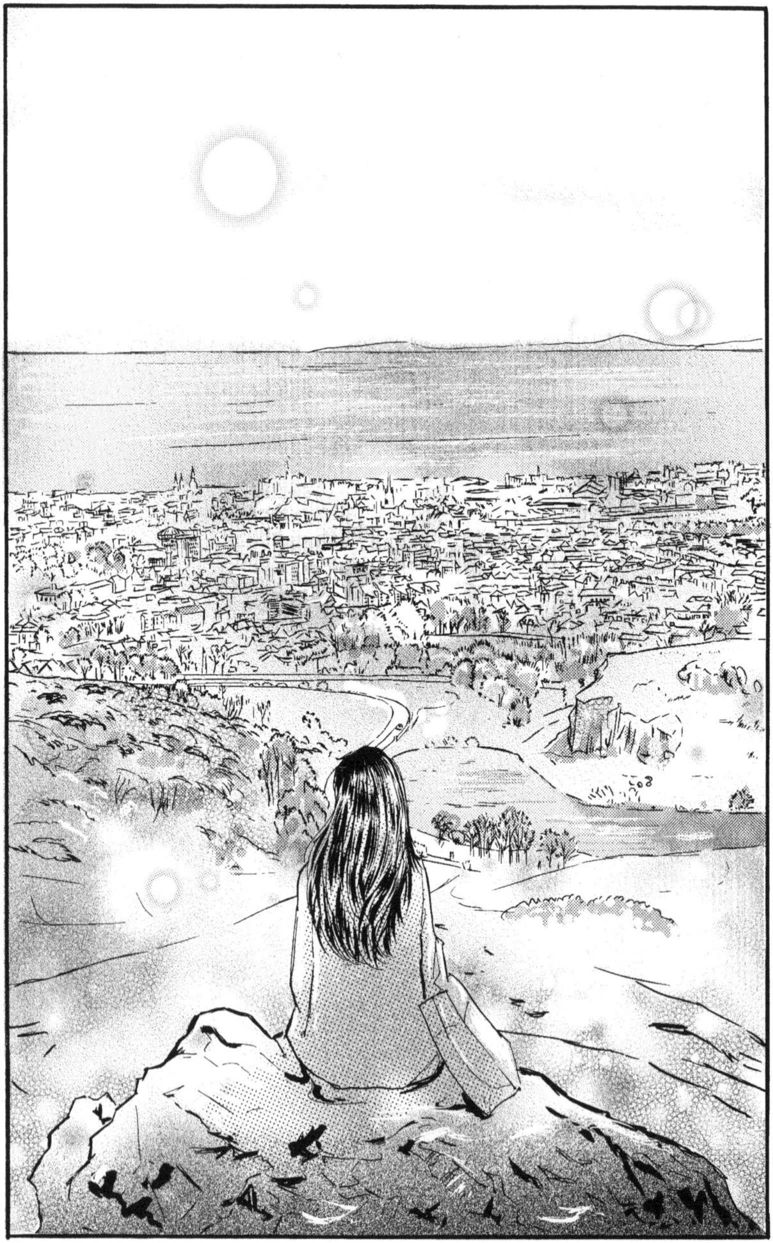

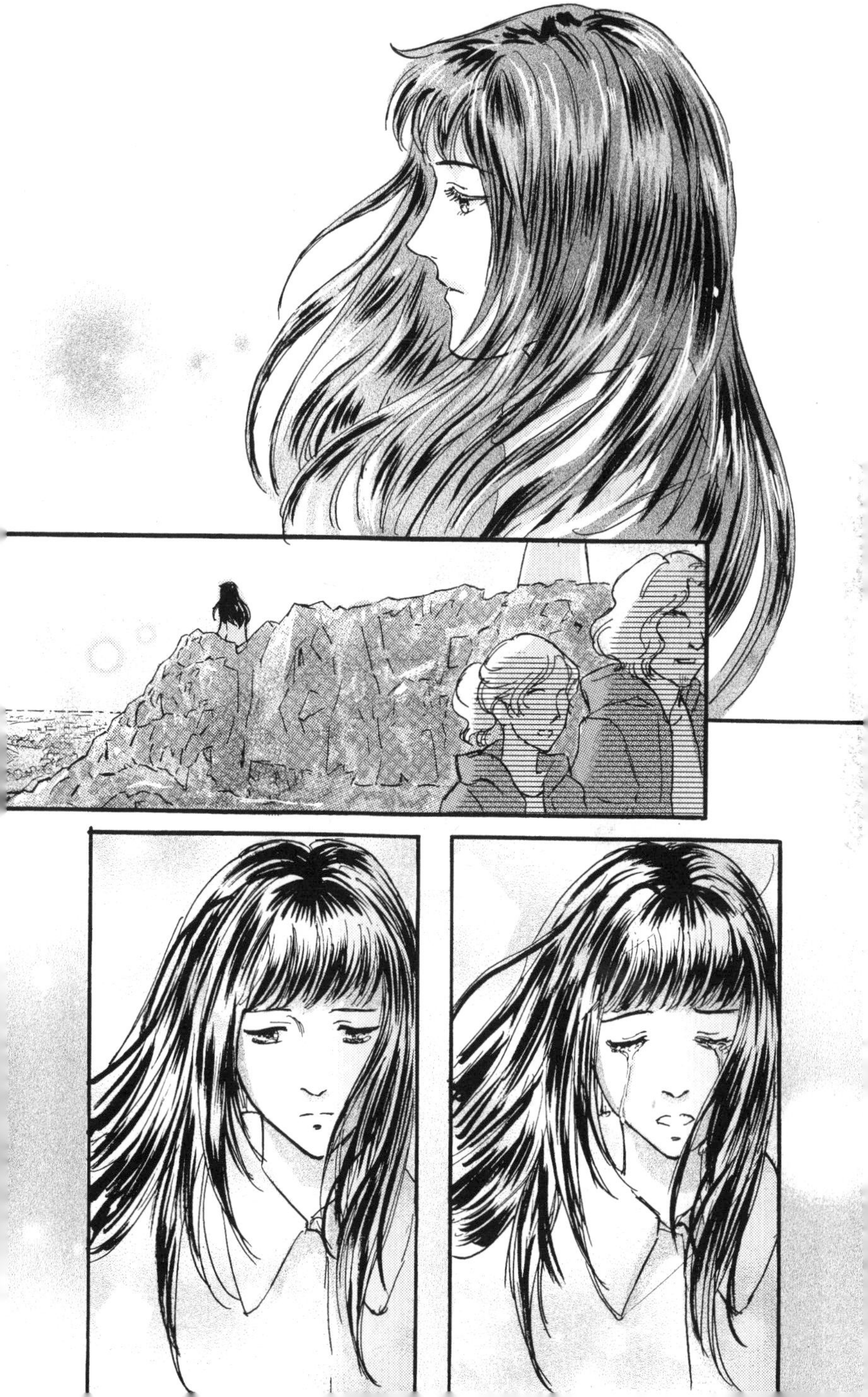

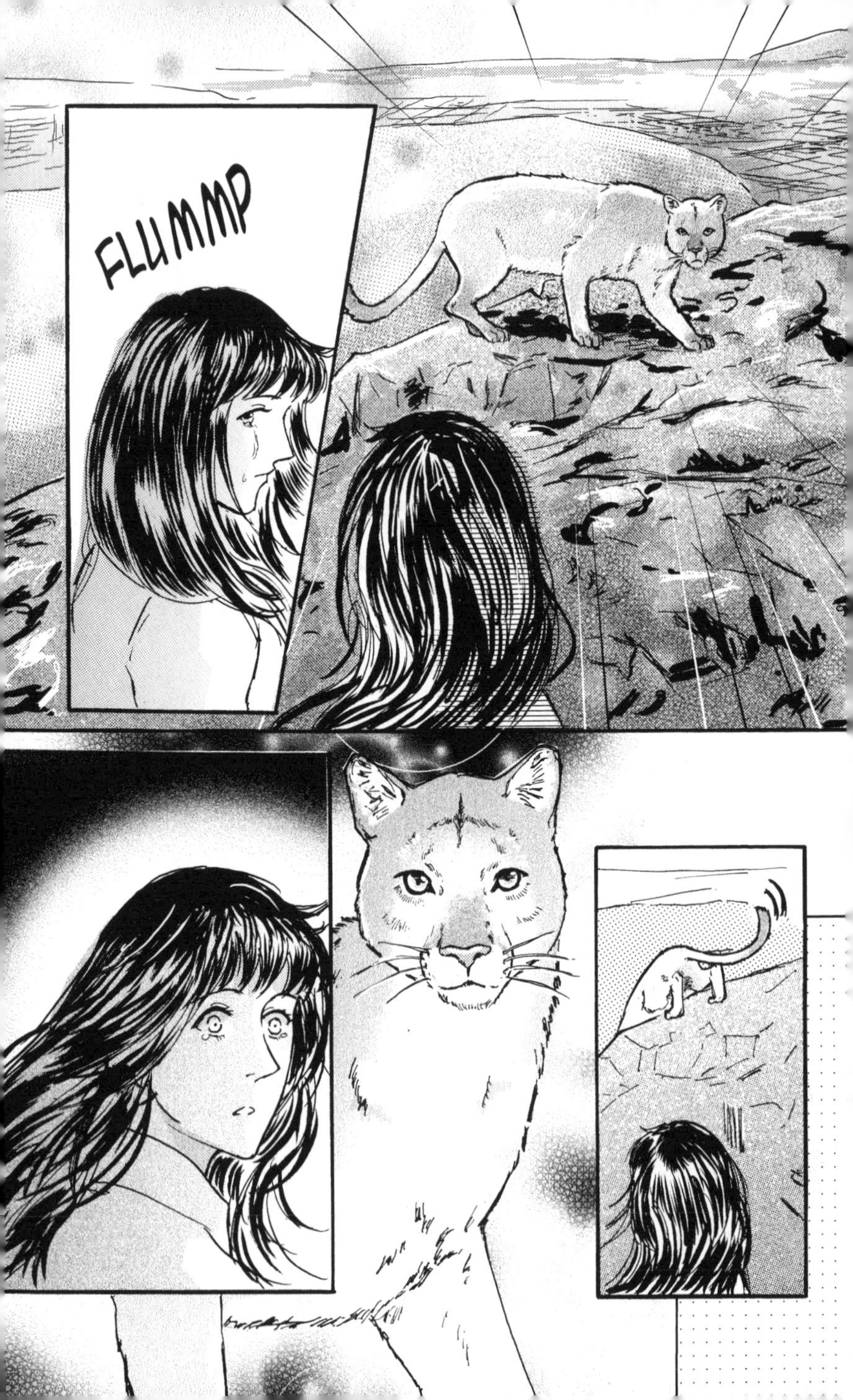
FLUMMP

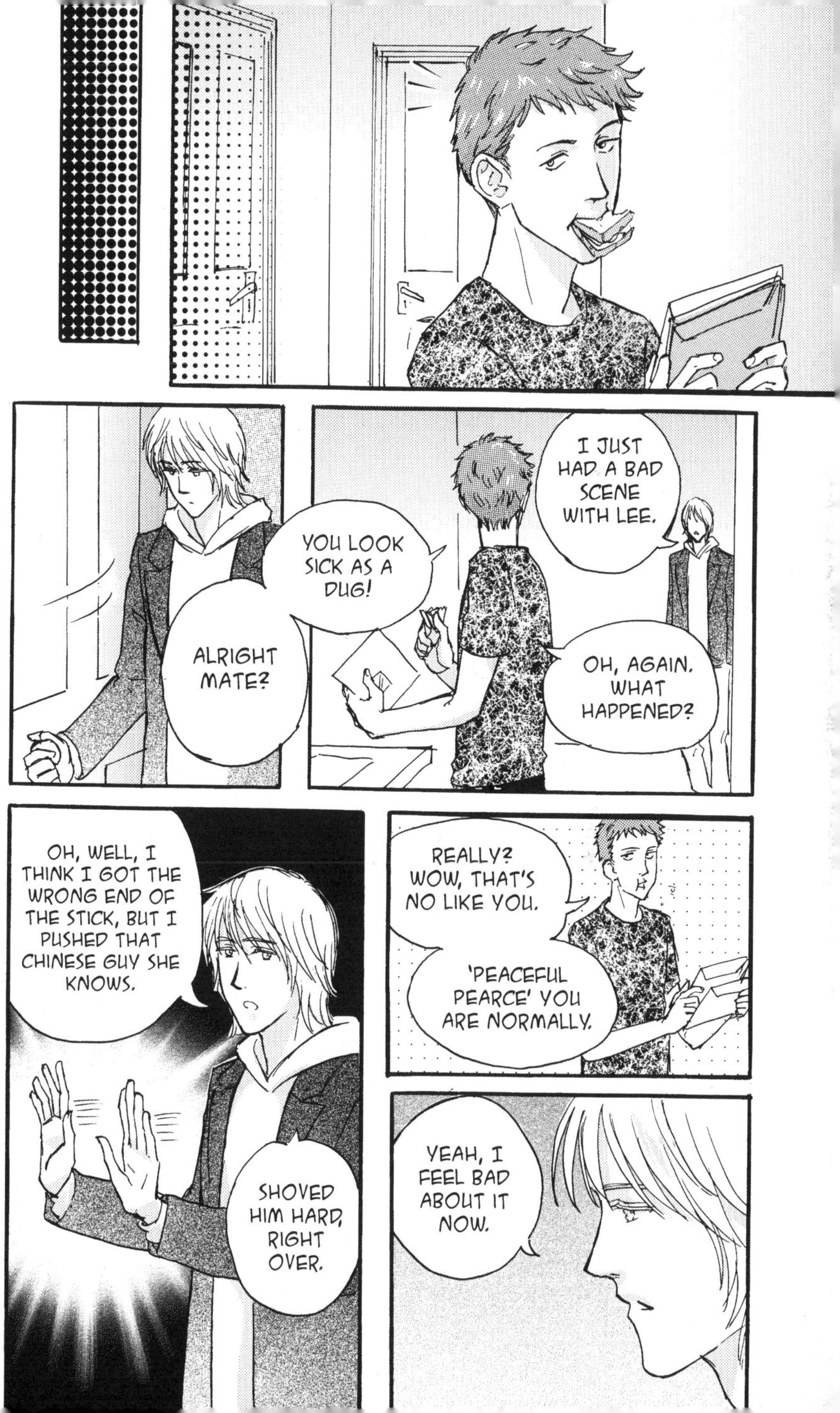
ALRIGHT MATE?
YOU LOOK SICK AS A DUG!
I JUST HAD A BAD SCENE WITH LEE.
OH, AGAIN. WHAT HAPPENED?
OH, WELL, I THINK I GOT THE WRONG END OF THE STICK, BUT I PUSHED THAT CHINESE GUY SHE KNOWS.
SHOVED HIM HARD, RIGHT OVER.
REALLY? WOW, THAT'S NO LIKE YOU.
'PEACEFUL PEARCE' YOU ARE NORMALLY.
YEAH, I FEEL BAD ABOUT IT NOW.

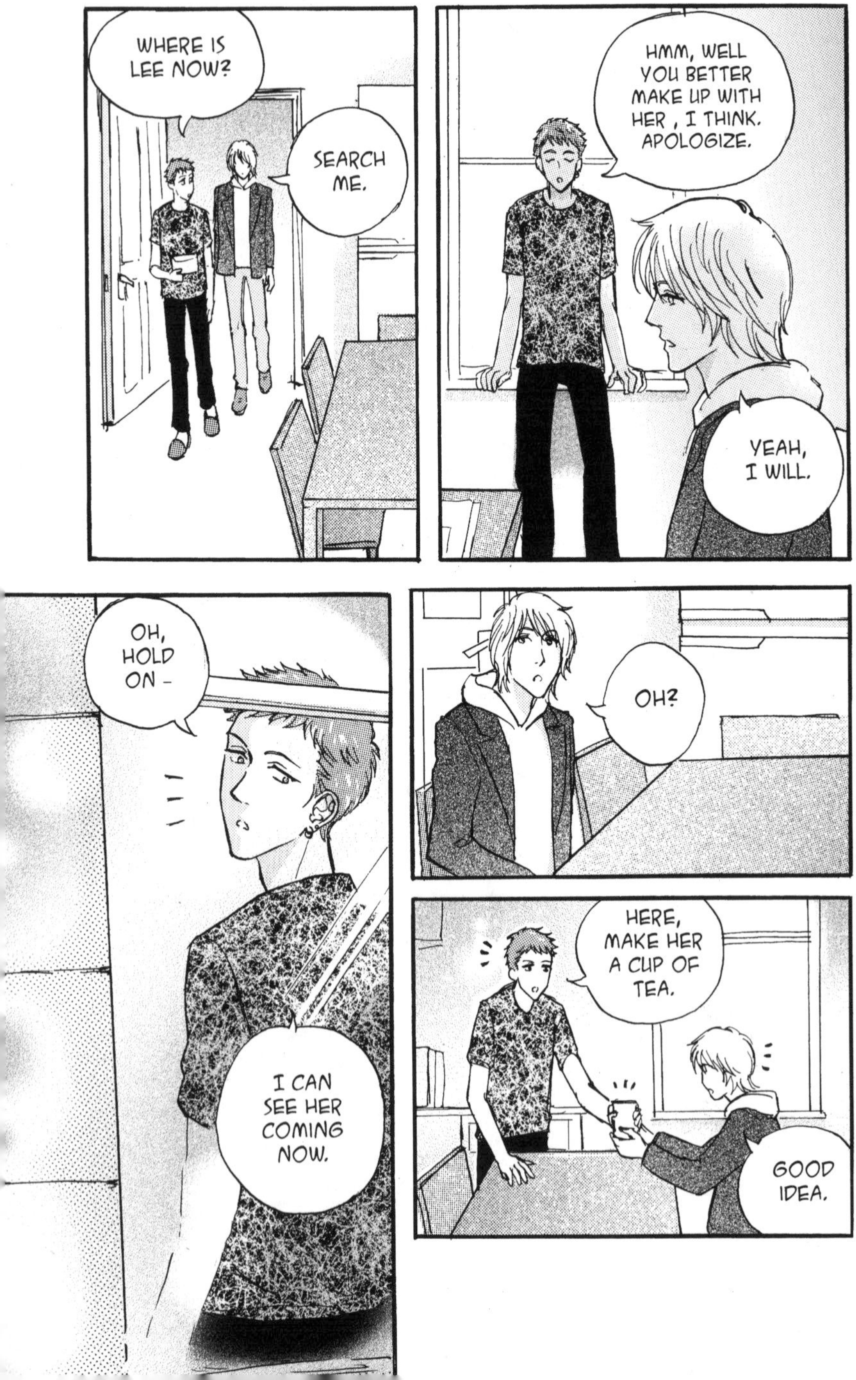
WHERE IS LEE NOW?
SEARCH ME.
HMM, WELL YOU BETTER MAKE UP WITH HER, I THINK. APOLOGIZE.
YEAH, I WILL.
OH, HOLD ON –
I CAN SEE HER COMING NOW.
OH?
HERE, MAKE HER A CUP OF TEA.
GOOD IDEA.

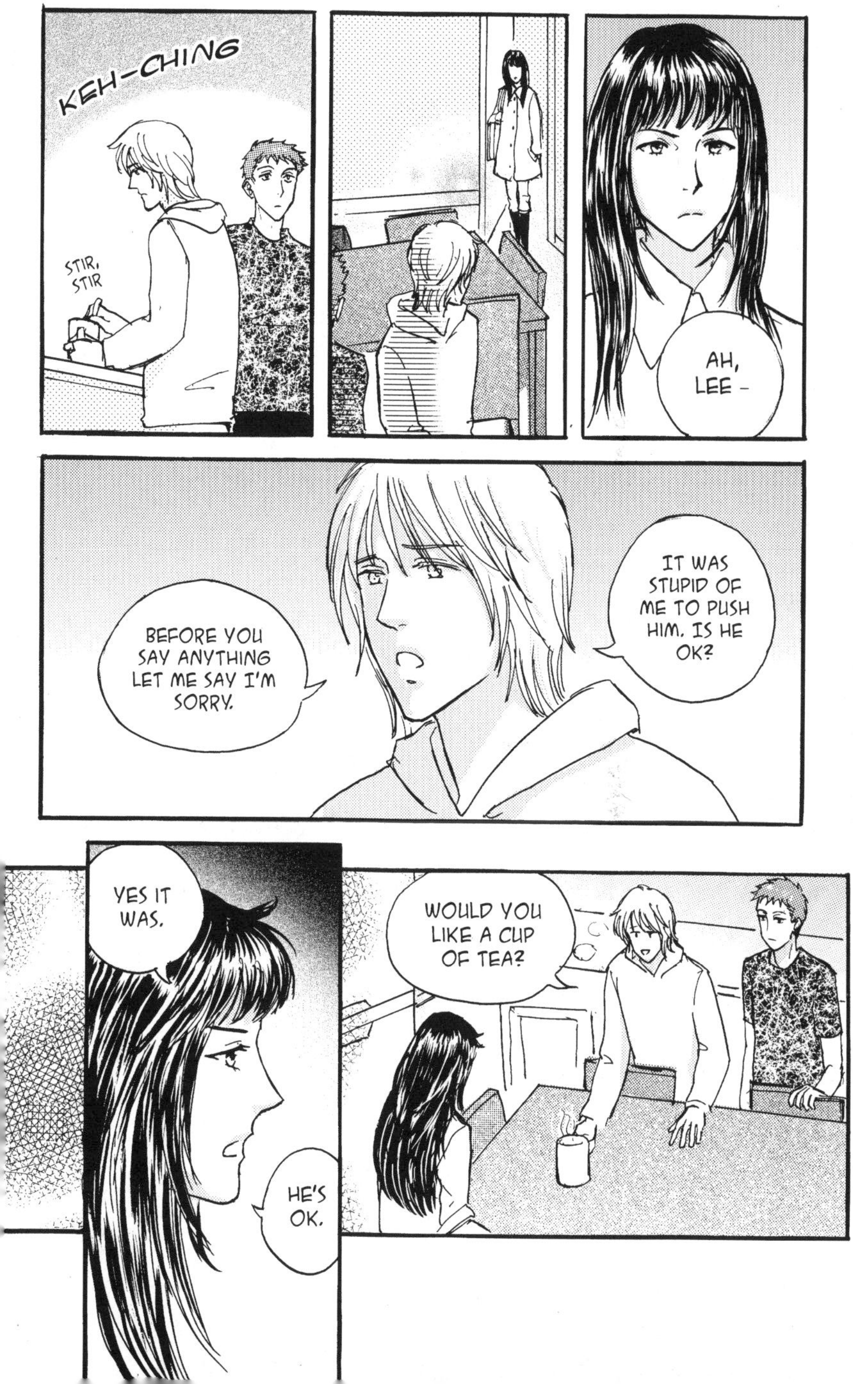
KEH-CHING
STIR, STIR
AH, LEE -
BEFORE YOU SAY ANYTHING LET ME SAY I'M SORRY.
IT WAS STUPID OF ME TO PUSH HIM. IS HE OK?
YES IT WAS.
HE'S OK.
WOULD YOU LIKE A CUP OF TEA?

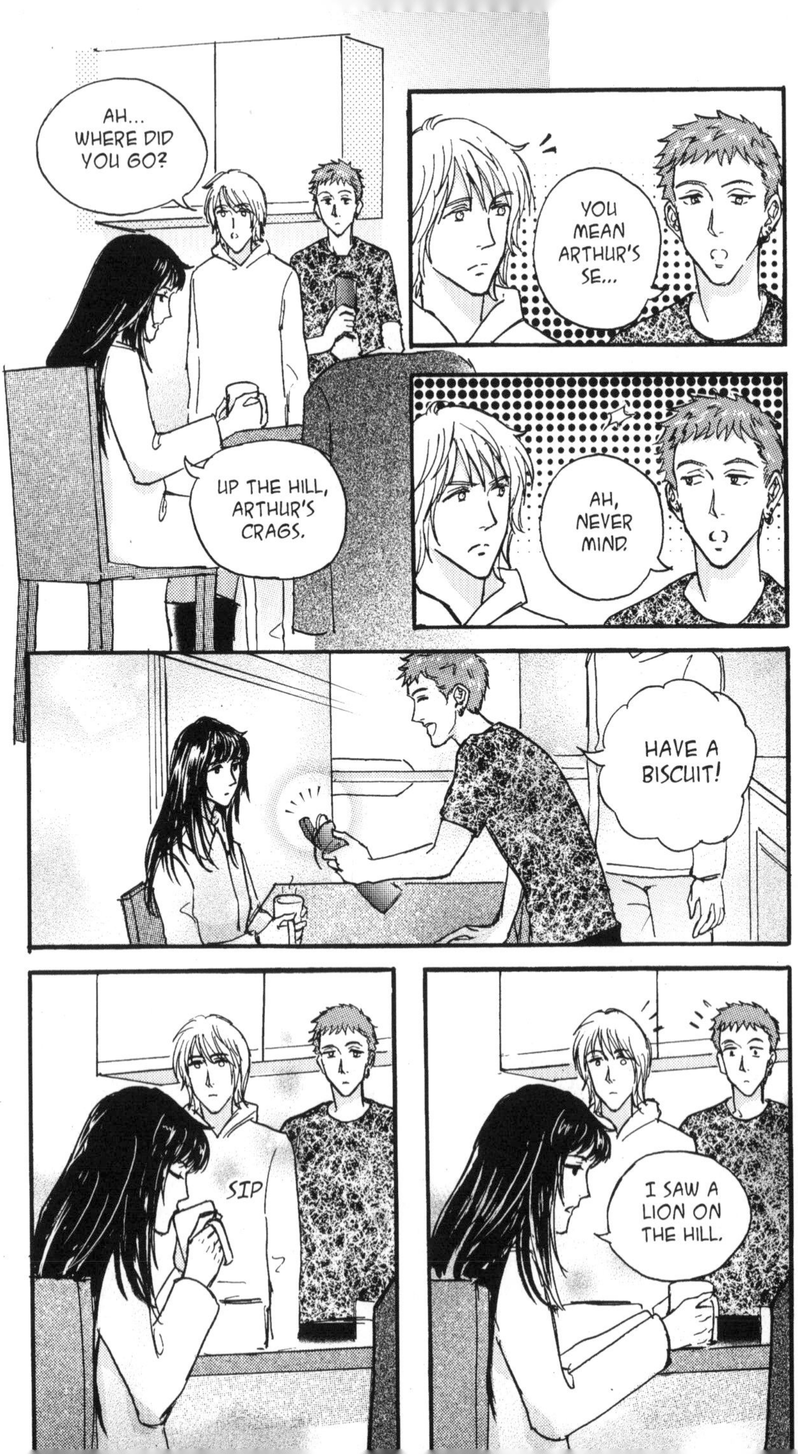
AH... WHERE DID YOU GO?
YOU MEAN ARTHUR'S SE...
UP THE HILL, ARTHUR'S CRAGS.
AH, NEVER MIND.
HAVE A BISCUIT!
SIP
I SAW A LION ON THE HILL.

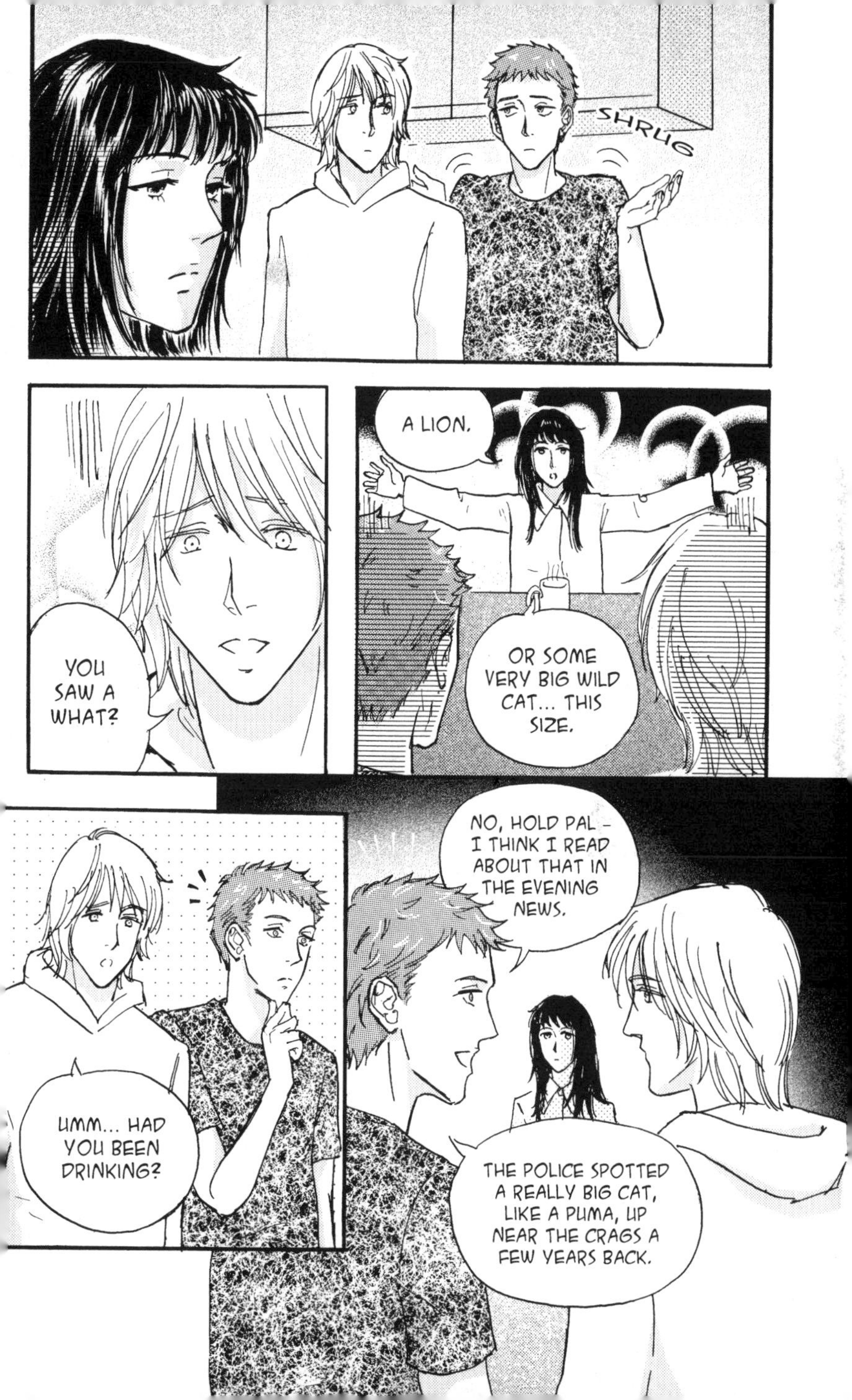
SHRUG
YOU SAW A WHAT?
A LION.
OR SOME VERY BIG WILD CAT... THIS SIZE.
UMM... HAD YOU BEEN DRINKING?
NO, HOLD PAL - I THINK I READ ABOUT THAT IN THE EVENING NEWS.
THE POLICE SPOTTED A REALLY BIG CAT, LIKE A PUMA, UP NEAR THE CRAGS A FEW YEARS BACK.

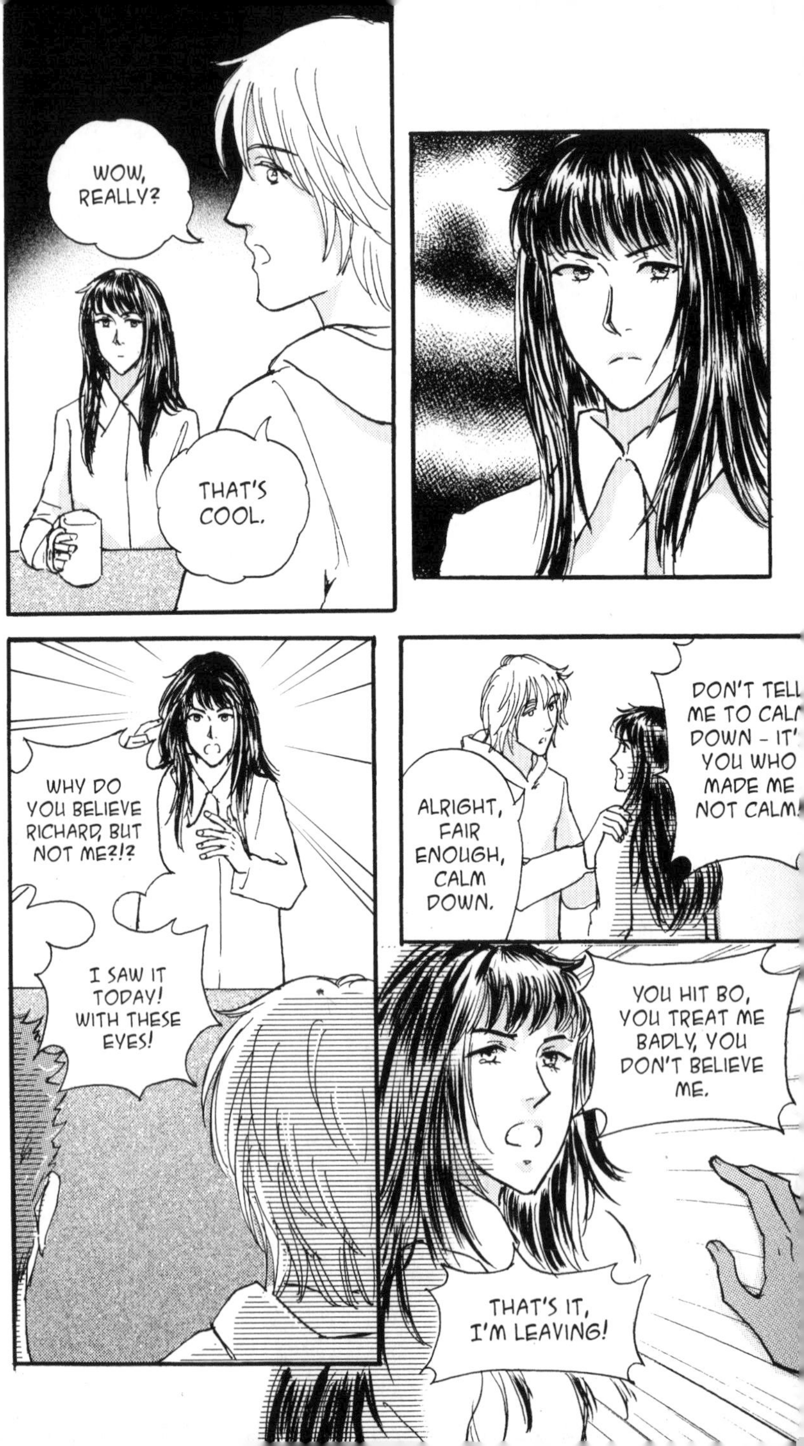
WOW, REALLY?
THAT'S COOL.
WHY DO YOU BELIEVE RICHARD, BUT NOT ME?!?
ALRIGHT, FAIR ENOUGH, CALM DOWN.
DON'T TELL ME TO CALM DOWN - IT'S YOU WHO MADE ME NOT CALM!
I SAW IT TODAY! WITH THESE EYES!
YOU HIT BO, YOU TREAT ME BADLY, YOU DON'T BELIEVE ME.
THAT'S IT, I'M LEAVING!

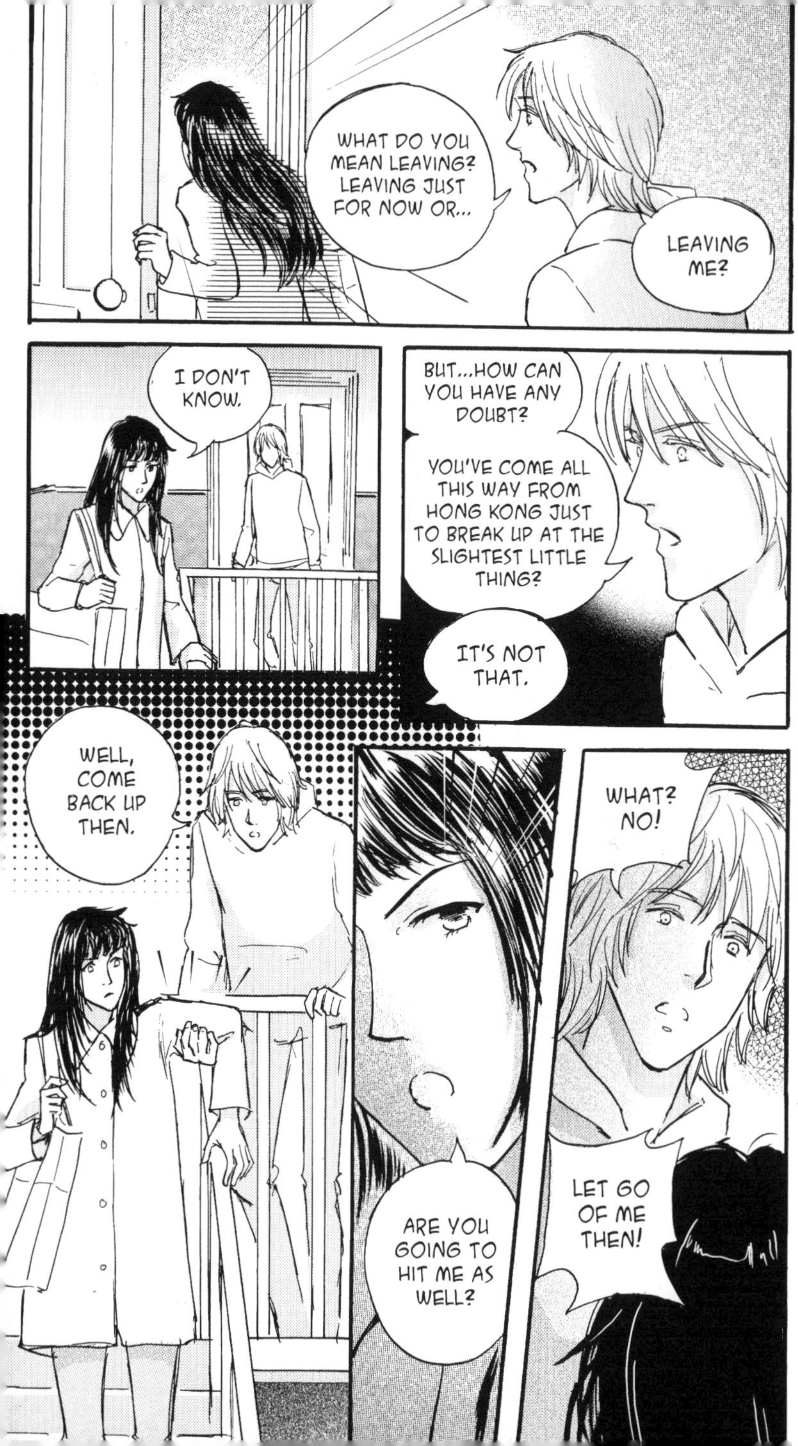
WHAT DO YOU MEAN LEAVING? LEAVING JUST FOR NOW OR...
LEAVING ME?
I DON'T KNOW.
BUT...HOW CAN YOU HAVE ANY DOUBT?
YOU'VE COME ALL THIS WAY FROM HONG KONG JUST TO BREAK UP AT THE SLIGHTEST LITTLE THING?
IT'S NOT THAT.
WELL, COME BACK UP THEN.
ARE YOU GOING TO HIT ME AS WELL?
WHAT? NO!
LET GO OF ME THEN!

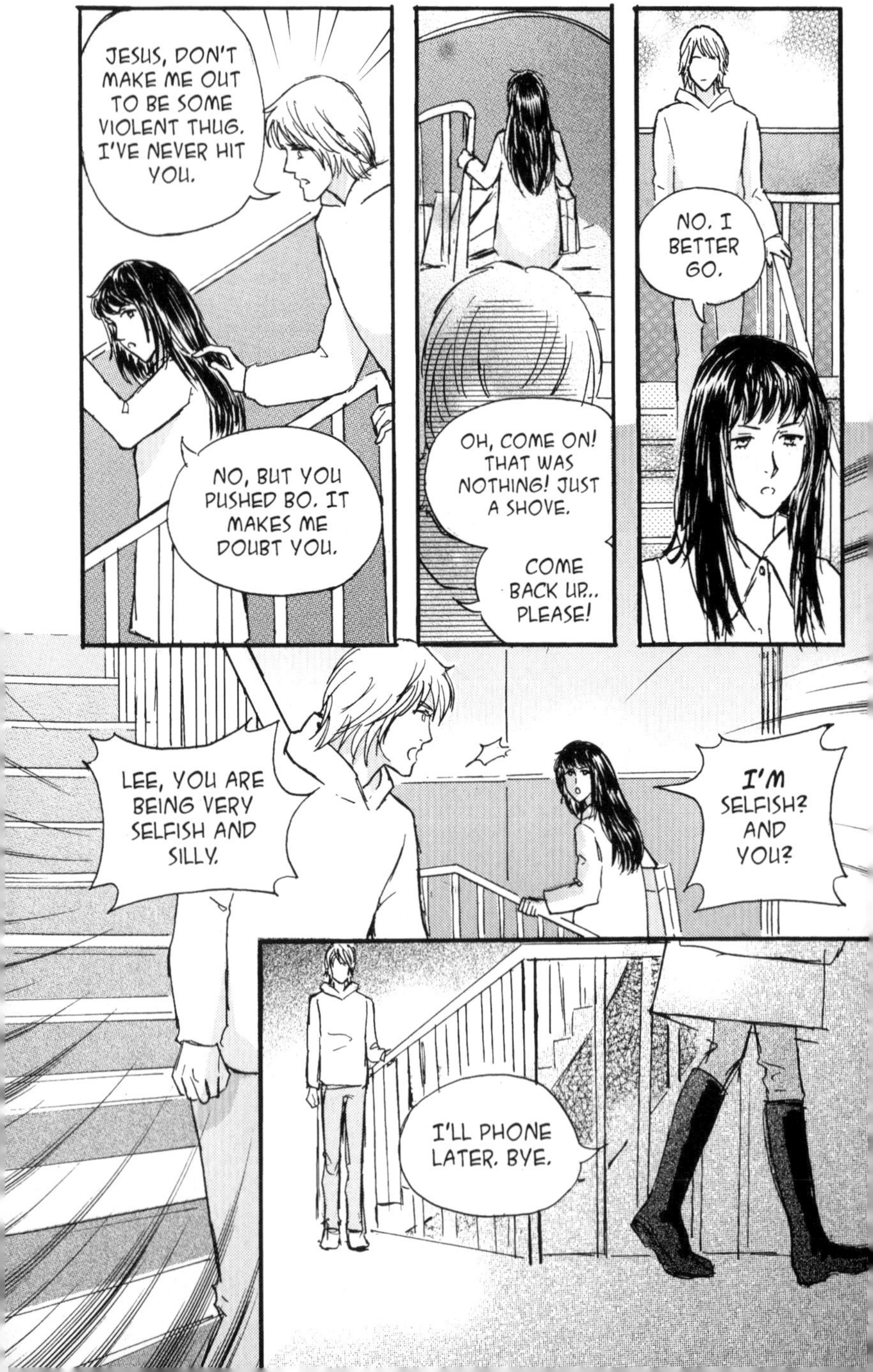
JESUS, DON'T MAKE ME OUT TO BE SOME VIOLENT THUG. I'VE NEVER HIT YOU.
NO, BUT YOU PUSHED BO. IT MAKES ME DOUBT YOU.
OH, COME ON! THAT WAS NOTHING! JUST A SHOVE.
COME BACK UP... PLEASE!
NO. I BETTER GO.
LEE, YOU ARE BEING VERY SELFISH AND SILLY.
I'M SELFISH? AND YOU?
I'LL PHONE LATER. BYE.

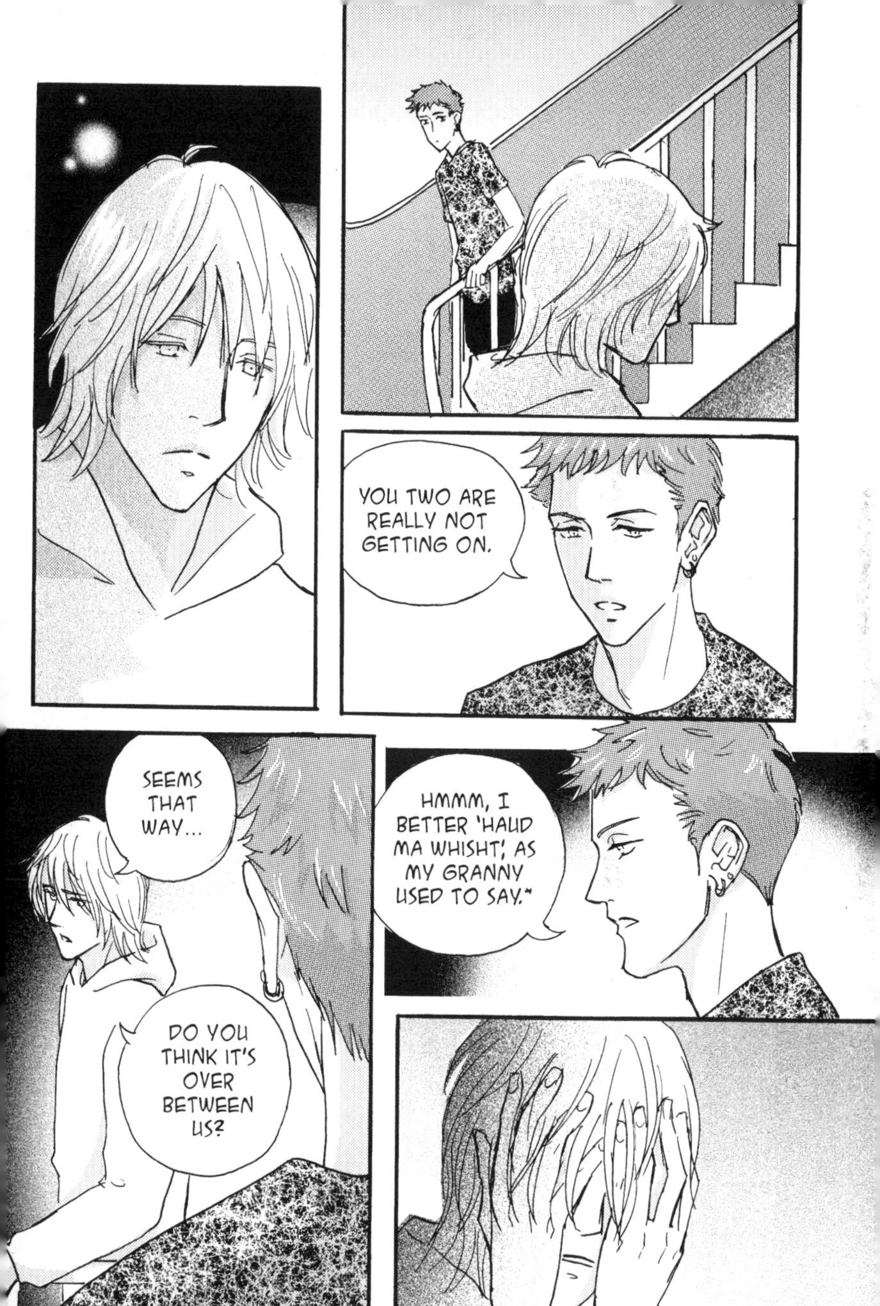
YOU TWO ARE REALLY NOT GETTING ON.
SEEMS THAT WAY...
HMMM, I BETTER 'HAUD MA WHISHT', AS MY GRANNY USED TO SAY.*
DO YOU THINK IT'S OVER BETWEEN US?

*HAUD MA WHISHT OR HAUD YER WHISHT MEANS TO NOT SAY ANYTHING, TO KEEP QUIET, IN SCOTS

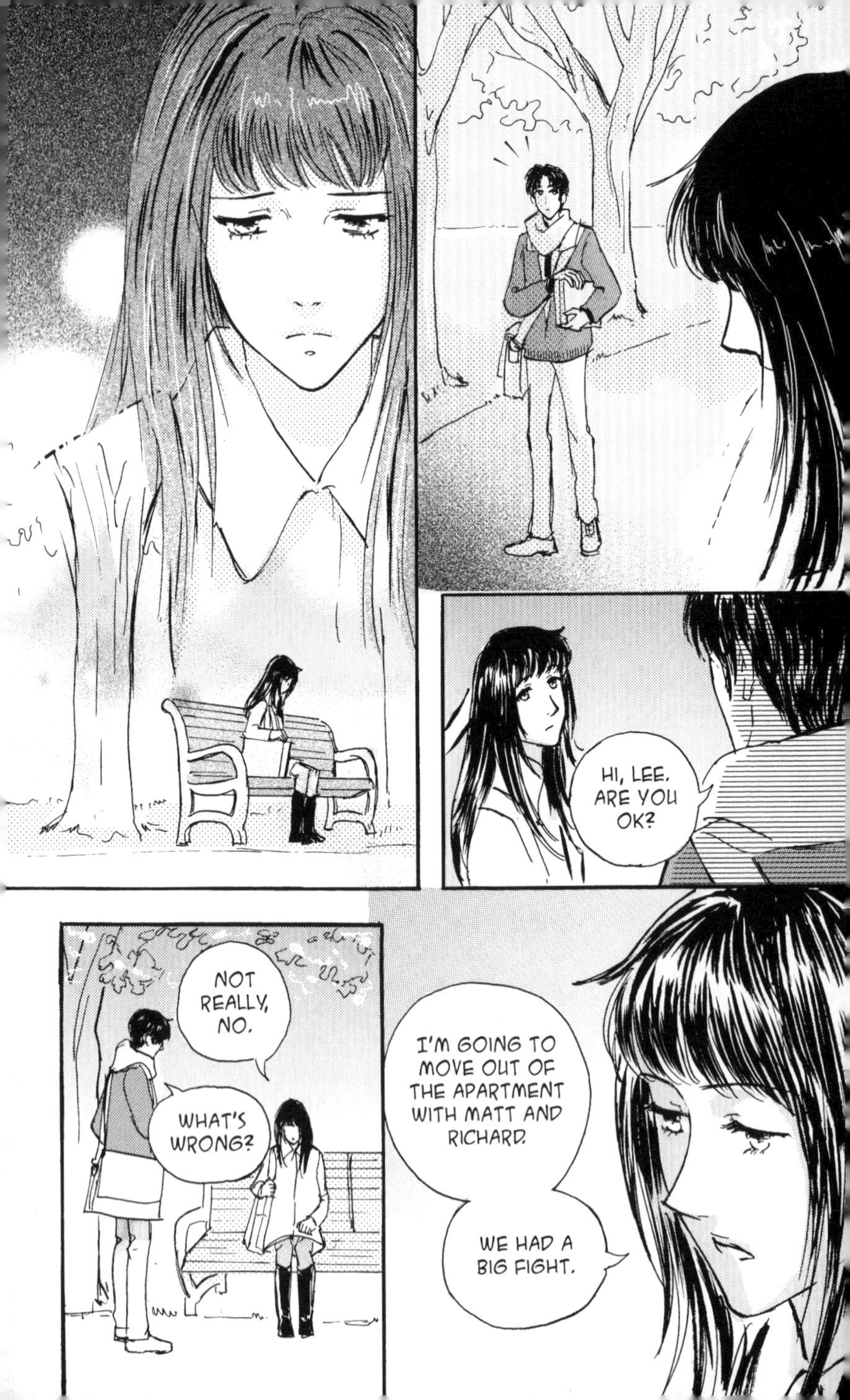
HI, LEE. ARE YOU OK?
NOT REALLY, NO.
WHAT'S WRONG?
I'M GOING TO MOVE OUT OF THE APARTMENT WITH MATT AND RICHARD.
WE HAD A BIG FIGHT.

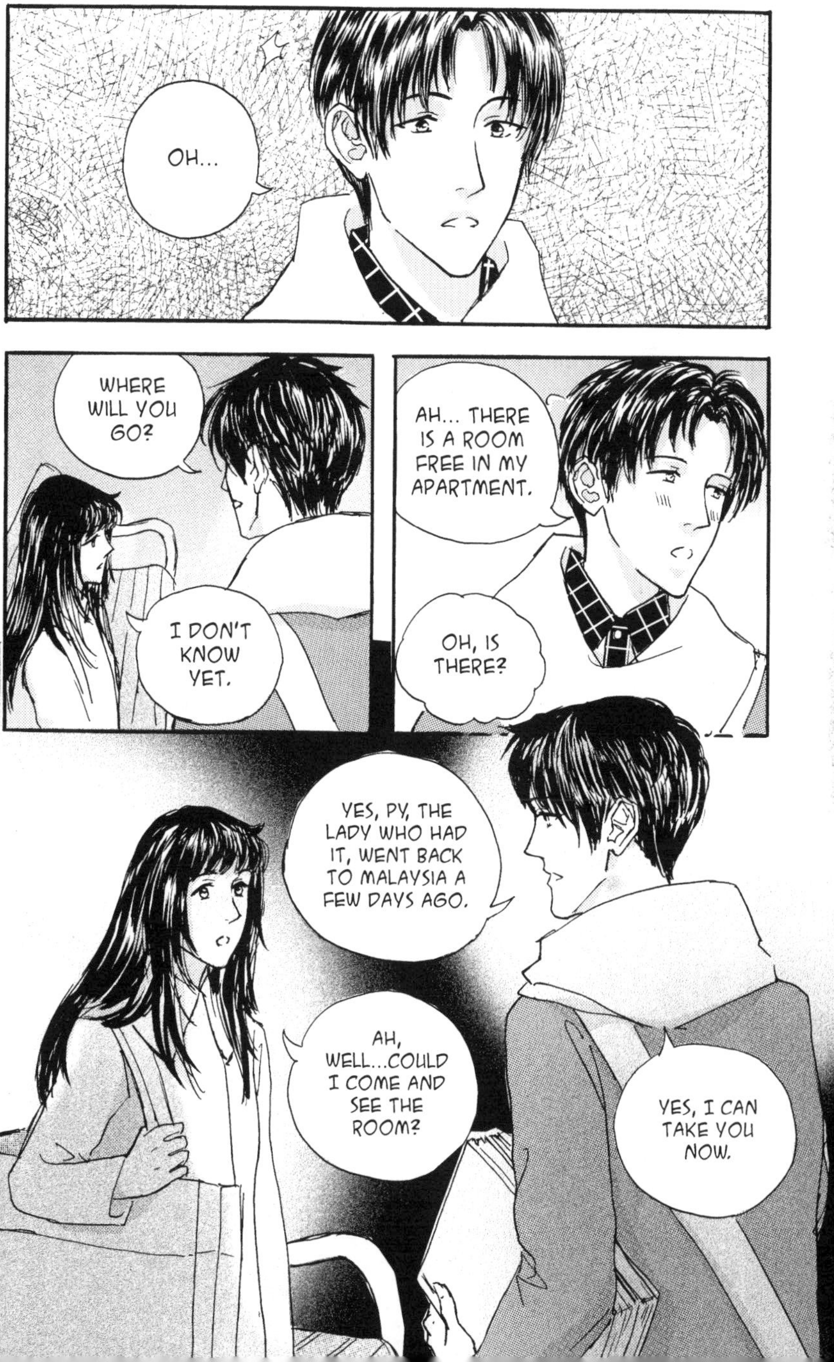
OH...
WHERE WILL YOU GO?
I DON'T KNOW YET.
AH... THERE IS A ROOM FREE IN MY APARTMENT.
OH, IS THERE?
YES, PY, THE LADY WHO HAD IT, WENT BACK TO MALAYSIA A FEW DAYS AGO.
AH, WELL...COULD I COME AND SEE THE ROOM?
YES, I CAN TAKE YOU NOW.

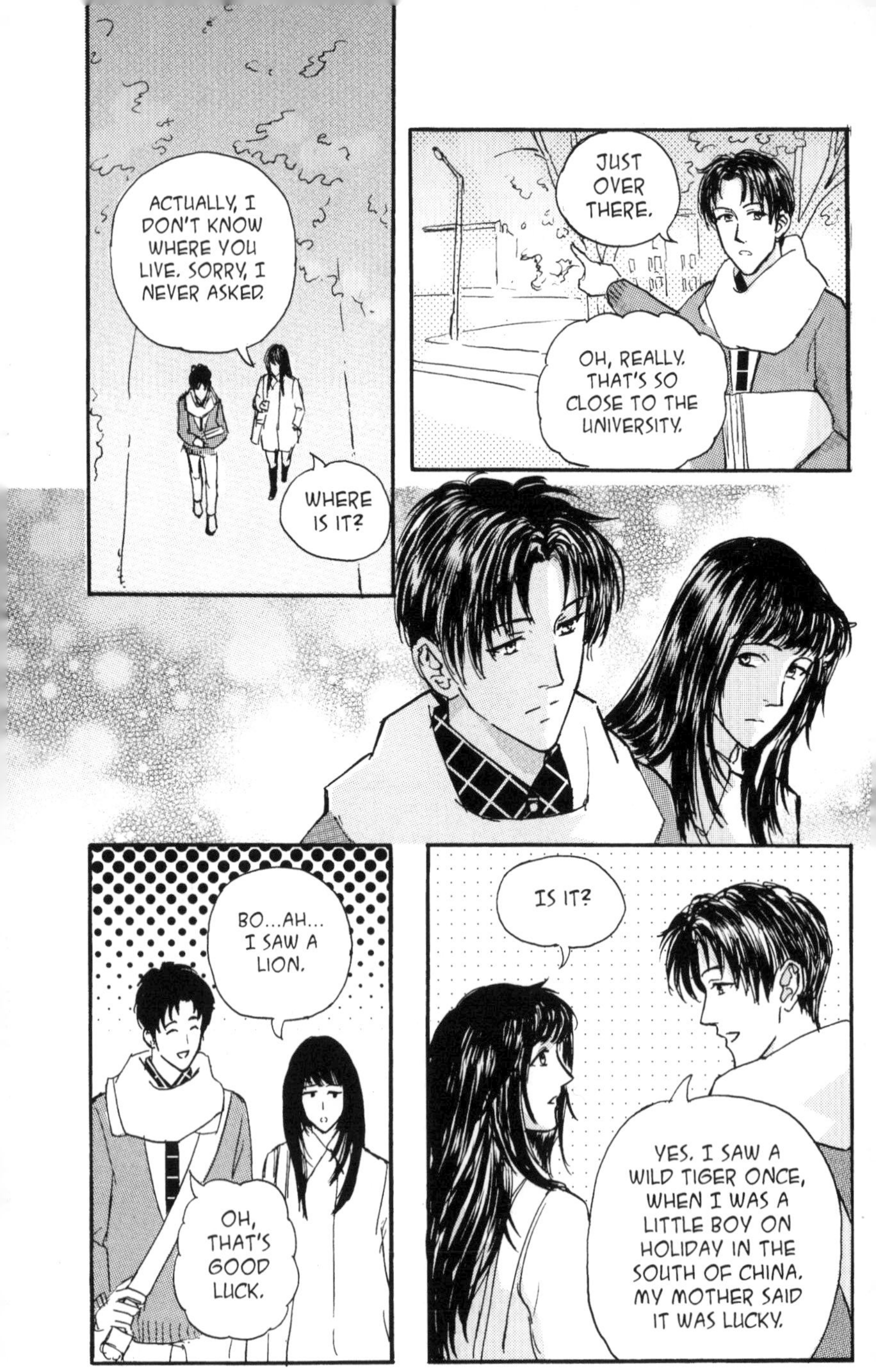
ACTUALLY, I DON'T KNOW WHERE YOU LIVE. SORRY, I NEVER ASKED.
WHERE IS IT?
JUST OVER THERE.
OH, REALLY. THAT'S SO CLOSE TO THE UNIVERSITY.
BO...AH... I SAW A LION.
OH, THAT'S GOOD LUCK.
IS IT?
YES. I SAW A WILD TIGER ONCE, WHEN I WAS A LITTLE BOY ON HOLIDAY IN THE SOUTH OF CHINA. MY MOTHER SAID IT WAS LUCKY.

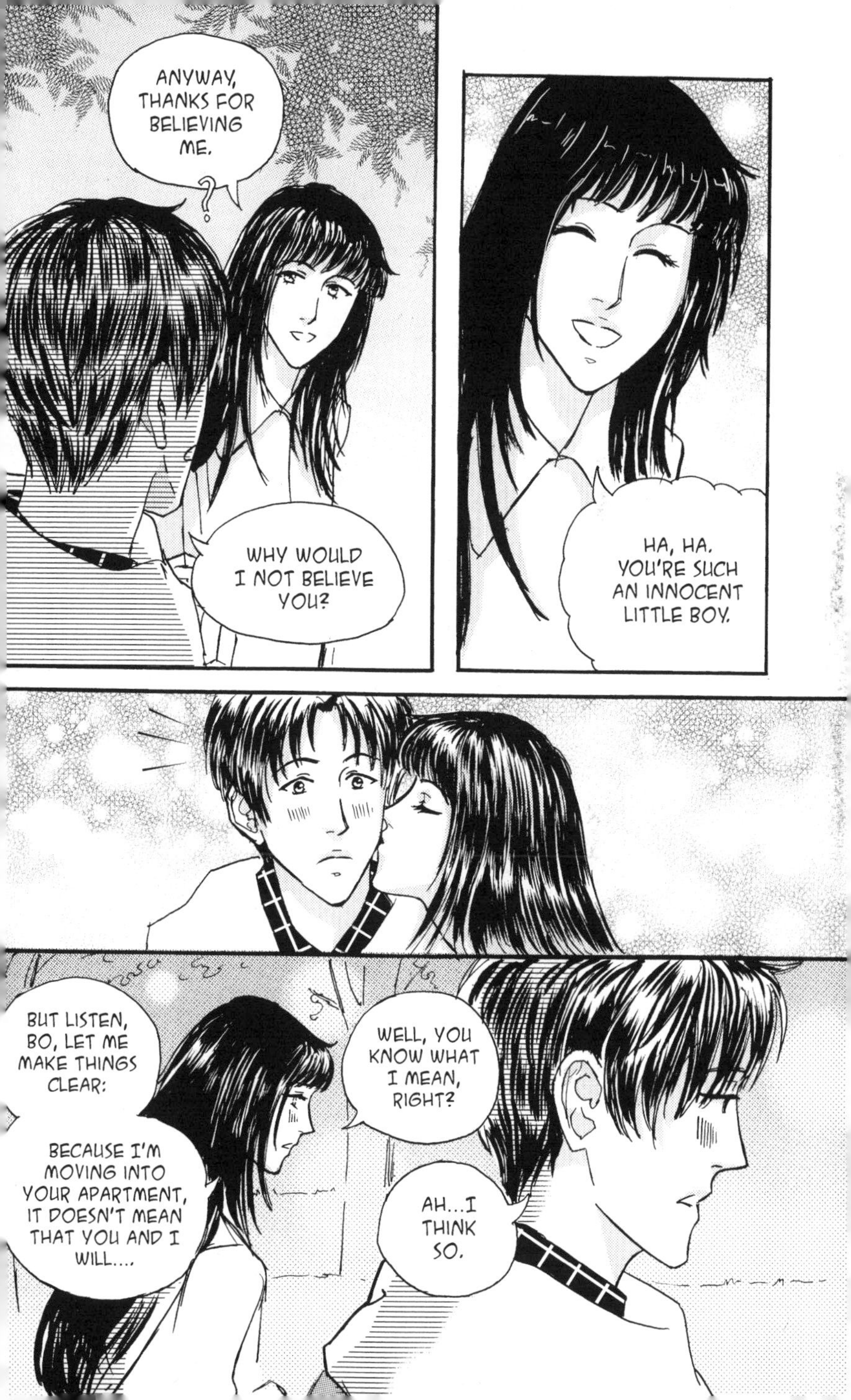

ANYWAY, THANKS FOR BELIEVING ME.
?
WHY WOULD I NOT BELIEVE YOU?
HA, HA. YOU'RE SUCH AN INNOCENT LITTLE BOY.
BUT LISTEN, BO, LET ME MAKE THINGS CLEAR:
BECAUSE I'M MOVING INTO YOUR APARTMENT, IT DOESN'T MEAN THAT YOU AND I WILL....
WELL, YOU KNOW WHAT I MEAN, RIGHT?
AH...I THINK SO.

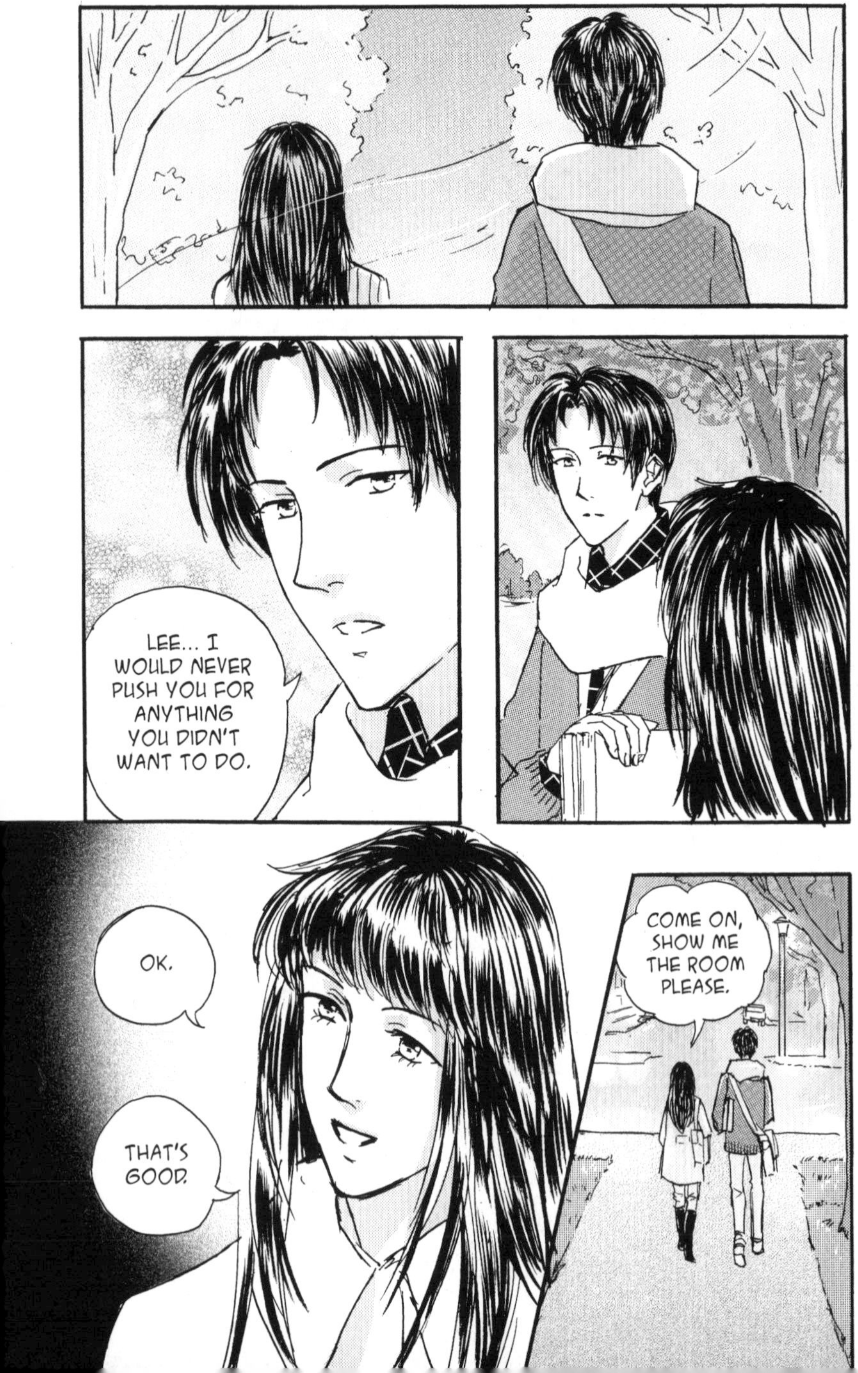
LEE... I WOULD NEVER PUSH YOU FOR ANYTHING YOU DIDN'T WANT TO DO.
OK.
THAT'S GOOD.
COME ON, SHOW ME THE ROOM PLEASE.

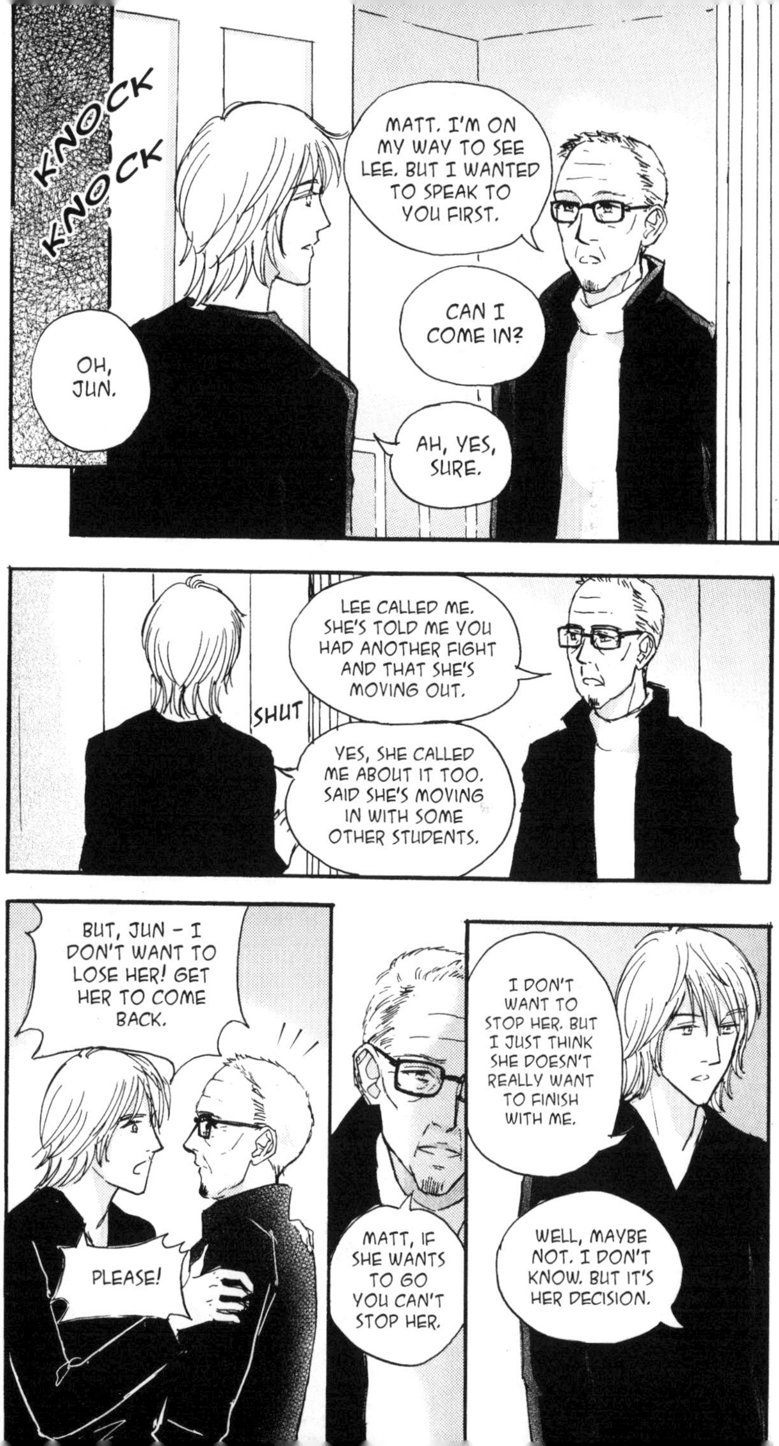
KNOCK
KNOCK
OH, JUN.
MATT. I'M ON MY WAY TO SEE LEE. BUT I WANTED TO SPEAK TO YOU FIRST.
CAN I COME IN?
AH, YES, SURE.
LEE CALLED ME. SHE'S TOLD ME YOU HAD ANOTHER FIGHT AND THAT SHE'S MOVING OUT.
SHUT
YES, SHE CALLED ME ABOUT IT TOO. SAID SHE'S MOVING IN WITH SOME OTHER STUDENTS.
BUT, JUN – I DON'T WANT TO LOSE HER! GET HER TO COME BACK.
PLEASE!
I DON'T WANT TO STOP HER. BUT I JUST THINK SHE DOESN'T REALLY WANT TO FINISH WITH ME.
MATT, IF SHE WANTS TO GO YOU CAN'T STOP HER.
WELL, MAYBE NOT. I DON'T KNOW. BUT IT'S HER DECISION.

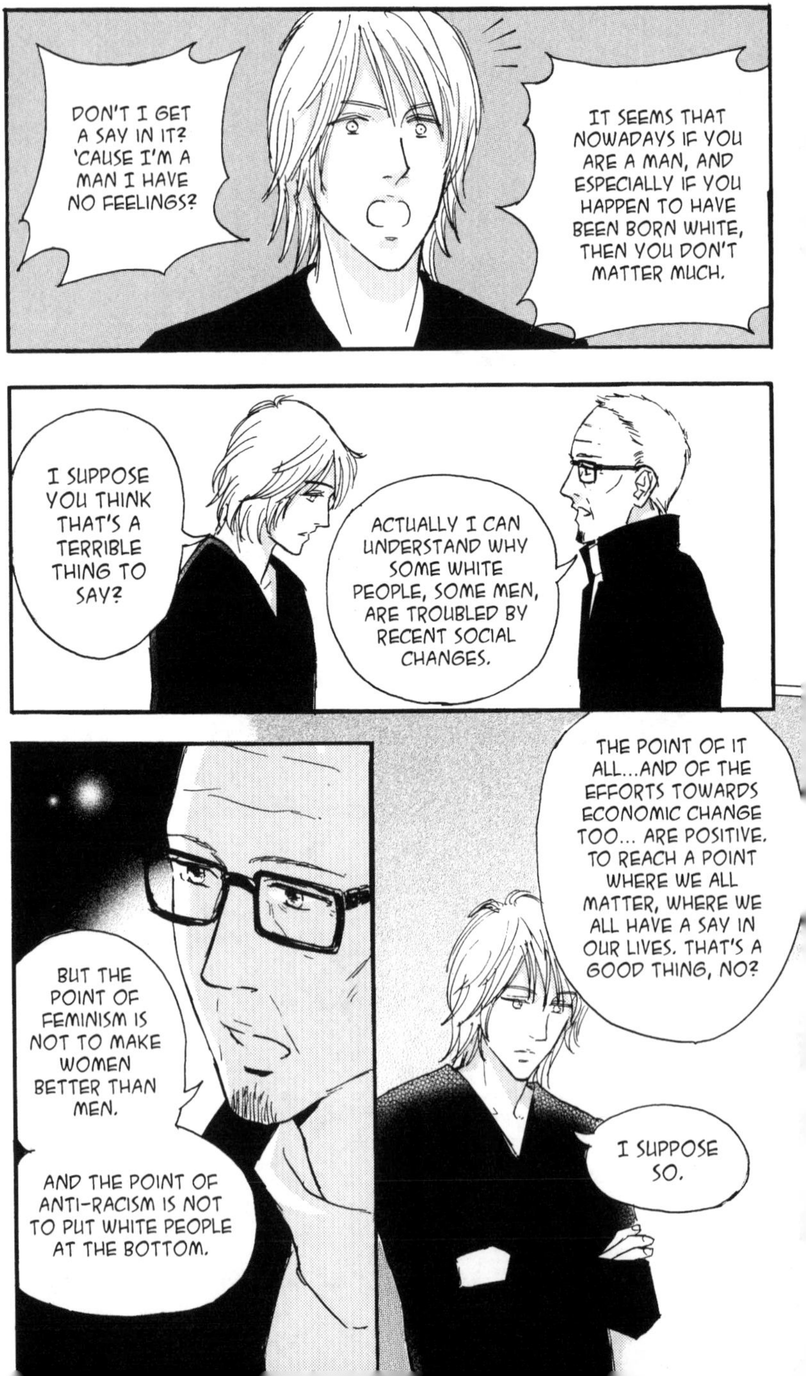
DON'T I GET A SAY IN IT? 'CAUSE I'M A MAN I HAVE NO FEELINGS?
IT SEEMS THAT NOWADAYS IF YOU ARE A MAN, AND ESPECIALLY IF YOU HAPPEN TO HAVE BEEN BORN WHITE, THEN YOU DON'T MATTER MUCH.
I SUPPOSE YOU THINK THAT'S A TERRIBLE THING TO SAY?
ACTUALLY I CAN UNDERSTAND WHY SOME WHITE PEOPLE, SOME MEN, ARE TROUBLED BY RECENT SOCIAL CHANGES.
BUT THE POINT OF FEMINISM IS NOT TO MAKE WOMEN BETTER THAN MEN.
AND THE POINT OF ANTI-RACISM IS NOT TO PUT WHITE PEOPLE AT THE BOTTOM.
THE POINT OF IT ALL...AND OF THE EFFORTS TOWARDS ECONOMIC CHANGE TOO... ARE POSITIVE. TO REACH A POINT WHERE WE ALL MATTER, WHERE WE ALL HAVE A SAY IN OUR LIVES. THAT'S A GOOD THING, NO?
I SUPPOSE SO.

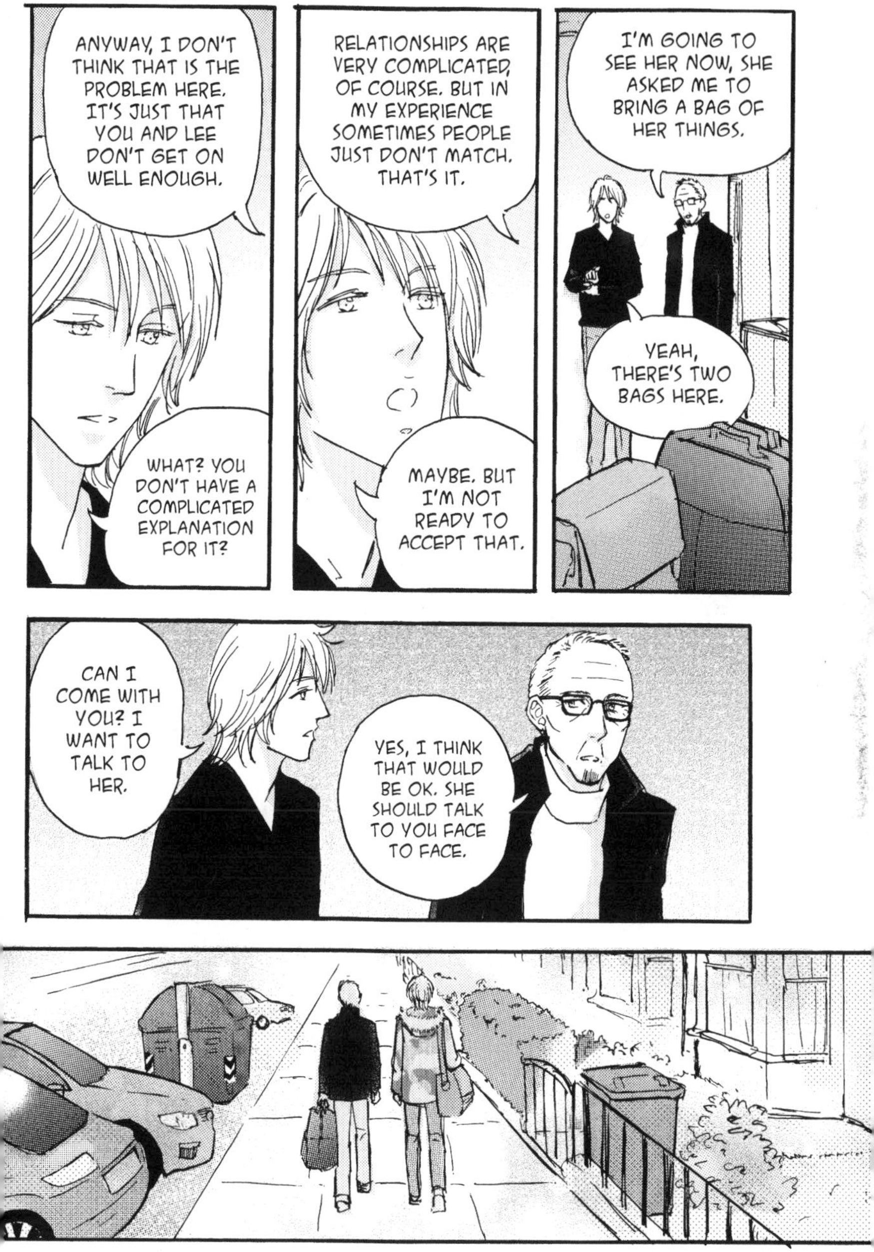
ANYWAY, I DON'T THINK THAT IS THE PROBLEM HERE. IT'S JUST THAT YOU AND LEE DON'T GET ON WELL ENOUGH.
WHAT? YOU DON'T HAVE A COMPLICATED EXPLANATION FOR IT?
RELATIONSHIPS ARE VERY COMPLICATED, OF COURSE. BUT IN MY EXPERIENCE SOMETIMES PEOPLE JUST DON'T MATCH. THAT'S IT.
MAYBE. BUT I'M NOT READY TO ACCEPT THAT.
I'M GOING TO SEE HER NOW, SHE ASKED ME TO BRING A BAG OF HER THINGS.
YEAH, THERE'S TWO BAGS HERE.
CAN I COME WITH YOU? I WANT TO TALK TO HER.
YES, I THINK THAT WOULD BE OK. SHE SHOULD TALK TO YOU FACE TO FACE.

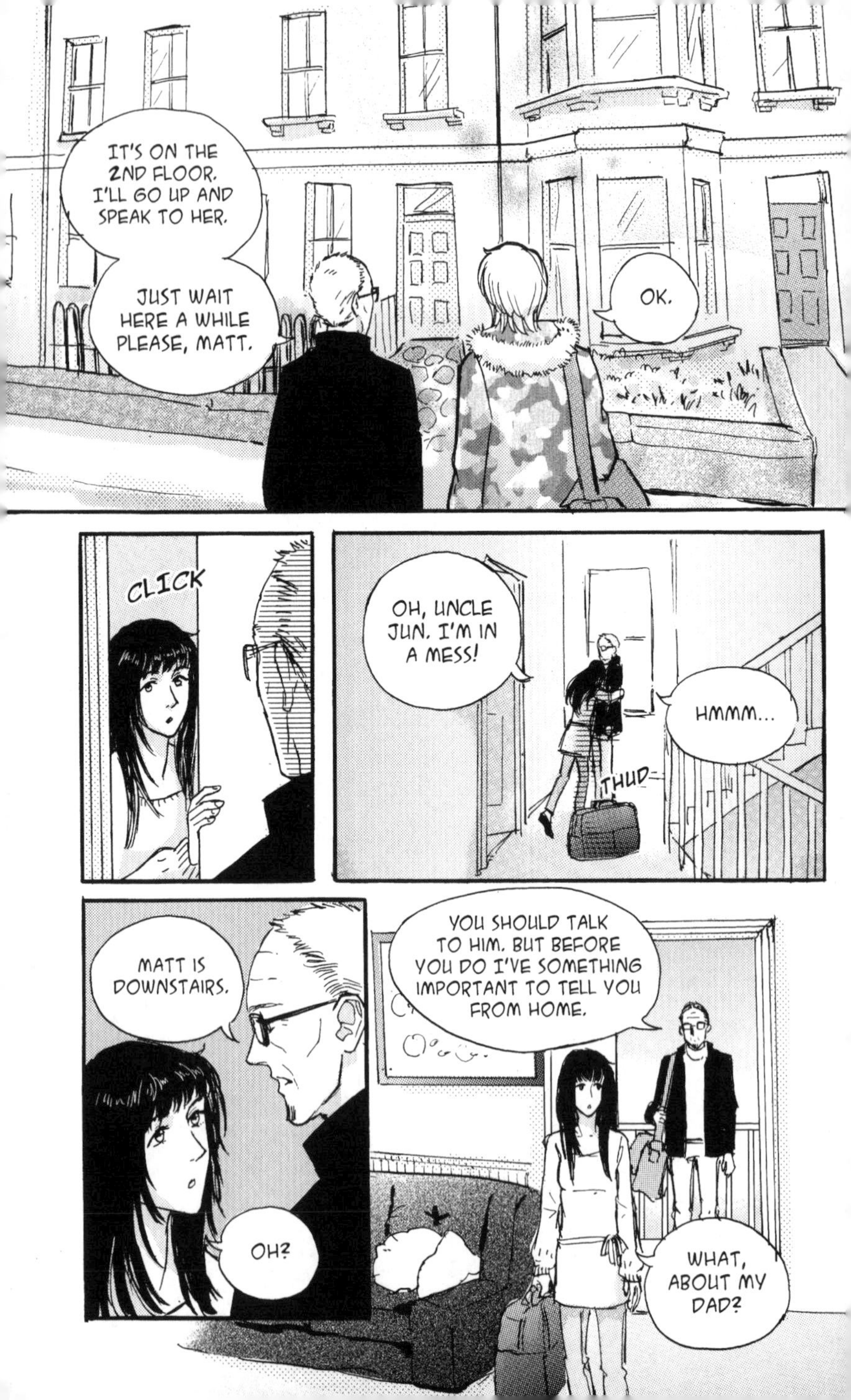
IT'S ON THE 2ND FLOOR. I'LL GO UP AND SPEAK TO HER.
JUST WAIT HERE A WHILE PLEASE, MATT.
OK.
CLICK
OH, UNCLE JUN. I'M IN A MESS!
HMMM...
THUD
MATT IS DOWNSTAIRS.
OH?
YOU SHOULD TALK TO HIM. BUT BEFORE YOU DO I'VE SOMETHING IMPORTANT TO TELL YOU FROM HOME.
WHAT, ABOUT MY DAD?

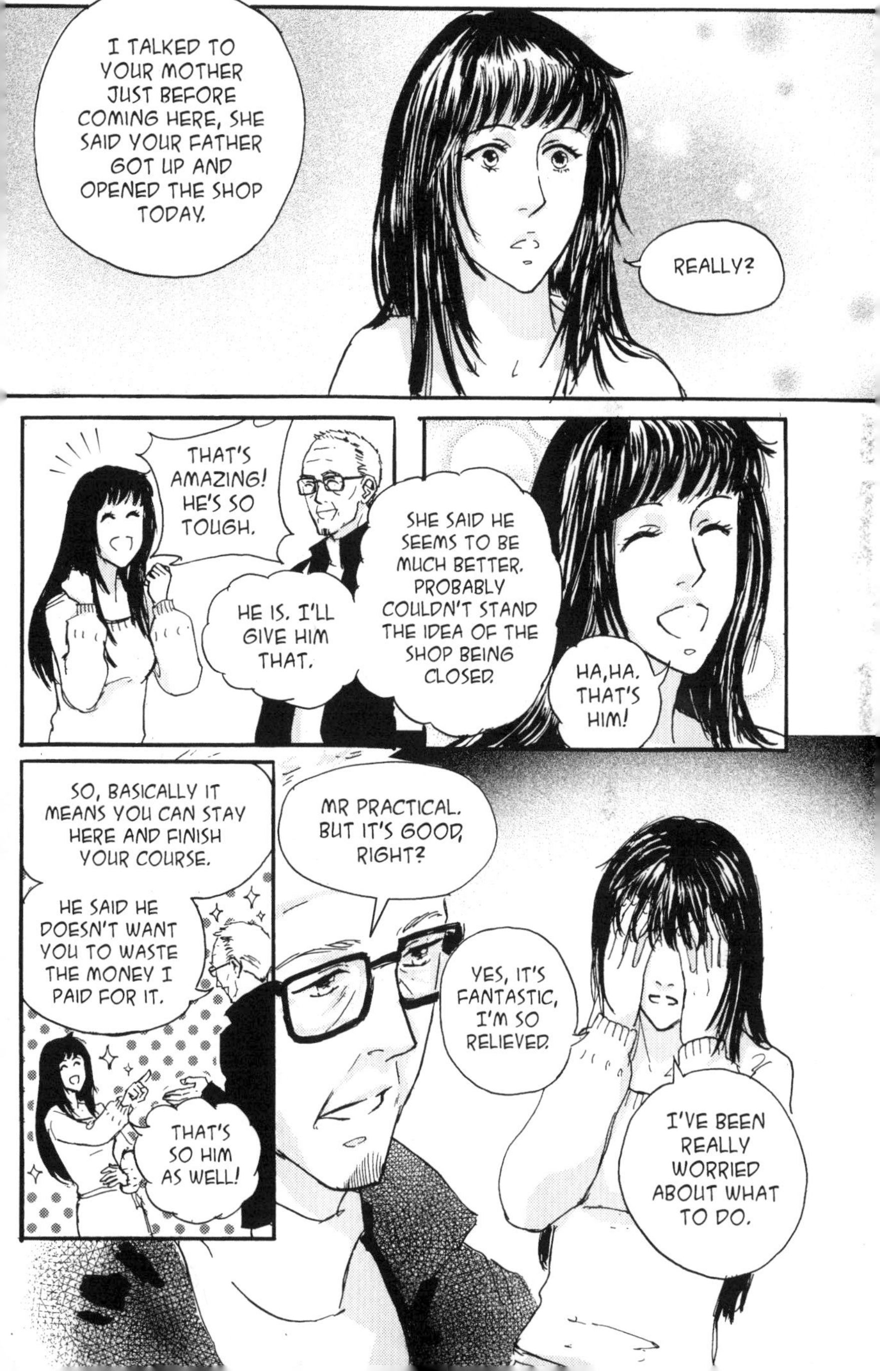
I TALKED TO YOUR MOTHER JUST BEFORE COMING HERE, SHE SAID YOUR FATHER GOT UP AND OPENED THE SHOP TODAY.
REALLY?
THAT'S AMAZING! HE'S SO TOUGH.
HE IS. I'LL GIVE HIM THAT.
SHE SAID HE SEEMS TO BE MUCH BETTER. PROBABLY COULDN'T STAND THE IDEA OF THE SHOP BEING CLOSED.
HA,HA. THAT'S HIM!
SO, BASICALLY IT MEANS YOU CAN STAY HERE AND FINISH YOUR COURSE.
HE SAID HE DOESN'T WANT YOU TO WASTE THE MONEY I PAID FOR IT.
THAT'S SO HIM AS WELL!
MR PRACTICAL. BUT IT'S GOOD, RIGHT?
YES, IT'S FANTASTIC, I'M SO RELIEVED.
I'VE BEEN REALLY WORRIED ABOUT WHAT TO DO.

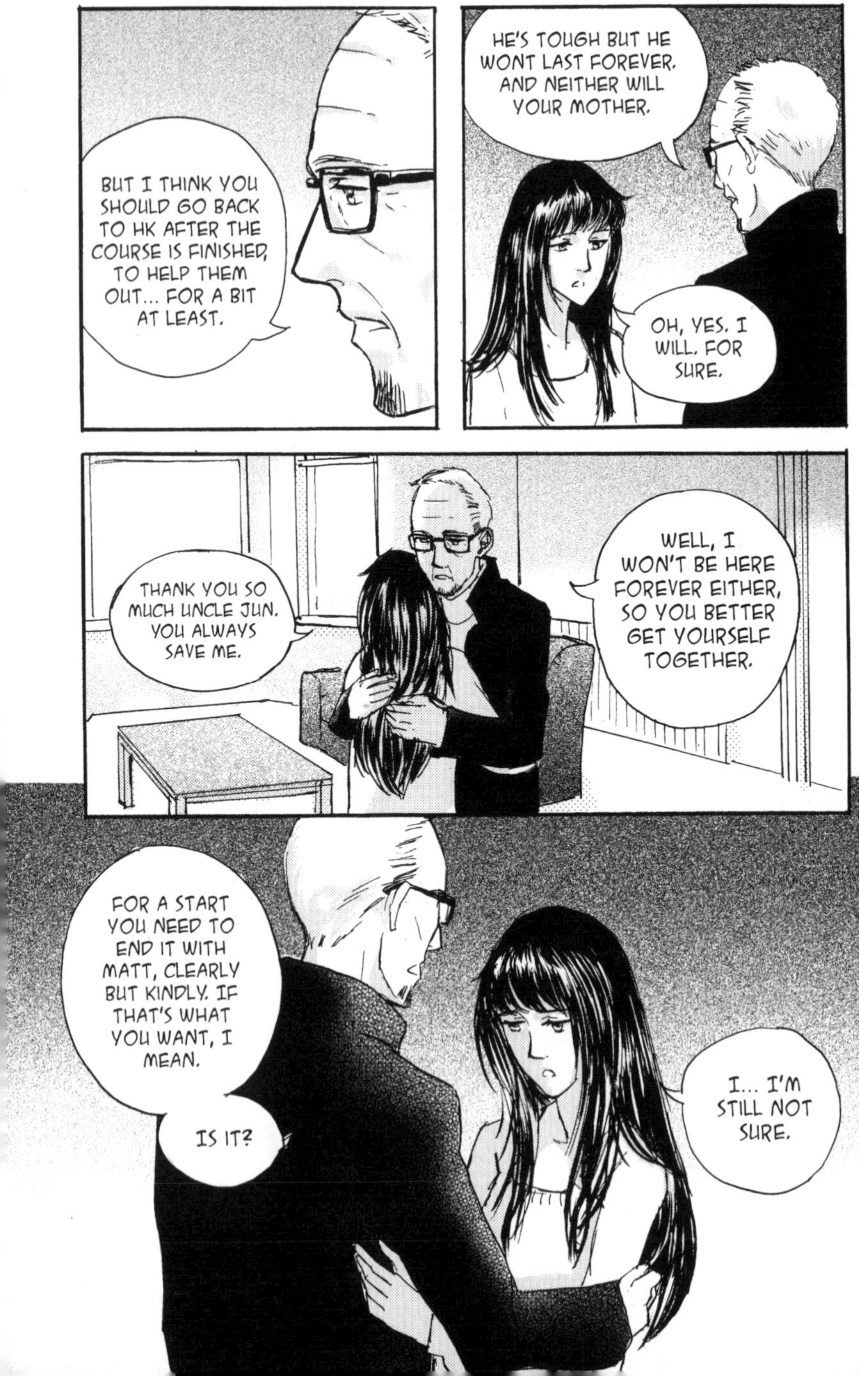
BUT I THINK YOU SHOULD GO BACK TO HK AFTER THE COURSE IS FINISHED, TO HELP THEM OUT... FOR A BIT AT LEAST.
HE'S TOUGH BUT HE WONT LAST FOREVER. AND NEITHER WILL YOUR MOTHER.
OH, YES. I WILL. FOR SURE.
THANK YOU SO MUCH UNCLE JUN. YOU ALWAYS SAVE ME.
WELL, I WON'T BE HERE FOREVER EITHER, SO YOU BETTER GET YOURSELF TOGETHER.
FOR A START YOU NEED TO END IT WITH MATT, CLEARLY BUT KINDLY. IF THAT'S WHAT YOU WANT, I MEAN.
IS IT?
I... I'M STILL NOT SURE.

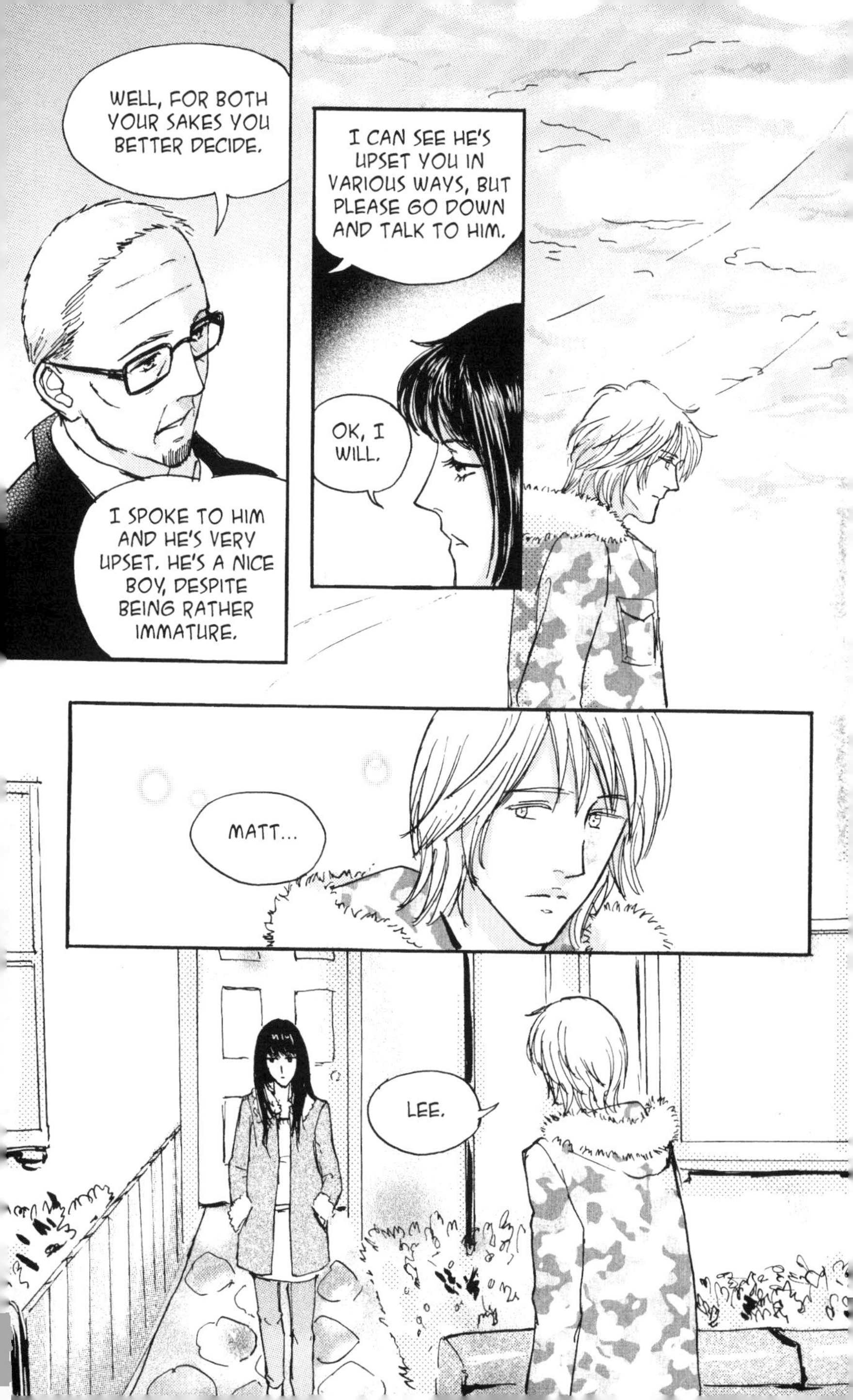
WELL, FOR BOTH YOUR SAKES YOU BETTER DECIDE.
I SPOKE TO HIM AND HE'S VERY UPSET. HE'S A NICE BOY, DESPITE BEING RATHER IMMATURE.
I CAN SEE HE'S UPSET YOU IN VARIOUS WAYS, BUT PLEASE GO DOWN AND TALK TO HIM.
OK, I WILL.
MATT...
LEE.

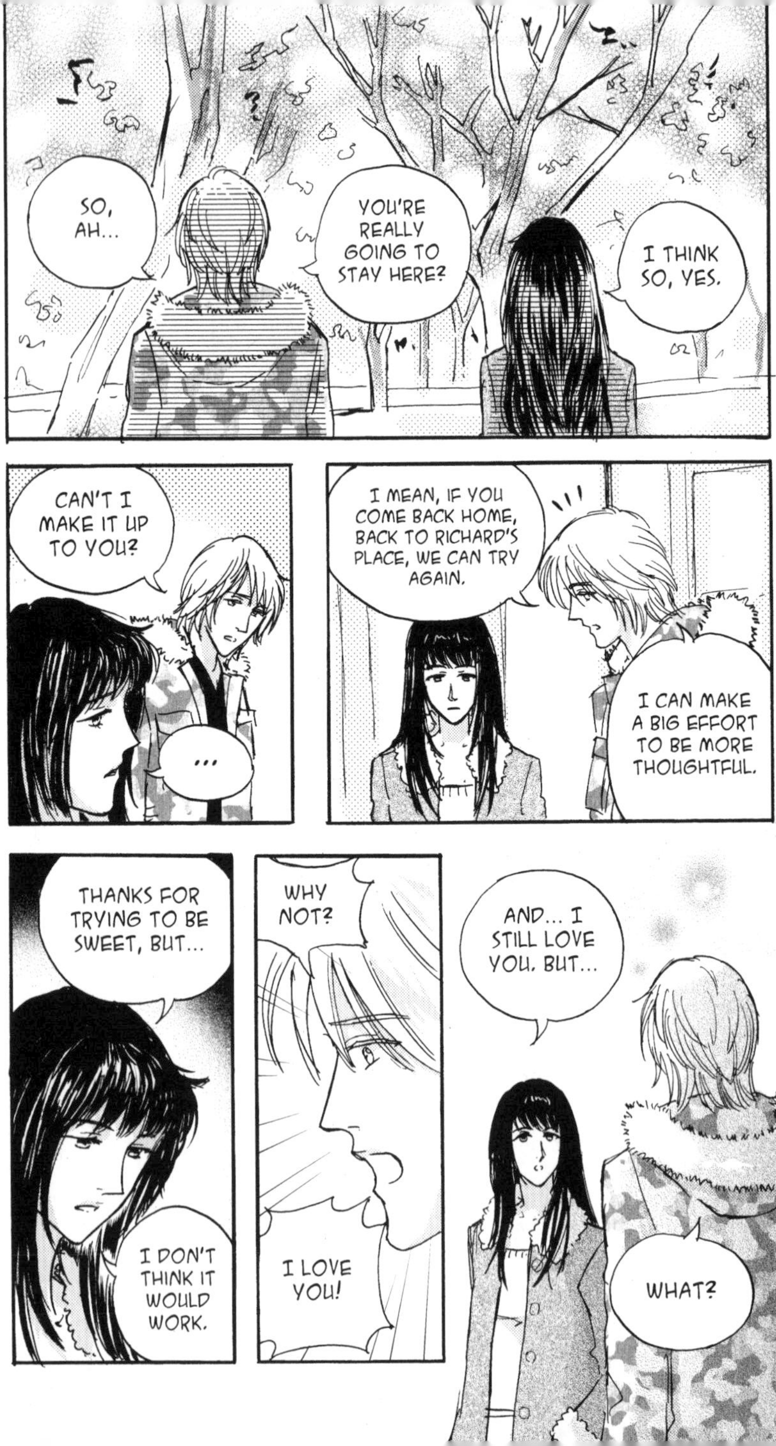
SO, AH...
YOU'RE REALLY GOING TO STAY HERE?
I THINK SO, YES.
CAN'T I MAKE IT UP TO YOU?
...
I MEAN, IF YOU COME BACK HOME, BACK TO RICHARD'S PLACE, WE CAN TRY AGAIN.
I CAN MAKE A BIG EFFORT TO BE MORE THOUGHTFUL.
THANKS FOR TRYING TO BE SWEET, BUT...
I DON'T THINK IT WOULD WORK.
WHY NOT?
I LOVE YOU!
AND... I STILL LOVE YOU, BUT...
WHAT?

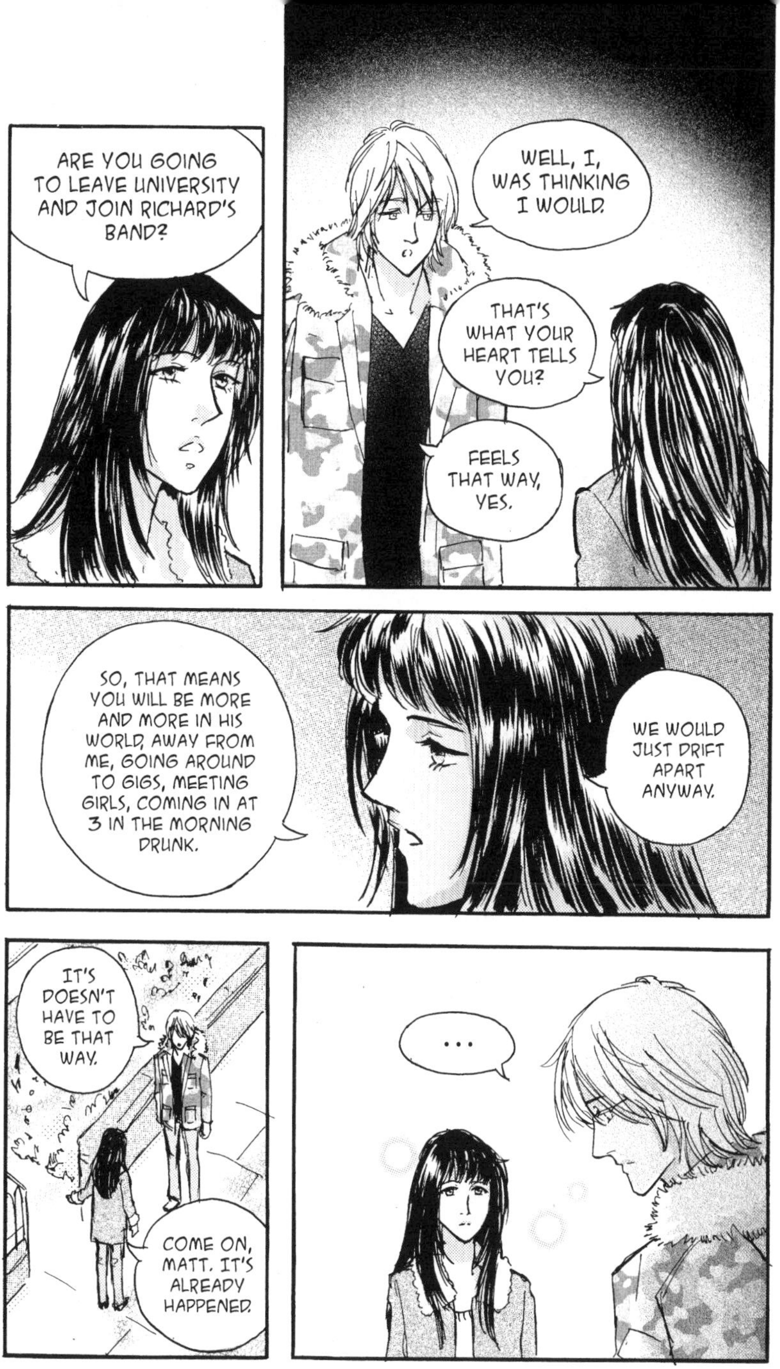
ARE YOU GOING TO LEAVE UNIVERSITY AND JOIN RICHARD'S BAND?
WELL, I, WAS THINKING I WOULD.
THAT'S WHAT YOUR HEART TELLS YOU?
FEELS THAT WAY, YES.
SO, THAT MEANS YOU WILL BE MORE AND MORE IN HIS WORLD, AWAY FROM ME, GOING AROUND TO GIGS, MEETING GIRLS, COMING IN AT 3 IN THE MORNING DRUNK.
WE WOULD JUST DRIFT APART ANYWAY.
IT'S DOESN'T HAVE TO BE THAT WAY.
COME ON, MATT. IT'S ALREADY HAPPENED.
...

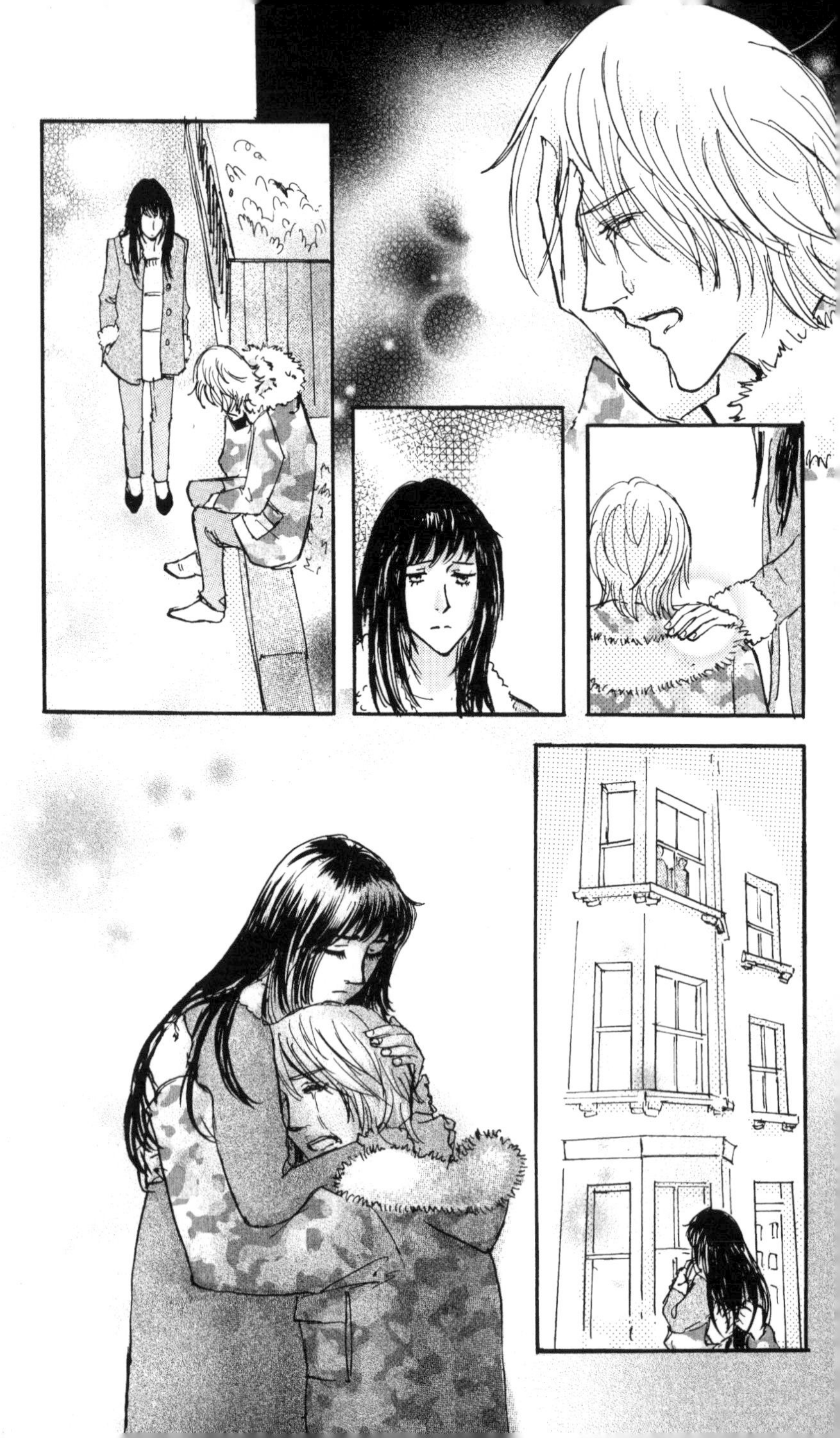

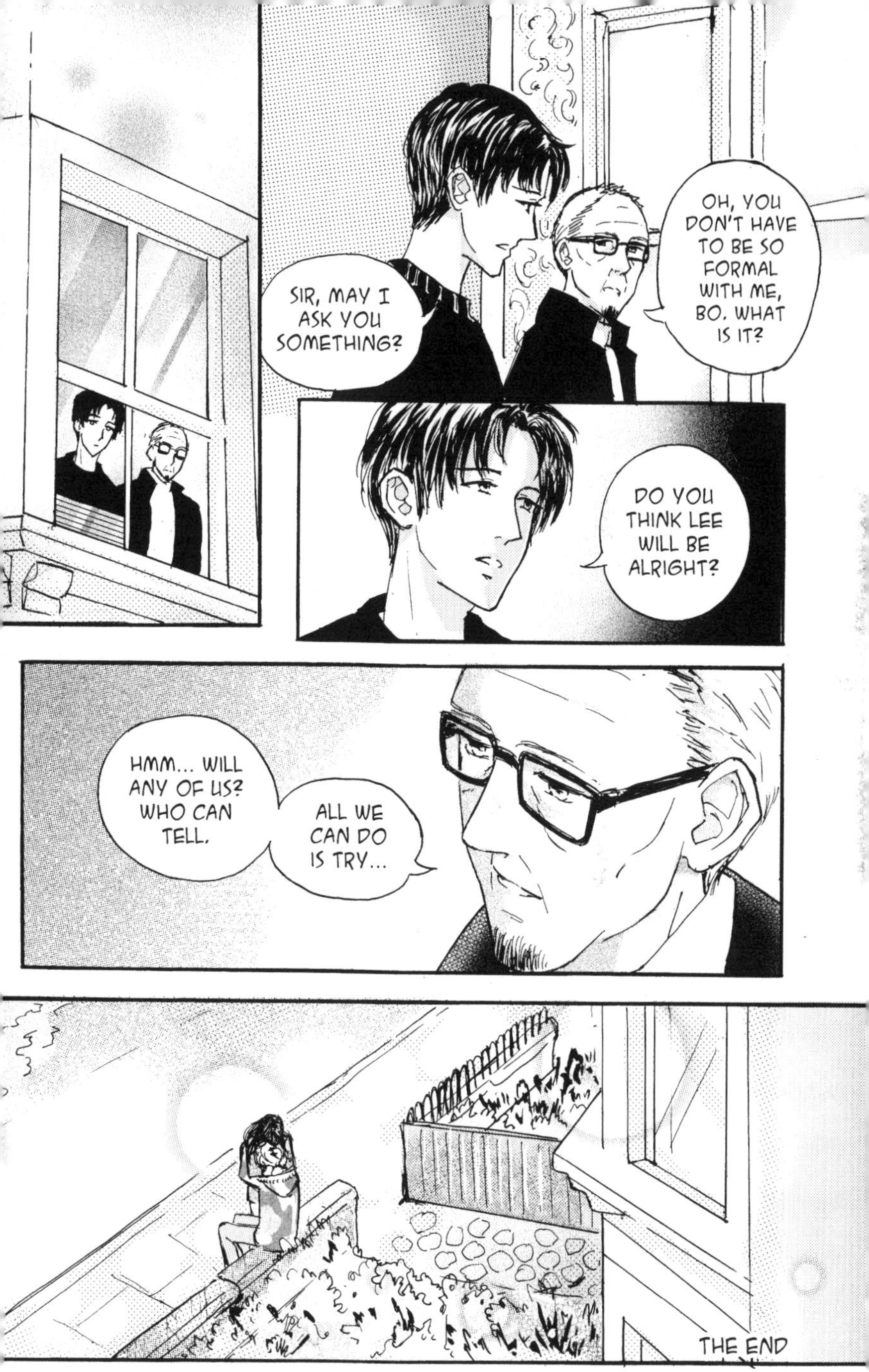
SIR, MAY I ASK YOU SOMETHING?
OH, YOU DON'T HAVE TO BE SO FORMAL WITH ME, BO. WHAT IS IT?
DO YOU THINK LEE WILL BE ALRIGHT?
HMM... WILL ANY OF US? WHO CAN TELL.
ALL WE CAN DO IS TRY...
THE END

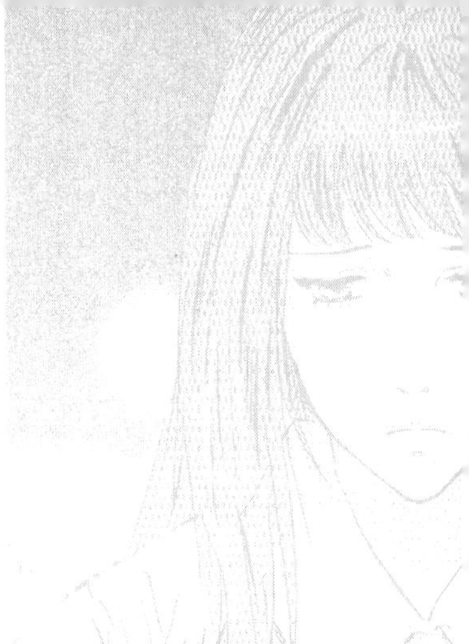

Glossary & Notes

Page 2 - The character Xavier is based on an international student who was in my masters degree program in Edinburgh University. The kind of person who is smart but can't resist showing off about it. We had all agreed not to show the results of our first essay, as it was immature to compare marks and not the point of learning. But as soon as he saw that his result was good he showed it off to any one he could. Haha! He is probably the head of a department of sociology now somewhere.

Page 5 - Despite studying and teaching these things for years, I STILL sometimes forget what things like 'ethnomethodology' mean! That is them walking in the George Square area of Edinburgh University, as we saw in volume 2, going towards the library (where I worked part time for a year after finishing my studies).

Page 9 - More Scott Walker! He has been mentioned in all 3 of the volumes of The Story of Lee. A huge influence on me, both for the quality and beauty of his songs and also the attitude of the artist trying to do something meaningful with them, rather than chase fame. He was extremely famous in the mid and late 60s but gave that up in order to do very odd, unsettling but wonderful music that had no chance of large sales. Much as the comic book writer Alan Moore has given up on a lot more fame and money to do work he finds meaningful. Admirable!

Pages 16 and 17 - 'Lassies' is a Scots word meaning young women especially but women in general. 'Aye, nah danger' is a common Scots phrase meaning 'Yes, no problem, don't worry, that's ok.' There is a habit in Scotland to call people 'wee man' or 'big man' - and not necessarily in connection to their body size!

Page 19 - 'Shaky Jakes' is a real bar/club in Edinburgh (and a cool song from 1969 by the band Humble Pie) but 'Radges' is a made up one by me. 'Range' or 'raj' is a Scots word, used largely in the east coast, to mean 'idiot/fool/bad behaviour.'

Page 21 - As it says there 'ken ye fine' means 'I know your personality'. 'Ken' means know, 'ye' means you.

Page 22 - 'Eejit' is the Irish and Scottish pronunciation of idiot.

Page 26 - Uncle Jun, literate person that he is, reads that classic of Scottish literature 'Sunset Song' (1932) by Lewis Grassic Gibbon while actually in Scotland. It was a set text when I was in school in Scotland, and very moving it is - a portrait of the rural North East area.

Page 38 - A song by the wonderful garage punk band, *The Seeds* 1966. In 2004 the singer Sky Saxon, suddenly came into my friend's house in London, totally unexpected. I thought I was dreaming - a 60s hero was suddenly sitting next to me! He told me wild stories about the 60s, like when he threatened to beat up Jack Nicholson and left by saying "I love you Sean, man!"

Page 41 - 'The Pride of Miss Jean Brodie' (1961) is a classic novel by Edinburgh writer Muriel Spark, and the school it takes place at is just a few minutes away from where our characters live.

Pages 51 to 55 - With the old Scottish lady: The phrase 'wit are ye daeing' means what are you doing. 'Chinky' and 'chink' are racist terms for Chinese…used to be very common but are said much less often now, i think… 'Awa wae ye' means go away… 'ach' is oh…'auld' is old…'awful' is awful… 'bairn' is a child…'frae' is from…'dinae fancy it meself' is I dont like it myself…'Glasgea' is the big city Glasgow (and by the way, lovely Americans, the city is not pronounced 'Glas-GOW', the correct way is 'GLAS-go' or, in the local accent more like 'GLAS-gay')… 'ony' is any… 'guid' is good…'oor' is our… 'mare' is more… 'skelped' is slap or smack…. 'hae' is have… 'wis quite richt' is quite right… 'wimmin' is women.

Page 56 - The well-known phrase expressing egalitarianism 'A man's a man for a' that' are from a Robert Burns song 'Is There for Honest Poverty' (1795). A simple but powerful message of the universal connection of all people that has strongly influenced Scotland and many other countries but which we are still far off from achieving!

Page 71 - As they walk home, they pass the new Edinburgh tram/street car, that started in May 2014. Trams used to run in Edinburgh until they were closed down in 1956. So, it's an interesting reflection on city public transport trends that they decided to 're-tram' again more than 50 years later.

Page 73 - They pass the statue of publisher and politician William Chambers, on Chambers Street. I used to park my scooter there!

Page 97 - Lee goes off on her own up Arthur's Seat and the Crags (she gets the name wrong later on page 104), the beautiful hill and nature reserve near the centre of Edinburgh.

Pay 101 - 'dug' means dog. Though a cat is just a cat.

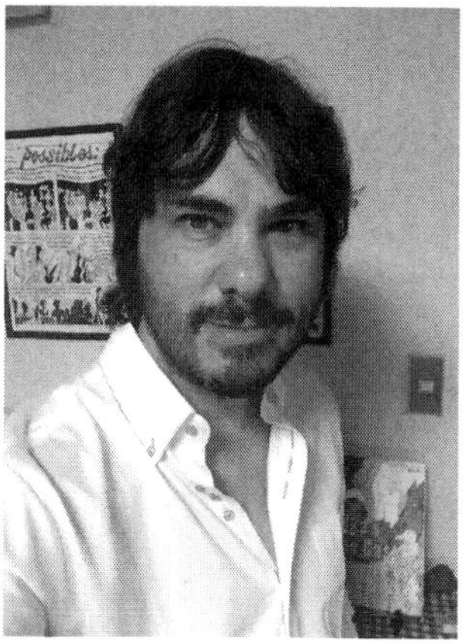

Sean Michael Wilson is a comic book writer from Scotland. He has had many books published with a variety of US, UK and Japanese publishers, such as 'A Christmas Carol' (Sunday Times 'Best of 2008'), 'The Book of Five Rings' (Shambhala Publications) and edited the critically acclaimed 'AX:alternative manga' (Publishers Weekly's 'Best Ten Books of 2010'). In 2016 his book 'The Faceless Ghost' was nominated for the prestigious Eisner Book Awards. In 2017 his book 'Secrets of the Ninja' won an International Manga Award from the Japanese Ministry of Foreign Affairs - the first time a British person has received this award. seanmichaelwilson.weebly.com

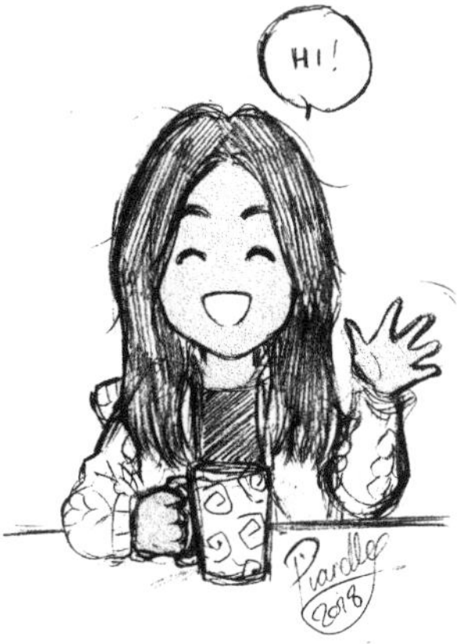
HI!

Piarelle (a.k.a. Pamela Lokhun) is a British comic artist/illustrator, based in London. Having loved drawing since she first scribbled crayon to wallpaper, her work has since won various competitions (notably shortlisted in the UK's annual Manga Jiman competition a few times), been featured in NEO magazine and has even been exhibited as far as Tokyo, Japan. 'The Story of Lee' volume 3 is her debut work as a graphic novel artist. pencilled-dreams.co.uk

Also by Wilson from NBM:
The Story of Lee, vol.1 and vol.2
Breaking the Ten (2 volumes)

Other manga from NBM:
In the Louvre collection:
Rohan at the Louvre by Araki
Guardians of the Louvre by Taniguchi

We have over 200 titles.

See our complete list, Wilson's blog and order at:
NBMPUB.COM

NBM Graphic Novels
160 Broadway, Suite 700, East Wing,
New York, NY 10038
Catalog available by request

Sean Michael Wilson & Chie Kutsuwada
The Story of Lee

Sean Michael Wilson & Nami Tamura
The Story of Lee
Volume 2

BREAKING
THE
10

BREAKING
THE 10
Volume 2
nbm

Rohan at the Louvre
Hirohiko
Araki

GUARDIANS
OF THE
LOUVRE

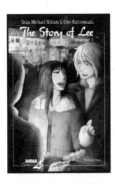

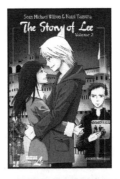

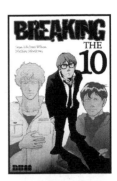

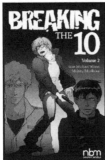

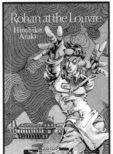

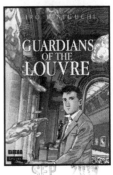